METATAXIS

Distributed Language Translation

The goal of these series is to publish texts which are related to computational linguistics and machine translation in general, and the DLT (Distributed Language Translation) research project in particular.

Series editor
Toon Witkam
B.S.O./Research
P.O. Box 8348, NL-3503 RH Utrecht
The Netherlands

Other book in this series:
1. B.C. Papegaaij, V. Sadler and A.P.M. Witkam (eds.)
   Word Expert Semantics

Klaus Schubert

METATAXIS

Contrastive dependency syntax for machine translation

1987
FORIS PUBLICATIONS
Dordrecht - Holland/Providence R.I. - U.S.A.

Published by:
Foris Publications Holland
P.O. Box 509
3300 AM Dordrecht, The Netherlands

Sole distributor for the U.S.A. and Canada:
Foris Publications USA Inc.
P.O. Box 5904
Providence R.I. 02903
U.S.A.

CIP-DATA

Schubert, Klaus

Metataxis: Contrastive Dependency Syntax for Machine Translation / Klaus Schubert. -
Dordrecht [etc.]: Foris. - (Distributed Language Translation; 2)
With ref.
ISBN 90-6765-358-6 bound
ISBN 90-6765-359-4 paper
SISO 807 UDC 681.3.053:801.56
Subject headings: machine translation / computer linguistics.

In co-operation with BSO, Utrecht,
The Netherlands

ISBN 90 6765 358 6 (Bound)
ISBN 90 6765 359 4 (Paper)

Printed in the Netherlands by ICG Printing, Dordrecht.

Contents

Foreword

This book has come about within the Distributed Language Translation project, a major research and development effort of the BSO software house in Utrecht for advanced semi-automatic multilingual machine translation. The body of this study deals with the theoretical foundation of the translation process in language science and presents the involved problems and a suggested solution in an application-oriented shape.

This study is an account of two years of intensive work within the DLT team on topics of machine translation-oriented monolingual and contrastive syntax. The models of dependency syntax and metataxis described in this study have come about in a process of fruitful mutual exchange of ideas, suggestions and counterproposals with all members of the DLT team and a number of external scholars. Today I can say that the models suggested here are not only mere theoretical constructs, but have already been tested and improved in practical work.

In this context, I should like to express my gratitude to all those who have agreed to plunge into the notorious grammatical details of various languages, applying to them the principles formulated in my models of syntax and metataxis. Their work, their criticism, and their questions have in many ways helped me to formulate the basis of our common work more precisely.

My thanks are due to the writers of dependency syntaxes: Luc Isaac (Archennes) and Dorine Tamis (Utrecht) for French, Dan Maxwell (Utrecht) and Bieke van der Korst (Amsterdam / Utrecht) for English, Henning Lobin (Bonn) for German, Prof. Kalevi Tarvainen (Jyväskylä) for Finnish and Ingrid Schubert (Utrecht) for Danish. I should also like to thank those whose work is still in progress, namely Prof. Eva Hajičová and associates (Prague) for Czech and Ilona Koutny, Gábor Prószéky and Balázs Wacha (Budapest) for Hungarian.

Building on these dependency syntaxes, the first metataxis rule systems have been worked out, and I am grateful to the two authors, Dan Maxwell for English-Esperanto and Dorine Tamis for Esperanto-French. The pioneer formaliser of metataxis in DLT, Job van Zuijlen, must not be forgotten.

The grammatical work within the DLT project would not have been possible without the inspiring collaboration with all project colleagues, both computer scientists and linguists. They all have their part in this book. I am especially grateful to Toon Witkam for many critical remarks on a draft manuscript of this study, and to Dan Maxwell for smoothening my English.

Also on the occasion of a treatise about contrastive dependency syntax, I should like to mention my gratitude to Hans Robert Mehlig (Kiel), who introduced me to contrastive linguistics, and Ingeborg Zint-Dyhr (Copenhagen), who guided my first acquaintance with dependency grammar.

Utrecht, September 1987 Klaus Schubert

Chapter 1

Metataxis between theoretical and computational linguistics

Metataxis is a new word in English. It denotes the structural change which a text or sentence undergoes when being translated. The term derives from Lucien Tesnière's "**métataxe**" (1959/1982: 283) and signals that the present study belongs to the realm of **dependency grammar**.

This book is the result of work on both the theoretical foundation and the practical realisation of one of the major **machine translation** projects at present under development, called Distributed Language Translation (**DLT**). This study is written with an eye on both language theory and its computational application. I therefore spend a couple of chapters on constructing and theoretically motivating a metataxis system and only thereafter take the step towards the computer. It is my hope that such an approach not only makes most of this study readable also for readers interested in language theory and not so much in machine translation, but that it in addition enhances the practical application. Indeed, modular thinking seems to me to be of utmost import for the quality of practical results in natural-language processing. The description of regularity in language should not be tailored to fit the possibilities and restrictions of machines and algorithms, but to fit language. Even an application-oriented investigation profits from being directed mainly towards a self-contained language theory. When such a theory yields the desired results, a formalised process of analyses and syntheses can be shaped in accordance with the theory.

The present study is arranged along these lines of modularity. In chapter 2., I give some basic definitions, paying special attention to the concept of **dependency** which is essential to the whole theory. As dependency grammar is less known - especially to those who rely mainly on works written in English - I try in chapter 3. to give a brief introduction to the theory, naming the main research centres and referring to specialised literature.

The two major chapters are dedicated to **metataxis** (5.) and, as the basis on which metataxis rests, **dependency syntax** (4.). In chapter 4. a strictly form-oriented model of dependency syntax is designed. The accent is on applicability: I set up and motivate the principles of the syntax model in such a way that the chapter can be read as a guideline for writing a dependency syntax of a language. Chapter 5. is the core of the study. On the basis of the model of dependency syntax described here, I devise a metataxis system, that is, a system for translation syntax. Again the principles and choices are described in such a way that the reader is invited to make practical use of the system.

Metataxis is strictly form-oriented contrastive syntax. But of course syntax is part of grammar. In chapter 6. the link is established: I review related models of dependency **semantics** and **pragmatics** and discuss possible connections to metataxis. Chapter 7. finally takes up the **computational application** of metataxis and dependency syntax in general. I discuss to what extent dependency syntax can be handled with standard parsing techniques and outline a few problems of formalising metataxis towards an implementation in computer programs. Chapter 8. looks ahead to prospects and future developments of metataxis.

The following two sections take up the purpose of this study in somewhat more detail (1.1.) and provide brief information about the DLT machine translation system with which this study is closely linked (1.2.).

1.1. **Metataxis - for what purpose?**

Metataxis is structural change in translation. Every translation process brings about structural change, but it is not self-evident that, when the step-by-step process of translating is made explicit in machine translation, the transfer step from source to target language should actually be taken at a level of structure. In other words, when a machine translation system contains metataxis as one of the subprocesses of its overall translation procedure, this is a deliberate choice. Calling metataxis translation **syntax**, I have in mind a wide definition of syntax (given in 2.1.) that includes all levels between morpheme and text. But even with such a large definition of syntax, transfer at the syntactic level remains a choice. Early attempts tried to achieve translation at the word level, considering structure more or less redundant, and today efforts are being made to find a breakthrough at the other extreme: totally semantics-based translation in which structure is in another sense taken to be redundant. I return to these alternatives in 6.2.

In this study, I quite often use words like "choose", "decide" etc. In my view, designing a grammar is devising a model that describes language, and model design allows for choices. If a model is meant to have psychological reality, observations and proofs are required, but if a model is meant just to account for the facts without rendering language-related activities in the human brain, it is enough to motivate decisions of system design as being purposeful, but it cannot be ultimately proven that they are the best possible.

I design a metataxis system for machine translation with a particular machine translation system in mind, but I do not in the following chapters so much adhere to peculiarities of the DLT system to make my ideas feasible for that system only. As a consequence, I hope that the present model of dependency syntax and of metataxis will be useful for those interested in translation between arbitrary languages. Because of this **cross-linguistic scope**, I sometimes have to describe my line of reasoning at a rather abstract level. I try in appropriate cases to illustrate my ideas with concrete examples from a few different languages, but I beg the reader's pardon for not having been able to supply illustrations in some places where they may seem called for.

1.2. The DLT machine translation system

The present study is based on the DLT machine translation system. A full account of that system cannot be included here, but a few design characteristics may be worthwhile for a better understanding of the applicational background of this study.

Distributed Language Translation is the name of a major research and development project of Buro voor Systeemontwikkeling (BSO/Research), a software house at Utrecht in the Netherlands. DLT was initiated around 1980 by Toon Witkam. In 1983 he completed a feasibility study, funded by the European Communities (Witkam 1983). The feasibility study contains a comprehensive account of the linguistic, computational and commercial aspects of the machine translation system. Since the beginning of 1985 the DLT project has been in a six-year period of research and development with the aim of delivering a complete prototype for a single language pair (English to French) by the end of the period. A restricted prototype is scheduled to be demonstrated in late 1987. The period 1985-1990 is jointly funded by the Netherlands Ministry of Economic Affairs and BSO, and has a total budget of 17 million guilders. Commercialisation of the DLT system is scheduled for about 1993.

DLT is a system for semi-automatic machine translation with a monolingual interactive dialogue with the user. It is designed for use in personal computers in data communication networks and is therefore set up to work **without post-editing**. The basic idea, from which the epithet "distributed" derives, is that the translation process is split up in two parts: The text is entered in, say, English and immediately translated into an **intermediate language**. Problems that cannot be resolved by the system are submitted to the user in an interactive dialogue. The dialogue is exclusively in the source language, in the example in plain English, so that the user need not have command of the target or the intermediate language and need not even know to what languages the text is going to be translated. The intermediate-language form is sent to receivers in the network, and only there the text is translated on into the final target language(s), without a dialogue with a user being possible in the second half of the process. The system is **modular** in the sense that the intermediate form of a text lends itself for further translation to any target language. DLT is designed as a **multilingual** machine translation system which is easily **extendable** to include more languages. It is not restricted to typologically similar languages. These requirements presuppose a fully expressive intermediate language, and the need of translating **from** the intermediate language into the target language **fully automatically** presupposes an extremely clear and translation-friendly intermediate language. DLT therefore uses a slightly modified version of Esperanto for this purpose.

The Esperanto-based intermediate language, which in the feasibility study (Witkam 1983: II-15) was designed to be not much more than a compact half-way text notation, has during the development since then acquired a more and more crucial role in the design of DLT (cf. also Schubert 1986b). This is due to the fact that the DLT developers are striving to concentrate in the kernel of the system all difficult and computationally time-consuming functions, so that they have to be devised only once, for the intermediate language, and not again and again for all the source and target languages that might be added to the system. This is most essential for the **lexical knowledge bank** where **knowledge of the world** is stored, and for the **word expert system** that makes use of the knowledge bank. The entire **semantic** and **pragmatic** processing has been concentrated in the the kernel, so that **Esperanto** has become **the language of Artificial Intelligence** in DLT. The principle is to transport all semantic and pragmatic decisions from the source language analysis into the intermediate form and to resolve them there. They arrive in the Esperanto kernel in the form of **syntactically possible translation alternatives**. In a similar way the translation from intermediate into the target language is substantially prepared in the Esperanto kernel.

The **extendability principle**, together with the desire to concentrate complicated processings in the kernel of the system, assigns an essentially important role to **metataxis**. Given the idea of choosing among syntactically possible alternatives, there are indeed only two interfaces which connect any source or target language to the kernel of the DLT system:

- a bilingual dictionary and
- a metataxis rule system.

Both these interfaces are described in this study. It is noteworthy that, although the work during the present period is concentrated on English, French and Esperanto, the DLT developers are interested in testing and refining the definitions for these two interfaces already now, because the cross-linguistic extendability of the system essentially depends on them. For this purpose, a number of preparatory studies as to the dependency syntax and metataxis of typologically diverse languages have been initiated, partly in collaboration with universities and external contractors. These investigations follow the principles outlined in chapters 4. and 5.

Metataxis is a contrastive rule system that links two languages. It is built on dependency syntaxes of both languages. When proposing dependency syntax for the DLT system, I therefore already sketched metataxis (Schubert 1986a: 166ff.). Since then, a number of dependency syntaxes have been written in accordance with the principles set up in that study. Also two metataxes have been worked out and implemented (English to Esperanto and Esperanto to French; see the Foreword). The experiences won in this work and the need of making its guiding principles more explicit than they were in my previous study (Schubert 1986a) have resulted in a refined and theoretically founded account which is given in this book.

More details about the DLT system are found in a variety of publications from the DLT team and from outside observers. The most comprehensive account is the feasibility study (Witkam 1983). A description of the overall translation process is given in a more recent article (Schubert 1986c). The semantic-pragmatic processing is in detail discussed by Papegaaij (1986) and in a very concise version by Papegaaij, Sadler and Witkam (1986). The quality test of the lexical-transfer capacity of DLT's word expert processing announced by Alan Melby (1986) has in the meantime been accomplished successfully. Melby is an outside observer, and so is John Hutchins, who gives a good brief overview of the state of DLT at the end of 1985 (Hutchins 1986: 287ff.).

Chapter 2

Some fundamentals of grammar

Metataxis is the structural change a text undergoes when being translated. As such, it is a topic of **contrastive syntax** - dependency syntax as will turn out in a moment. Translation involves a source and a target language, so a metataxis description typically concerns **a pair of languages** and presupposes syntax descriptions of both languages. Before entering a discussion of any details about metataxis, it therefore seems worthwhile to give an overview of what syntax is, especially in the framework of dependency grammar, and what the possible alternatives would be. As this study is written with a practical application (machine translation) in mind, I also motivate the preference given to dependency grammar (as opposed to constituency grammar) for this particular purpose. In order to approach these subjects, a few fundamentals need to be taken up.

2.1. A general view of grammar

The study of language is an old science. A very huge number of scholars have been and still are engaged in the field, speaking and writing in hundreds of different languages, and by now there is no consensus about the precise meaning of the most basic terms. Their meaning has become or has probably always been vague and they are often used contradictorily by different authors. This puzzling situation has definitely not improved since computer scientists started using many terms of linguistics, not always realising that they were using them in a metaphorical way. When the two only apparently equivalent terminologies merge in computational linguistics, complete conceptual clarity should be established before entering any discussion. As this book deals with topics of linguistics directed towards a computational application, concise definitions of the fundamental notions, as I use them here, are called for.

> **Language** is a system of signs for human communication. The signs consist of **form** and **content** (Saussure 1916: 32). **Grammar** is the theory about the internal system of language. Grammar contains the study of both the formal

and the content side of the linguistic sign. The theory about the formal side is **syntax**, the one about the content is **semantics**. Language is not a closed system, but is subject to influence from outside factors. The theory about extra-linguistic influence on language is **pragmatics** (with **sociolinguistics** as an important sub-branch).

I do not maintain that these definitions are exhaustive, nor that they are the only suitable ones. There are other opinions, some of them perhaps better substantiated than mine. It is possible to give more complete and precise definitions and compare them with other authors' approaches, but that is far beyond the scope of this book. In this context, two supplementary remarks may, however, be appropriate.

The first one is about the concept of **grammar**. It is worth noting that within the same branch of language theory in which this study is placed, i.e. within dependency syntax, the notion of grammar is sometimes defined in a larger sense than I do here, namely including pragmatics. Ulrich Engel (1982: 17) gives this a ready formulation: "Grammatik ist Theorie der Sprache."

The second remark concerns the term **syntax**, which is crucial for metataxis. While my definition of grammar is narrower than Engel's, I am using the word syntax in a much larger sense than many other authors do. In many contexts the notion of syntax is confined to the sentence and words as its elements. Metataxis, however, presupposes a description of the entire formal side of the linguistic sign both below and above sentence level. I have therefore adopted the term syntax in this larger meaning, giving it a scope that is parallel to the one of semantics. Syntax, defined in this way, contains at the word level morphology and a good deal of word formation, and on text level the formal characteristics of text structure.

This view of grammar can be depicted in the following figure. That I establish three levels is a choice, not a theoretical requirement. One may find it appropriate for other purposes to establish more levels in between, e.g. a syntagma level, a clause level, etc.

[1]

	GRAMMAR		
	SYNTAX	SEMANTICS	
WORD LEVEL			
SENTENCE LEVEL			
TEXT LEVEL			
	FORM	CONTENT	

2.2. Dependency and constituency

Given the extended definition of syntax suggested in 2.1., metataxis lies totally within the realm of syntax. More precisely, it is a subject of **contrastive dependency syntax**. The present section is therefore clearly about syntax, not about grammar as a whole. The link to **dependency semantics** is established in chapter 6.

Dependency syntax is a theory of the formal side of the linguistic sign, based on one of two possible fundamental grammatical concepts: **dependency**. What is, then, dependency, what is the alternative, and how does dependency apply to syntax?

Language is a **system** of signs, and, as any system, it can be described in terms of its **elements** and the **relationships** that hold among them. The smallest signs are per definition **morphemes**, but grammatical reasoning can and should often be based on higher-level groups of morphemes such as words, phrases, clauses, sentences or texts. The perhaps most self-evident element for a syntactic analysis is the **word**. Units that are not signs, e.g. sounds, letters or syllables, are not relevant here.

Although there has been much discussion about the precise definition and identification of **word**, **sentence** and other syntactic units, the assumption that they are elements of the language system is hardly controversial. But the description of the relationships among the elements can be based on either of two fundamental grammatical concepts, **constituency** or **dependency**. Besides combinations of the two, there is no third possibility (Mel'čuk 1979a: 4).

A **constituency syntax** describes a sentence (in practice normally not a whole text) by grouping adjacent words into abstract, higher-level units. (This approach has therefore also been termed "grouping", Hays 1961). A typical example is the denotation of the combination of <u>blue</u> and <u>chair</u>, an adjective and a noun, in <u>blue chair</u> as a "noun phrase" (NP). The analysis proceeds by grouping the words into ever higher levels, until the highest-level unit is reached, usually the sentence (S). The basic relationship among the elements on different levels is "is a" upwards and "consists of" downwards.

A **dependency syntax** describes a sentence by establishing lines of syntactic relation among words. In such an analysis, <u>blue</u> is said to be related to <u>chair</u>, but no abstract higher-level name is given to the word pair. The two words are not looked upon as interdependent, but one of them is assigned the role of **governor** (chair), whereas the other one is the **dependent** (blue). The analysis links up the whole sentence by defining a governor for each word, except for one word which is the main governor of the whole sentence. The relationship is "depends on" upwards and "governs" downwards.

Of course these clear-cut definitions leave many questions open, and as far as dependency is concerned, more details are given in 4.1.

In view of the fact that much (but by no means all) of the grammatical work done in natural-language processing, and especially in machine translation, is based on the constituency approach, a closer look at the value and status of the two concepts of constituency and dependency may be interesting. Klaus Baumgärtner (1970: 52) points out that the two concepts have been competing with each other ever since language has been reflected about in a scientific way. Baumgärtner (1970: 53) emphasises that the constituency principle comes down to grouping on the basis of **contiguity**, which means that two words cannot be considered to form a higher-level unit, unless they occur **adjacent** in the sentence. A contiguity-based analysis appears to him as the guarantee for capturing a basic property of linguistic utterances: **linearity**. Baumgärtner then defines a type of dependency which is also contiguity-based. For such a dependency it is easy to show that it is a special case of constituency (Baumgärtner 1970: 54). But is contiguity really needed in a definition of dependency? After all, syntactic relationships, whether termed dependency or not, can be established between any two words of a sentence, without adjacency being required. However, Baumgärtner's paper was written in 1967. It is interesting to see how the text, and in particular the footnotes, are full of the spirit of those years, when the findings of what we now call early computational linguistics and early transformational grammar sometimes were believed to be the observable facts of an exact science. In the light of today's knowledge it is easier to see that this extraordinary emphasis on linearity has much to do with the possibilities and restrictions of the computational facilities that were available twenty years ago. As the input procedure most naturally worked left to right, the most straightforward manner of analysing a sentence was proceeding in the same way from a handled word on to its right neighbour (either in a single or in several passes). The whole discussion about whether or not such an analysis could be done in a "context-free" way has much to do with this method. And of course the syntax of the language most computational linguists worked with in those days, English, lends itself quite well to a procedure that takes into account first of all the adjacent word.

Dependency, however, is a notion that certainly is not bound to any one language, let alone to any one parsing method. Dependency and constituency are, as Baumgärtner (1970: 52) acknowledges, the fundamental principles of grammar. Baumgärtner's link between dependency and linearity must therefore be considered inspired by the state of the art of the mid-sixties in two branches of science that have developed rapidly since then. This can also be traced to an earlier article in which Baumgärtner (1965: 46) directly takes up the early computational applications of dependency grammar. But linearity is not in any theoretically justified way essential to the concept of dependency. Indeed Baumgärtner (1970: 57) himself mentions that Tesnière's (1959/1982: 13) dependency concept allows for more than two dependents under one governor. This means that Tesnière's dependency cannot be based on contiguity, because in a linear string a governing element can at most have two dependents: its right and its left neighbour.

As the present study is based on Tesnière's concept, dependency as it is understood here cannot be seen as a special case of constituency.

Ten years later, discussions of grammar are much less influenced by the way computers work. Richard Hudson (1980) assesses constituency and dependency in a much freer way than Baumgärtner. Hudson's conclusion is clear-cut: "I argue that dependency is necessary in syntax, but constituency is not" (Hudson 1980: 179). I return to his ideas in 5.6. and 8.

2.3. The contrastive capacity of dependency and constituency

Which one of the two, constituency or dependency, is better? I do not think this is a meaningful question. Concepts as fundamental as these cannot be good or bad in an absolute sense. When a choice has to be made, the guiding arguments should be whether one of the two ideas lends itself better or worse than the other one to resolving the particular problem one is interested in. The present study is aimed at syntactic analysis, transfer and synthesis for machine translation. The choice between a dependency and a constituency approach should therefore be made on the basis of the qualities of the two approaches in a **translation grammar**. The aim is not syntax per se, but **contrastive syntax**.

Writing under the heading of metataxis, I have obviously chosen the dependency approach, and this decision needs to be motivated. Discussion of such motivation can, however, yield better insight into the advantages and disadvantages of the two competing principles if proceeded by an explanation of a few more details of dependency syntax in general and of the version of dependency syntax which I have adopted for machine translation. I therefore return to this question in 5.6.

Chapter 3

Streams of development in dependency grammar

The present study contains the theoretical foundation of work within applied grammar for machine translation, and it is my hope that it will contribute to a more general linguistic discussion also among those who are not engaged in this particular application. Metataxis is a subfield of dependency syntax, and dependency grammar for at least a few decades has been outside the scope of research done by many linguists, especially those trained in English-speaking countries. In this short chapter, I try to provide a historical orientation to this field of study and also to provide a road guide to related work by other scholars.

3.1. The reception of Tesnière's work

The concept of dependency has, often tacitly, every now and then been at issue in grammatical scholarship throughout the centuries. Much of what is known as traditional grammar is based on ideas about grammatical dependency relations, which, like many other concepts in language science, are derived from the classical Greek school of Stoic philosophy with its Latin successors. Also Pāṇini (5th-4th century B.C.) makes use of the concept of dependency (Maas 1974: 257). In medieval scholastic grammar, there is a period in which the concept of dependency and verb-centred syntax play an important role. Richard Baum (1976: 29) mentions especially Martinus of Dacia, Thomas of Erfurt and Siger of Courtrai, who lived in the 13th and 14th century.

In modern times, the idea of dependency has reappeared on the scene in one of the branches of Structuralism, namely in the work of **Lucien Tesnière**. Tesnière's own term is "**syntaxe structurale**", the name "Dependenzgrammatik" or "dependency grammar" has been attached to the theory by German and English-speaking scholars. Tesnière did not manage to publish the full description of his ideas within his own lifetime, but applied them freely in numerous works (for bibliographies of Tesnière's publications, see Tesnière 1959/1982: 671ff.; Baum 1976: 159f.). For some years, the main publication dedicated to the new theory itself was his "Esquisse d'une syntaxe structurale" (1953), a thin booklet that was much too concise and preliminary to make his ideas clear to unacquainted readers, as reviews show (e.g. Garey 1954; cf. Baum 1976: 17 n. 17). Not earlier than five years after Tesnière's death, Jean Fourquet succeeded in publishing Tesnière's principal work, **"Éléments de syntaxe structurale"** (1959), which gives a comprehensive account of Tesnière's revolutionary ideas on syntax and many related fields of language theory. His "Éléments", as well as some of his other other works, have a special value for linguistics, partly because of Tesnière's unusual knowledge of languages, both classical and modern, among which even remote ones were included. This broad range of linguistic evidence which Tesnière had readily available is incorporated into his work which includes a good deal of what later would be made explicit in language typology and the research into language universals.

The three main parts of Tesnière's "Éléments" are entitled "La connexion", "La jonction" and "La translation", which in today's terms may be translated as 'dependency', 'coordination' and 'word class transformation'. "La connexion" is divided up into five subparts, three about the fundamentals of dependency syntax and two more specific ones, "Valence" 'valency' and "Métataxe" 'metataxis'. The parts of the huge work have been read by different scholars with various degrees of intensity, which will become more obvious in the following paragraphs.

For understanding the current status of dependency research in the world of linguistics and its computational applications, it is instructive to follow the lines along which the reception of Tesnière's work has spread. Tesnière's "Éléments" can be said to have become a quite often-quoted book in the French and other Romance language areas. However, the acquaintance with his work has not brought about a revolution there. In works written in French, Spanish, Italian and other Romanic languages, Tesnière is referred to as a classic of linguistics, but hardly anybody has taken up the essence of his ideas and written for example a dependency syntax of French or a valency dictionary of Spanish.

The works by Maurice Gross (especially 1975) are sometimes mentioned in the context of dependency grammar, and in particular of valency dictionaries, but the connection seems rather to lie in the person of Gross, who was involved in early computational dependency grammar (e.g. Gross 1964), than in the principles and the content of his method.

3.2. Leipzig and Mannheim

It is in Germany, both the Federal Republic of Germany and the German Democratic Republic, that Tesnière's theory has had a much more striking effect. Its main ideas were in the early sixties taken up in current grammatical discussion by scholars such as Johannes Erben (1958/1972), Hennig Brinkmann (1962) and Gerhard Helbig (1965).

One of the first authors who attempted writing a complete syntax of a language by applying dependency principles was Hans-Jürgen Heringer. However, his German syntax is not a pure dependency syntax, but combines constituency and dependency elements. Unfortunately, Heringer's book (1970a) is very difficult to read and to understand, as he has overformalised his reasoning and representations, while abandoning all the simple elegance that is so characteristic of Tesnière's writing. If Tesnière is mainly interested not in the **theory** of grammar, but in the **results**, as Baum (1976: 5) says, Heringer approached the problem rather the other way round. Although he at the same time published a simplified, more result-oriented, account of his thoughts (Heringer 1970b), he has not been understood by many. The intertwined use of constituency and dependency can be traced in Heringer's work starting from an overview of his entire grammatical model (Heringer 1970b: 32). A critical summary is supplied by Jarmo Korhonen (1977: 38ff., 49ff.).

More decisive for the development of dependency grammar became two schools that arose in the sixties in Leipzig and Mannheim, respectively. The leading persons are Gerhard Helbig in Leipzig and Ulrich Engel in Mannheim. Both schools focus primarily on one of Tesnière's central notions: **valency** (see 3.5.).

The Leipzig school issued the first valency dictionaries, namely for German verbs (Helbig / Schenkel 1969/1980), adjectives (Sommerfeldt / Schreiber 1974/1983) and nouns (Sommerfeldt / Schreiber 1977/1980). The Leipzig authors have been so much concerned with the notion of valency that they almost always speak of valency theory, valency grammar and valency research, but do not place their valency theory in the wider framework of a dependency grammar. Nikula (1986: 110) points out that Helbig and Schenkel (1969/1980: 36) in their first valency dictionary placed their theory within a transformational grammar of Noam Chomsky's Standard-Theory type (Chomsky 1965). They do not discuss the opposition dependency - constituency.

Mannheim seems to have been less concerned with Chomsky's constituency-based grammar. Although even the Mannheim works focus on valency in the early stages, the step towards a more complete dependency grammar was taken soon. A group around Engel and Schumacher has published an alternative valency dictionary of German verbs (Engel / Schumacher 1976), Wolfgang Teubert (1979) has investigated the valency of nouns and Engel has written a German dependency syntax (Engel 1977, revised edition 1982), the first dependency syntax of an entire language.

From these two centres, dependency grammar has spread throughout the linguistics of German. It can be noted that in a number of language areas besides German, the interest in dependency grammar has first arisen in the German language institutes of the universities, e.g. in Scandinavia through the Danish Germanists in Copenhagen (Fabricius-Hansen 1977, 1979a, 1980), through Kalevi Tarvainen in Jyväskylä, who wrote the first introduction to dependency grammar in Finnish (Tarvainen 1977), or through Henrik Nikula in Turku for Swedish (Nikula 1976, 1986). Where dependency-oriented approaches have spread into the linguistics of other languages than German, this has in many occasions taken place either in Germany or in German language institutes. Examples are the works on English valency by Rudolf Emons (1974, 1978) and Thomas Herbst (1983). As far as I can see, Allerton (1982) in Basel has also worked in close contact with German centres of dependency theory. Contrastive linguistics with German as one counterpart is another area which has contributed to spreading dependency grammar to other groups of linguists and other fields of linguistics. Nikula (1976) compares German and Swedish, Krystyna Smereka (1986) German and Polish.

Even the first French valency dictionary is a contrastive one with German as the counterpart (Busse / Dubost 1977). Although the authors criticise Gross (Busse / Dubost 1977: VIII), their dictionary follows works such as Gross (1975) by going directly to syntactic form rather than from function to form (see the discussion of this distinction in 5.6.). Therefore their dictionary is not the type of bilingual valency dictionary needed in the present metataxis model (see 5.1.). Corpus materials for a machine translation-oriented French-German valency dictionary have been collected by Monika Weissgerber (1983: 139ff.).

3.3. Other readers of Tesnière

However, not all work within dependency grammar is linked to the two German schools in Leipzig and Mannheim. Tesnière has been read in other countries as well, and not all of the current developments have come about through German mediation.

An independent approach is forwarded by Richard Hudson (1980, 1984) which is in the tradition of Tesnière (Hudson 1984: 76), but lacks direct links to Leipzig or Mannheim.

Also some of the scholars involved in early computational dependency grammar (see 3.4. and 7.1.) have carried on: Igor' Mel'čuk and Nikolaj Percov have recently published a very original dependency grammar of English (Mel'čuk / Percov 1987). This grammar is no longer explicitly linked to the authors' earlier work on computational applications.

Heringer (see 3.2.) has also stayed active in the field. He is the co-author of a "formal" dependency grammar (Heringer / Strecker / Wimmer 1980: 167ff.) and regularly publishes articles on dependency, valency etc. (e.g. Heringer 1985; cf. Eckert 1985).

3.4. Early computational applications

In the context of the present study it is also important to note the discussions of dependency in **computational linguistics**, which took place earlier than the German blossoming of dependency grammar. These developments can be traced to the two main countries of early computational linguistics, the United States and Soviet Union. The American direction of dependency grammar is linked to the names of David Hays (1961, 1964a,b) and Jane Robinson (1970), whereas works from the Soviet school come for instance from Lejkina (1961: 1ff.), Zasorina and Berkov (1961: 139ff.) and Igor' Mel'čuk (1964 and other works). The early dependency attempts in computational linguistics were made during a culmination period of transformational grammar and accordingly could not gain much of a following. This situation may be the reason for the negative judgements on dependency grammar in natural-language processing that are found in various overview accounts (e.g. Winograd 1983: 75; Hutchins 1986: 49). These judgements refer to unelaborated experimental dependency grammars of the early sixties and fail to take into account later developments.

The developments that since the early experiments in the sixties have caused dependency grammar to spread increasingly in computational linguistics are taken up in 7.1.

3.5. Not only Tesnière

Tesnière did not invent dependency. It is much too fundamental a concept in grammatical theory and has, tacitly or explicitly, been used virtually as long as there are records of linguistic scholarship. There is, however, some discussion about the question to what extent Tesnière can be said to be the inventor of the term of **valency**, his most famous term.

Tesnière speaks about valency already in his "Esquisse" (1953: 9). Baum (1976: 32) mentions that Charles Hockett (1958: 249) uses the term "valence" apparently independently of Tesnière. Van Megen (1985: 170 n. 1) points to de Groot (1949: 111ff.), who used the term "syntactische valentie" before Tesnière, and Smereka (1986: 4) claims that Kacnel'son (1948) is the originator of the term. Indeed Kacnel'son's (1948: 132) "sintaksičeskaja valentnost'" is the earliest use of the term in linguistics I am aware of, but perhaps someone will find a still earlier one.

As the discussion in 4.4.3. shows, valency is defined in many different ways. It is, in the way Tesnière uses it, a fundamental phenomenon of grammar and has therefore of course been used and defined by quite a few authors in many different ways that are more or less similar to Tesnière's. The discussion can therefore ultimately only concern the question who coined the **term** valency, or, more precisely speaking, who took it over from chemistry or atom physics. More interesting to the history of linguistic thought is the question how the **concept** of valency arose and spread, whether or not it is termed valency. Good overviews of this development are given by Helbig and Schenkel (1969/1980: 12ff.) and by Baum (1976: 28ff.).

Baum's book is interesting also because he is one of the few readers of Tesnière who do not concentrate on valency. Instead, Baum has chosen another major concept of Tesnière to focus on, namely word class transformation (French "translation").

Readers interested in more details on the history of dependency grammar and of linguistic scholarship based on it are referred to Helbig (1973: 198ff.), Baum (1976: 7ff., 27ff.) and Eroms (1981: 9ff.). Comparative reviews of various approaches to dependency, and in particular to valency, are given by various authors, e.g. Korhonen (1977: 40ff.), Herbst (1983: 1ff.), Nikula (1986: 107ff.), Smereka (1986: 35ff.). Much further reading is referred to in Tarvainen's (1981) introductory book and in Engel's (1982) chapter bibliographies. An account mainly dedicated to formal properties of dependency grammar is supplied by Maas (1974) and a recent, computationally oriented one originates from Somers (1987: 4ff.).

Chapter 4

Dependency syntax

This chapter describes a model of dependency syntax that, in my opinion, is well suited for the machine translation purpose I have in mind. However, the model is not meant to meet the needs of this particular application only, but is general in scope. Yet, since syntactic theory in many details requires arbitrary choices among equally feasible alternatives, I have to make decisions. The options I choose in this study have to do with the requirements of translation, and in particular, of machine translation. The goal of designing a metataxis-oriented syntax model makes it desirable not just to take over any existing version of dependency syntax, but to develop a version that meets the requirements of formal stringency and reliability that a computational application presupposes. Using the word **formal**, I do **not** mean **formalised**. I strive not to mix up grammar with its possible formalisations or with implementations in the form of computer programs (see 7.2.). I call this type of dependency syntax **formal** or **form-oriented** because it is in a strict way bound to the definition of syntax, given in 2.1.: Syntax is grammar about the **form** of the linguistic sign.

This chapter consists of thirteen sections. The first four of them (4.1. to 4.4.) establish the foundation of the present model of dependency syntax. They describe the basic notion, dependency, and apply it to the two fundamental concepts that describe a syntactic system: the elements of the system and the relations among them. The next seven sections (4.5. to 4.11.) describe cross-linguistically relevant problems that arise when specific languages are analysed in accordance with the present syntax model. Section 4.12. outlines the generative productivity of this model, and 4.13. summarises the principles applied.

4.1. A definition of dependency

Syntax is essentially concerned with the problem of how words combine to form correct sentences. The extended meaning assigned to the term syntax in this study (2.1.) in fact entails more than that, but nevertheless the notion of a sentence as a set of structurally linked words is the basic concept of syntax. Dependency syntax describes sentence structure in terms of a specific type of syntactic relation among words.

The syntactic relationship used in the present model is **dependency**. It can be defined as **directed co-occurrence**. This definition contains two main ideas, co-occurrence and directedness.

In order to substantiate this definition I discuss in the following three subsections details about co-occurrence and directedness and then give a few practical guidelines about how to apply the model in less obvious cases.

My definition of dependency is partially based on other scholars' work. I refer to them in the next section (4.2.), at the same time reviewing some alternative definitions.

4.1.1. Co-occurrence

Given the emphasis on form that is characteristic of the present model, **co-occurrence** is defined in terms of syntactic **distribution**. What this means can perhaps be shown in a hypothetical example from linguistic field work. Imagine you are a linguist who wants to analyse the syntax of an undescribed language. You have collected a large corpus of texts and written them down divided up into words. Of course your decisions about the word boundaries crucially influence the whole analysis, but once you have somehow made the critical decisions in this area, the following principles of analysis will be applicable. You do not know what the words or texts mean. Now you start analysing the distribution of words. You find that there are certain frequent words that do not occur unless there is at least one member of a certain large class of words in the same sentence. In making such a statement, you have begun classifying the words. You are establishing word classes (parts of speech). Your classification is based on co-occurrence of words. After having looked primarily at adjacent words, you eliminate this methodological restriction and discover that there are co-occurrence relations among distant words as well. Now you have given up the contiguity principle (see 2.2.).

Although this may sound like a Bloomfieldian dream, it is quite a practical guideline for those working according to the principles of the present model. The example tells us two things: First, word classes and co-occurrence relations are established on purely **formal** grounds, without reference to **meaning**. Second, the definitions of classes and relations influence each other. The decisions about how to delimit word classes are made on the basis of observed co-occurrences, but at the same time the exact definition and distinction of different co-occurrence relations depends on the particulars of how the word classes are marked off (For more about this mutual relatedness, see 4.3. and 4.4.).

The adherence to purely formal means notwithstanding, a structuralist field worker is allowed to have an informant who accepts or rejects sentences experimentally formulated by the field worker. The informant need not say anything about the meaning of the sentences, only about their correctness. With such an informant at hand, let us for a few moments continue the field worker's dream. The process of establishing word classes by virtue of their co-occurrence relations can be very useful, if the field worker can in corpus sentences replace words by other words and check with the informant whether the result still is a correct sentence. It will soon turn out that this sort of **paradigmatic** relation sometimes holds not between single words, but rather between a word and a word group, or between a word group and another word group. Since this word group as a whole enters into a paradigm, a natural conclusion is that there must be co-occurrence relations between the words of the group that link it up to a unit. These relations are **syntagmatic** and the word group can consequently be called a **syntagma** (or phrase). The relation that links the syntagma to something in the rest of the sentence is syntagmatic as well. On the other hand, within a syntagma it may be possible to form other paradigms, replacing words by other words or word groups. A syntagma can thus have subsyntagmata. I return to this idea in 4.12.

Isn't all this a bit too abstract? Aren't illustrations with concrete linguistic data finally called for? So far, I have deliberately refrained from presenting any examples, because in concrete data a specific property usually seems to suggest itself as most suited for establishing the lines of syntactic relations. I discuss some of these properties in the following paragraphs, especially with respect to practical analyses of particular languages, and I show there why these properties are less suited than they seem to be at first sight. My point here, however, is that **distributional co-occurrence** is a criterion that is cross-

linguistically applicable, whatever the formal characteristics of the language in question are.

The selection of distributional **co-occurrence** as a formal criterion is still at issue. I now look at a few alternative phenomena that might be considered candidates for the criterion on which to establish syntactic relations.

Dependency structures consist of governing and dependent elements. In traditional grammar there was also a concept of **government** (Latin <u>rectio</u>). In many cases this phenomenon suggests itself as a guideline for establishing lines of syntactic relations. In addition, it is often much more "visible" in language structure than distributional co-occurrence. It is therefore certainly worthwhile to ask whether this traditional government could be a workable criterion for the type of dependency syntax aimed at here.

Government, in the classical sense of the word, denotes the fact that sometimes the syntactic (mostly morphological) form of a word can be determined by another word in the sentence. In order to distinguish this phenomenon from government in the dependency-grammatical sense, I speak about **form government** throughout this study when government in the traditional sense is meant. I call the effect of form government **form determination**.

In German, for example, verbs and prepositions "govern" certain cases in the nouns and pronouns that co-occur with them:

[2]	**Sie**	**hilft**	**ihm.**
	nominative		dative
	'she	helps	him'

[3]	**Sie**	**unterstützt**	**ihn.**
	nominative		accusative
	'she	supports	him'

[4]	**Sie**	**kommt**	**mit**	**ihren**	**Büchern.**
				dative	dative
				plural	plural
	'she	comes	with	her	books'

[5]	**Sie**	**kommt**	**ohne**	**ihre**	**Bücher.**
				accusative	accusative
				plural	plural
	'she	comes	without	her	books'

In addition to government, traditional grammar makes use of the notion of **agreement** (or concord), i.e. formal coincidence of two words. Agreement is also a kind of form determination. This can be seen in [4] and [5] where the possessive pronoun (ihre) and the noun (Bücher) agree in case and number.

It will become evident in the whole body of this study that it is most desirable to let the lines of syntactic co-occurrence follow the lines along which **form determination**, thus form government and agreement, is effective. However, form determination should not be the criterion for establishing co-occurrence lines. There are at least two reasons for this. First, the form determination criterion can in some cases be equivocal. This can be seen in a Russian example:

[6]	**Iz ėtich**	**knig**	**kotoruju**		**vy voz'mëte?**
		feminine	feminine		
		plural	singular		
		genitive	accusative		
	'of these	books	which-one	[do]	you take'

The interrogative pronoun kotoruju carries three features whereof one, the singular, is a free semantic choice of the speaker and is not at issue here. The second, the feminine gender, is governed by the correlate, the feminine noun knig, and the third, the accusative, by the finite verb, voz'mëte. As far as form government is concerned, the relative pronoun can thus be said to be governed by two governors. In the present model, however, it is unadmissible that a word be governed by more than one governor. This is discussed in more detail in 4.7.

If this were the only objection against form government, one could calmly take it as a criterion and decide cases like [6] in an arbitrary way, choosing one of the possible governors. There is, however, a much more crucial argument against this candidate criterion: form determination can only be taken as a criterion where there are form changes. As the present model is intended to apply cross-linguistically, it should not rely on features that are absent in many languages. If form determination as a criterion is discarded on this grounds, this is done not only in order to be able to cope with isolating languages where there are no morphological forms at all, but also with regard to languages where there is not enough form determination among words to link up all the words of an arbitrary sentence. Very many languages with morphological marking have such areas of less elaborated formal paradigms in their structure. English is a good example. Form determination is just not sufficient for the objective.

Word order could be another candidate for a criterion for detecting syntactic co-occurrences, but as cross-linguistic comparisons show, the syntactic effect of word order is, so to speak, complementary to that of morphological marking. In languages with little or no morphological marking, word order plays an important role in the assignment of syntactic functions to words and syntagmata. But in highly inflectional or highly agglutinative languages, word order plays a small role or no role at all on a sentence-syntactic level (but see 5.4.).

I conclude that neither form determination nor word order alone can fulfil the required function. I return later to the question which role these two, apart and in combination, do play in the present model with regard to syntactic analysis and synthesis (see what is said about **syntactic form** in 4.4.1.; cf. also 5.2. and 5.5.1.). For the overall organisation of the model, however, form determination and word order cannot replace the cross-linguistically applicable criterion of **distributional co-occurrence**.

4.1.2. Directedness

Having chosen **co-occurrence** as the basic criterion of syntactic relations, I still need to deal with the second concept in the above definition of dependency: **directedness**.

In the second part of the field worker's dream (in 4.1.1.), I speak about **syntagmata** that as a whole have a paradigmatic relation to other words or syntagmata. An example is <u>very interesting people</u> in

[7] **Very interesting people arrive.**

This syntagma can be replaced by <u>they</u>.

[8] **They arrive.**

<u>They</u> and <u>very interesting people</u> form a paradigm. Between <u>very interesting people</u> and <u>arrive</u> there is a syntagmatic co-occurrence relation and - as far as one can tell before having examined the nature of co-occurrence relations more carefully - the same type of co-occurrence relation holds between <u>they</u> and <u>arrive</u> in [8] as between <u>very interesting people</u> and <u>arrive</u> in

[7]. For the question of directedness it is interesting to note that a syntagma like very interesting people can be replaced not only by totally different words (like they), but also by parts of the same syntagma:

[9] **Interesting people arrive.**

[10] **People arrive.**

But the choice is not totally free:

[11] *** Very people arrive.**

[12] *** Very interesting arrive.**

Large paradigm experiments of this type would show that the occurrence of certain words is made possible by the presence of other words. Very can occur by virtue of interesting and interesting by virtue of people. There is no direct link that would allow very or interesting to co-occur with arrive. The word that enables their co-occurrence with arrive is people. In other words, although the syntagma very interesting people as a whole co-occurs with the verb, it is not an unanalysable unit. There is a clear internal structure in the syntagma. The co-occurrence relation with the verb thus is not just

[13]

but rather

[14]

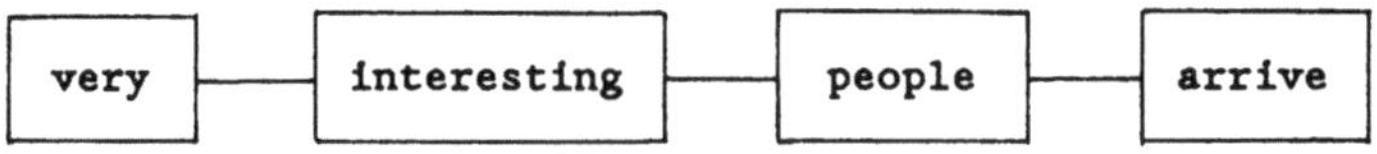

This diagram can still render the linear sequence of words, but in other cases this is no longer possible. An analysis of sentence [15] yields a diagram for which more than one dimension is needed, at least for drawing the lines showing the dependency relationships. This analysis of course presupposes a good deal of what I discuss below, and also a good deal of English dependency syntax:

[15] **The recently elected president of the local party committee gave some newspaper reporters a long interview.**

[16]

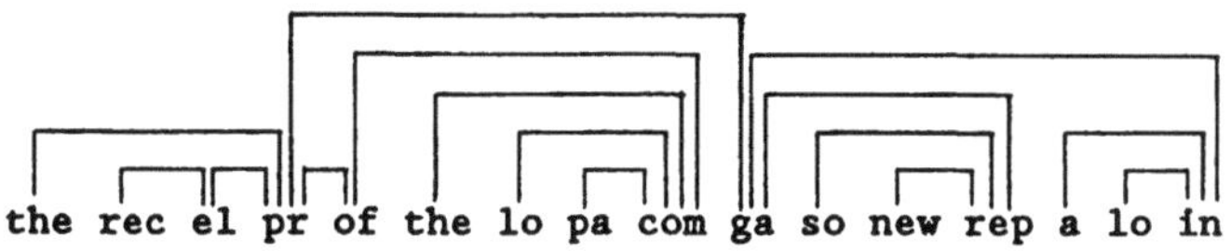

One can also use the second dimension for the words themselves:

[17]

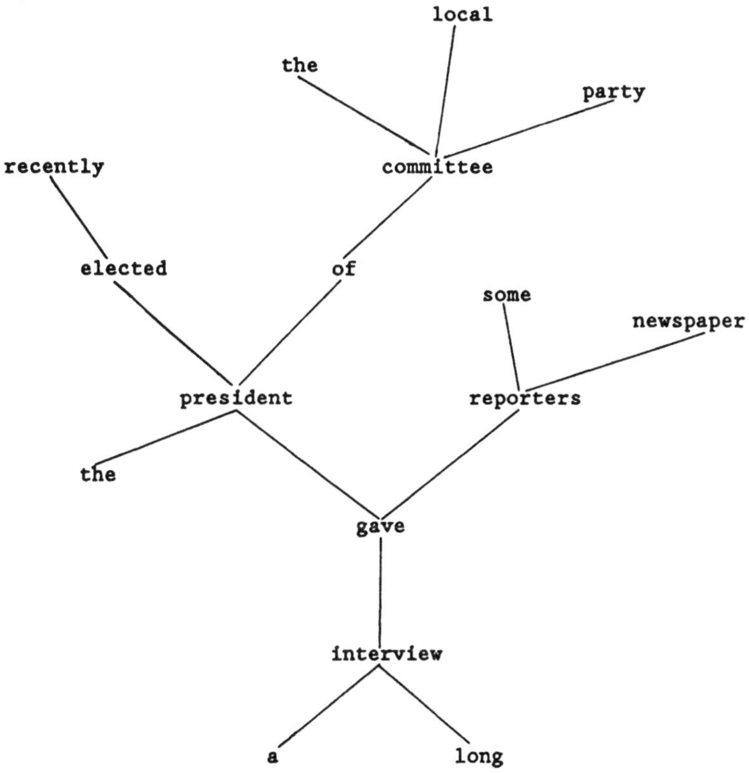

The positioning of a word higher or lower, or to the left or right of another word has no meaning in this diagram. The only things [17] should depict are co-occurrence relations. Words that are linked to a common co-occurrent have been grouped around that word. This is to show which words can be a structural centre for what sort of constructions.

In a structure like [17] one can thus say that a syntagma contains a word with all other words that are, directly or indirectly, linked to it by lines towards the periphery of the diagram. This description will soon be somewhat refined. But before going on, it should be noted that by arranging the diagram in such a way that seems to have some grammatical explanatory function, the concepts of **centre** and **periphery** have been introduced. This gives the syntactic co-occurrence lines a clear **direction**.

Of course a so essential concept as the directedness of co-occurrence relations is not introduced into the theory only because it accidentally came about in a rather intuitive diagram. But what is intuitive in [17] and what is not? The geometry of the diagram is certainly intuitive. [16] displays a totally different geometry, but the same connection lines as [17]. These lines have been drawn to depict an analysis of distributional co-occurrence. They have a function in grammatical explanation. The arrangement of diagram [17] suggest the concepts of centre and periphery, but the same arrangement could, in a graphically perhaps less perspicuous way, be found in [16]: Some words are linked by direct co-occurrence lines and others only indirectly. This observation, arrived at by reasoning over distributional co-occurrence only, can be formulated in a way that is somewhat less abstract and a bit closer to traditional syntactic thinking. As the co-occurence analysis shows, a syntagma is linked to the rest of the sentence via one word. This word - the structural centre of the syntagma - belongs to a word class and has additional syntactic features. The point now is that the syntagma as a whole, when combined with other words and syntagmata in a sentence, in its main syntactic functions behaves in accordance with the word class and the syntactic features of its structural centre.

These observations make the concept of syntagma recursive and thereby allow for a relatively simple structural description even of long and complicated sentences brought about by the generative productivity of language. In this simple description a sentence of arbitrary length consists of a word and possibly one or more dependent syntagmata. Each of these syntagmata in turn consists of a word and, possibly, a few dependent syntagmata. (The use of the relation "consists of" brings the discussion closer to the notion of constituency. Indeed the notion of syntagma is feasible for both constituency and dependency approaches, the main difference being that the syntagmata discussed here have been defined in terms of directed co-occurrence, thus dependency, relations.) In this way it becomes possible with a limited number of structural co-occurrence patterns to describe sentences of unlimited length and complexity.

It is a simple matter of convention that these directed co-occurrence graphs usually are not shown in the fashion of [17] with a centre and a periphery, but as tree structures with a governor at the top and dependents under it. [18] is equivalent to [17] and [16]:

[18]

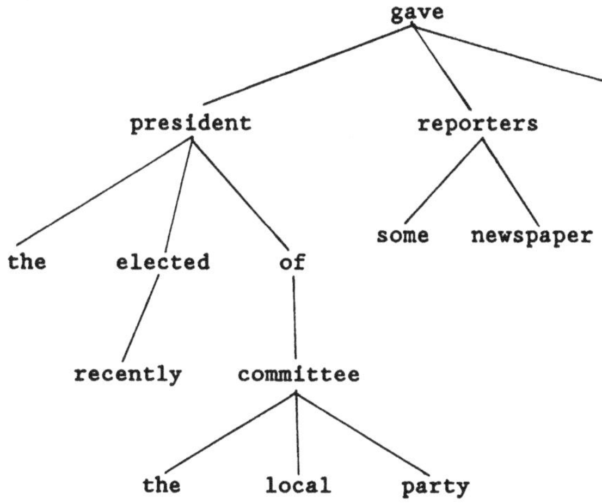

To sum up, the idea to consider the co-occurrence relations among words to be **directed** proves very fruitful. It yields a syntactic description tool that is at the same time elegant and powerful. This makes it desirable to work with **dependency**, defined as **directed co-occurrence**, as the fundamental principle of syntactic analysis.

4.1.3. How to detect dependency

There are alternative definitions of dependency that are based on other criteria than the definition given here. I review some of these definitions in 4.2. and I have already discussed some alternative criteria in 4.1.1. When the present model is used in practical syntactic work, such as writing a dependency syntax of a language or a metataxis for a language pair, it should be carefully kept in mind what the defining principles of dependency in the present model are. In analysing corpus texts and sentences, one always encounters cases where the principles that are so nice and elegant in theory appear to be doubtful or counterintuitive in practical application. A clear idea of the basic definitions is then essential.

Part of the possible hesitation about decisions on dependency relations is due to the fact that the fundamental criteria for dependency, distributional co-occurrence and directedness as defined by the idea of a structural centre, are so abstract. In many concrete cases other criteria, like form determination, almost impose themselves as at first sight more natural or more meaningful choices. **For a translation-oriented model**, however, **cross-linguistically valid concepts are indispensable**. A consideration of the degree of abstraction displayed by descriptions of tentative language universals shows that such language-independent criteria cannot be other than abstract. But since principles of this kind may entail difficulties for practical work, a somewhat more explicit account of some problematic choices should be given.

In 4.1.1. I discuss the sentence

[7] **Very interesting people arrive.**

and show that the noun people should be taken as the internal governor of the syntagma very interesting people because the syntagma as a whole combines with other words as if it were a noun. This is an argument for considering very and interesting (direct or indirect) dependents of people, but it does not yet say anything about whether people should depend on arrive or govern it. When discussing the sentence in 4.1.1., I use only the obvious cases, speaking only about those words that can be omitted, the sentence still remaining correct. Indeed, since very occurs only thanks to the presence of interesting, both the co-occurrence relation and its direction are quite obvious. But if the model is meant to be interesting at all (and, if it is meant to be workable in practice), of course the less obvious cases must be dealt with in a convincing way as well. That people and arrive are co-occurrent is not very doubtful. The question is which direction the co-occurrence relation has.

I have already decided not to use form determination as a criterion, but it may be interesting to recall that it would not solve this problem anyway. Very interesting people can be paradigmatically replaced by they, but not by them. This is due to form determination from the verb. But at the same time the verb does not carry the s ending of the third person singular, which is due to the pronoun or noun. In other words, there are two distinct form determinations with opposite directions.

According to the principles formulated above, the role of governor should be assigned to the word which is the structural centre of the sentence. By discussing only simple cases in my first approach (in 4.1.1). I may have created the impression that the role of dependent is always given to that one of two co-occurent words that can be omitted, still leaving a correct sentence. Normally this is a good guideline indeed, but it should be borne in mind that **omissibility** is not part of the definition of dependency. There are two reasons for this. Firstly, either word in a co-occurrent pair might be omissible if the other one is present, especially if constructions traditionally termed "elliptic" are taken into consideration (see 4.11.). Secondly, it often happens that neither of two co-occurring words are omissible. In English, the latter is normally true for the cases referred to above: a finite verb and its subject.

A solution might be found in formulating additional criteria for a dependency relation, although this entails the danger of ad hoc refinements of the definition. A solution may also be found in arbitrary decisions. But before these two possibilities are taken into consideration, maybe there is still a way to find evidence in the definition of dependency as given before. Such a solution, based on the unchanged definition only, would of course be by far preferable and would support this definition.

The field worker's dream (4.1.1.) shows how the two word groups discussed here have been arrived at: by forming syntactic paradigms. If carried out for English, this process yields a group of words that can be labelled subjects and another group that co-occur with subjects. The paradigm method also furnishes the model with the first classification of words: word classes. A closer look not only at the two groups of subjects and subject companions, but at all co-occurrence paradigms in the analysed English corpus, shows that the subject companions belong to one word class, verbs, whereas the subjects belong to several word classes, namely nouns, pronouns, gerunds, the internal governors of certain subordinate clauses (e.g. that clauses) etc. These words have been attributed to different word classes because they are not in all their occurrences paradigmatically interchangeable, but only in the subject constellation.

This is the cue that was being looked for. If the co-occurrence relation in question is characteristic for one word class, it is in fact part of the distributional pattern that is the definition of that class. The description becomes much simpler, if that word of the two candidates that is characterised by the given co-occurrence relation is taken as the governor. Therefore, in the given example the verb should be taken as the governor and the subject as a dependent. Co-occurrence with a subject is characteristic of a verb, but co-occurrence with a verb is not so characteristic of a noun, since also pronouns, etc. co-occur with verbs.

When motivating (in 4.1.2.) the need of directedness in the definition of dependency, I said that there is always one word in a syntagma that caters for the syntactic link to the outside structure. Why not simply apply this to the verb-subject problem? Indeed, as far as dependency structure is concerned - at the hardly detailed level of analysis reached so far - there is no fundamental difference between a sentence and a syntagma. They both consist of a word with dependent syntagmata. (These syntagmata may consist of one or more words, and there may even be no dependent syntagmata at all.) Applying the outside-link criterion to sentences, it is possible to ask how a sentence as a whole can combine with other words. In principle, this certainly is a good way of solving the problem, but in practice it leads deep into the discussions of a bundle of other problematic cases. I accordingly postpone this approach until later sections (especially 4.8. to 4.11.). The constructions in question are those with several finite verbs in one sentence, such as sentences with relative and other subordinate clauses, coordinated sentences and, especially in connection with coordination, elliptic constructions. And if the step beyond sentence boundaries is taken, a wide range of inter-sentence relationships can of course be studied at the text level.

The method sketched above works for English, but one cannot be sure that all co-occurrence relations in all languages happen to hold between members of a single word class on the one hand and members of several classes on the other hand. There must even be a way out when this criterion fails. In the above paragraphs and sections I have quite often used words such as "decide", "assign", "consider" and the like. These choices suggest that ultimately the direction of a co-occurrence relation is the result of an **arbitrary decision** taken by the grammarian. What I have given above are not so much proofs of objective facts, as motives for purposeful decisions. This insight makes it easy to postulate that in the present model **all syntactic relations are dependency relations**, in other words, there are no undirected co-occurrence relations and thus no relations involving **interdependency**. If no other help can be found, the grammarian has to decide arbitrarily. And often there are valid motives for several alternative decisions.

In the same sense, decision for the present model that **a word must not be governed by more than one governor** is arbitrary. The motivation for this decision is given in 4.7.

4.2. Alternative definitions of dependency

In the previous section I have totally refrained from referring to other scholars' findings, although my definition of dependency owes a lot to the work done by others. I now take up a few alternative dependency definitions and at the same time supplement the appropriate references.

In his characteristic style, Tesnière provides a very well illustrated "result grammar", but without much discussion (Baum 1976: 5). He then (1959/1982: 13) simply states that the "connexions" establish **dependency** relations ("dépendance") between words, and thus are directed. Again, he does not tell his readers how the direction is determined. A careful study of his work yields three criteria:

- form determination,
- analogy and
- semantics.

Normally Tesnière appears to decide on grounds of **form determination** such as form government and agreement (see 4.1.3.). This can be seen from his way of arguing, and it is explicit in a very few hidden instances where he says that there is a dependency relation between two words and in passing mentions that "l'accord l'indique" (e.g. Tesnière 1959/1982: 43). In cases where such influence is absent, as in many of his English examples, he apparently decides by analogy to languages that have such an influence in a comparable structure (see stemmas 12 [French] and 13 [English], Tesnière 1959/1982: 23).

In principle Tesnière conceives syntax and **semantics** as independent levels of language analysis (and his concept of semantics is even related to extralinguistic fields such as psychology and logic). But there is a parallelism between the two, says Tesnière (1959/1982: 41ff.), in such a way that the lines of semantic relations coincide with those of syntactic dependency, the difference being that the direction may differ. His example is:

[19] **Les petits ruisseaux font les grandes rivières.**
'the small brooks make the big rivers'

which he analyses as (Tesnière 1959/1982: 19):

[20]

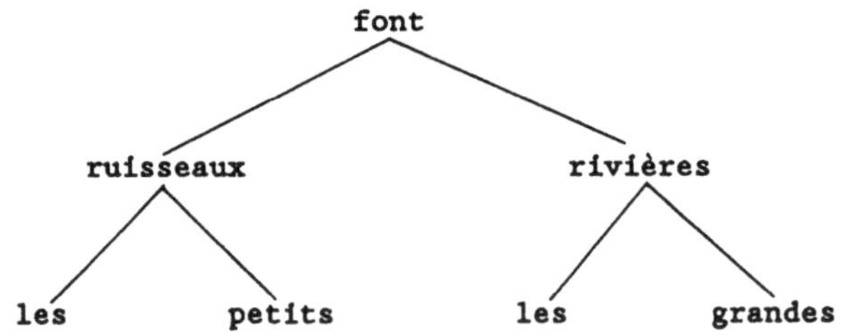

saying (Tesnière 1959/1982: 43) that syntactically <u>petits</u> depends on <u>ruisseaux</u> and <u>grandes</u> on <u>rivières</u> ("l'accord l'indique"), while semantically <u>petits</u> and <u>grandes</u> contain predications about <u>ruisseaux</u> and <u>rivières</u>, respectively, and thus take them as dependent arguments in a semantic structure.

In cases, however, where there is form determination from several sides (see 4.1.1.), Tesnière does not let a word depend on several governors, but on one only:

[21]	Latin:	**Romani**	**creauerunt**	**Ciceronem**	**consulem.**
		nominative		accusative	accusative
		'the-Romans	made	Cicero	a-consul'

becomes (Tesnière 1959/1982: 163):

[22]

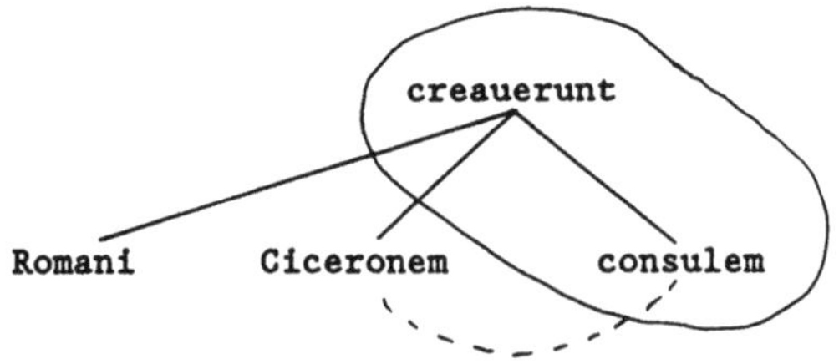

His decision has been brought about by analogy to other structures where the verb is the structural centre. One may also suppose that he was influenced by semantic or logical predicator-argument relations which made it preferable to take the verb as the predicator. But in these cases the precise role of semantic indications in Tesnière's thinking is not clear to me.

However, Tesnières decisions are certainly bound to predicator-argument considerations when he deals with sentences where the same two words without any morphological change can merely by means of sequential ordering (which is also a syntactic means) be arranged either as a sentence or as a syntagma without sentence status. There are Russian examples, although these do show some form difference, namely the alternation between the long and short forms of adjectives. The clearest example seems to be the one Tesnière (1959/1982: 156) quotes from Zyrian (also kalled Komi, a Finno-Ugric language) with the words bur 'bon' and ki̊v 'langue' (in order not to make the translation worse, I use Tesnière's French glosses):

[23] **bur** **ki̊v**
'une-bonne langue'

[24]

[25] **Ki̊v** **bur.**
'la-langue est-bonne'

[26]

Tesnières "Éléments" were first read in the early sixties, a period of vigorous activity in computational linguistics, especially machine translation (see 7.1.). In those years, mathematical exactitude was in vogue in linguistics. Klaus Baumgärtner (1970) tackles the definition of dependency in such a spirit. I have already mentioned (2.2.) that Baumgärtner links not only constituency, but also dependency to the idea of contiguity, which makes his dependency a special case of constituency (Baumgärtner 1970: 54). Baumgärtner's definition is because of this feature incompatible with Tesnière's. But apart from that, Baumgärtner adheres to the logical notions of necessity and sufficiency. He thus builds his system on the idea that one word (or morpheme) presupposes another one. Baumgärtner illustrates this only with pairs of words whereof one is omissible, but it appears that his definition is meant to apply to all dependency relations.

Several authors seem more or less explicitly to take omissibility as the deciding criterion for establishing dependency relations. The theoretical explanation in those works often in one way or other rewords the idea of words being either sufficient or necessary for their counterpart, but the illustrations and the practical application of the definition are in many works confined to cases of omissible words. Henrik Nikula's description (1986: 13) may be taken to represent this type of a very clear-cut, but maybe not always fully comprehensive account. Zellig Harris (1982: 2) formulates a similar definition, but after that point his grammar and dependency syntax diverge.

Many other authors write about dependency grammar taking the very definition of dependency for granted (most explicitly, e.g. Maas, 1974: 257). This need not necessarily be seen as a shortcoming, it can well have to do with the general Tesnière'ian tendency in this grammatical direction not to be at first hand interested in grammatical theory, but in results.

Igor' Mel'čuk (1979a: 10ff.; cf. Mel'čuk / Percov 1987: 53ff.) defines dependency as a binary relation that is based on **syntactic influence**. This is not exactly the influence I call form determination (see 4.1.3.). According to Mel'čuk (1979a: 7ff.), the grammatical means of language are lexical and non-lexical ones, and the lexical ones include linear order, prosody and inflection. They can be used both for semantic and for syntactic functions. Mel'čuk says that there are no other means besides these three. Mutual influence, the concept that defines Mel'čuk's notion of dependency, includes all three types of means together, provided that they are used syntactically. The problem of form determination from several sides is resolved by the remark that in such cases not all the influences are syntactic, but some may be semantic or morphological (Mel'čuk 1979a: 13). As far as I am acquainted with the numerous works with Mel'čuk as one of the authors, I am not aware of any answer to the following two questions: Is there any certainty that always exactly one of the detected influences is syntactic? And: Given that Mel'čuk makes only a binary distinction between syntactic and semantic means, what is the role of "morphological dependencies" (Mel'čuk 1979a: 13), if they are neither syntactic, nor semantic?

Mel'čuk's dependency lines are thus established by virtue of "mutual influence". In addition, Mel'čuk's definition (1979a: 11) requires that the relations be **directed**, which makes them true dependencies. Yet, the motive he gives for this need is quite different from that of other authors'. Mel'čuk removes all syntactic marking, such as word order or morphological forms, from the words in his dependency trees. These features were used for recognising one of two words as the dependent, and since the identifying features are thrown away, the dependence must be indicated in another way. This is done by making the relations directed. Thus we have a motivation for using directed relations in the first place, but not a procedure for saying how the choice of direction is made. I have not found any explicit ideas from Mel'čuk on this question.

My own definition of dependency (4.1.) relies mostly on the work of Ulrich Engel (1977/1982). Engel (1982: 29) starts out with the concept of "**Konkomitanz**". In the model I describe in this study, **co-occurrence** is defined in an attempt to make Engel's concomitance (and thereby also Tesnière's "connexion") more palpable and testable, especially with the aim of cross-linguistic applicability. Although the notion "dream" may seem to exclude the possibility of objectivity, the field worker's dream (4.1.1.) is meant as an objective description of the concept of co-occurrence. If it appears in the shape of a "dream", this is not because the working procedure described in it is subjective, but because it is so uncommon to take such an a priori look at language structure, in particular when the language in question is well-known.

Engel then (1982: 31) gives concomitance a direction, turning it into a **dependency** relation. Of all dependency grammarians whose works I have consulted, Engel is by far the most unequivocal and clear about the **arbitrariness** of the grammarian's decisions on the directedness of syntactic relations (Engel 1982: 32). Indeed, my work on the present model has profited much from the conceptual clarity in Engel's book.

Richard Hudson's definitions are very close to Engel's. He speaks about "companion-ship" and says that it "is more than mere co-occurrence: it is a matter of co-occurrence sanctioned explicitly by the grammar" (Hudson 1984: 76). The notion of distributional co-occurrence I am using is meant to capture this grammatical sanction (see 4.3. second step). Also Hudson gives his companionship relation a direction and speaks about "head" and "modifier" (rather than "governor" and "dependent"). In Hudson's description (1984: 77f.) the idea is found that the governor of a syntagma provides the outside link to the rest of the sentence (see 4.1.2.).

An overview of various definitions and systems of dependency is found in Jarmo Korhonen's book (1977: 40ff.).

4.3. Word classes

Word classes belong to those familiar things in grammar that are seldom defined. Most scholars tacitly take over the traditional system of word classes which exists at least for those languages whose grammarians have been under Greek-Latin influence. In principle there is not much reason to object to this procedure, but as the present model emphatically relies on form, and form only, there needs to be a guarantee that a traditional word classification does not import semantic imponderables into the model. This is important not only because a purely syntactic model is theoretically nicer, but to at least the same extent because semantic factors would introduce an element of uncertainty and vagueness that cannot be handled with the formal means available in this model. Since a dependency syntax written in accordance with the present model should be translation-oriented and ready to be linked to a complex rule system, called metataxis, unhandleable features that might have unforeseen consequences in the metataxis process should be kept out of the description.

But is a redefinition of word classes really necessary? As is shown in the field worker's dream (4.1.1.), the establishment of word classes is closely intertwined with the detection of dependency relations. These two can thus be taken as the fundamental categories of the syntax model, and as a weak fundament would make the whole building instable, some clarification seems expedient.

If made explicit at all, word class definitions often rely on a combination of criteria taken from different levels of grammar, such as morphology, syntax and semantics, and sometimes even extragrammatical indications, for instance from logic, are used. Tesnière (1959/1982: 52) points out that such competing criteria cannot lead to a good classification. Engel (1982: 86f.) especially criticises frequent attempts to define word classes semantically in terms of a basic meaning. A characteristic quotation from his argument takes up two nouns usually taken to describe the basic meaning of verbs: "Bezeichnet aber nicht auch das Wort _Tätigkeit_ eine Tätigkeit, das Wort _Vorgang_ einen Vorgang?" He is also critical of distributional definitions, but as he himself defines word classes in terms of combinability with morphemes and other words (which is a distributional approach as well), his criticism seems to be restricted to the more simplistic distributional definitions. The details of Engel's method are much too specific for the language he deals with,

German, to be taken as cross-linguistically valid criteria. I therefore base my metataxis-oriented solution on the notion of distributional co-occurrence.

In the present model, **word classes** are defined in terms of **paradigms of syntactic dependency patterns**. This has in a rough and preliminary manner been described already in 4.1.1., and the exact procedure of reasoning can now be spelt out in somewhat more detail.

First step: **Detecting mere co-occurrence**. The establishment of word classes is in 4.1.1. described in the imaginary situation of how a large corpus of texts in an unknown language is analysed. Word and sentence limits are taken for given. The field worker now at first hand makes lists of words that appear in the same sentence. These observations may be refined in several ways. For instance one could first look at two-word sets, then three-word sets etc. In addition, it may be interesting to check whether any meaningful results derive from distinguishing words that are adjacent or non-adjacent in a sentence, or one might measure the distance between two co-occurrent words, take into account whether they occur before or after each other and so on. The type of co-occurrence discovered in this way is indeed not yet what I termed co-occurrence in 4.1., but rather Hudson's "mere co-occurrence" (1984: 76). There are many ways to go on refining the analysis, depending on what forms and regularities are found in the first steps. An attempt may be made to analyse the words themselves and to establish morpheme boundaries; similar-looking words might be taken as forms of one root; and function morphemes may be identified (see 4.6.).

Second step: **Identifying grammatically significant co-occurrence**. The whole exercise of classifying words is interwoven with the search for co-occurrence relations (which in a later stage are viewed as dependencies). What one will discover first are "mere co-occurrences". As the analysis proceeds, a class of significantly frequent "mere co-occurrences" will emerge which - if the corpus is large enough and has a sufficient coverage of diverse text types - can in a first approach be considered to be the co-occurrences "sanctioned explicitly by the grammar" (Hudson 1984: 76). These are co-occurrences proper, or companion-ships as Hudson terms them.

Third step: **Establishing co-occurrence patterns**. When the co-occurrents (or companions) of a given word are studied, those that form a **paradigm** (see 4.1.1.) are grouped in one set of co-occurrents. As not all co-occurrents of a word have paradigmatic relations with each other, many words have not only one set of co-occurrents, but several distinct ones.

These sets may have common elements. The ensemble of sets of co-occurrents of one word is what I call the **co-occurrence pattern** of that word.

Fourth step: **Reviewing the half-way result.** Having dealt with all the words of the corpus, one can group those words together that have coincident co-occurrence patterns. If one carries out the sketched analysis very exactly, the result will be a huge number of different groups of words, characterised by common co-occurrence patterns. The number of such groups will be enormous, but the content of each group will be very small. Many groups will contain only one word. A grammar, however, that has to list nearly every word separately and give its combination rules, has failed to capture the **regularity** that makes language a system that can be productively used by humans. It is a characteristic of human languages that the combinatorial rules for different elements of the system have much in common. The structure of language is to a high degree regular.

Fifth step: **Accounting for regularity.** If the analysis described so far has yielded very many very small groups of words all with different co-occurrence patterns, in accordance with what was said about regularity, the co-occurrence patterns of different words nevertheless must have many common properties. The sets that make up the co-occurrence patterns of words will have common elements, and especially the frequent elements will occur in many sets. The next step is, therefore, accounting for regularity. The number of groups with common patterns is reduced by allowing not only for totally, but also for partially coincident patterns. Exactly what kinds of partial coincidence are to be preferred or to be tried first is a decision that plays an important role for the outcome of the process. In order not to drown in the details of a field worker's manual, however, I do not work out this here. If the reduction process is pursued until a number of groups approximately between ten and twenty is left, one has arrived at a system of word classes.

Sixth step: **Analysing the final results.** To review the results of the exercise, one can ask what has been obtained. The outcome is on the one hand word classes, i.e. groups of words that are characterised by similar, but not totally coincident co-occurrence patterns. On the other hand, another product is delivered: the co-occurrence patterns, and in particular the sets of words that make up the patterns. I return to these sets in 4.4. when defining dependency types.

As this procedure for defining word classes on distributional grounds is shown split up into a number of steps, an interesting feature comes into focus: The first three steps can be said to be relatively objective and not yet too much directed by the analyst's decisions. But as soon as the idea of **regularity** enters the reasoning, on cue the grammarian's **arbitrariness** turns up again. This is less surprising than it may seem to be. It goes without saying that there is regularity in grammar. But a human language is always changing and developing, so that hardly ever a major grammatical phenomenon exactly follows a single rule. Normally there are competing rules, relicts of older rules, interferences with rules on different levels, etc. What exactly the rules are that describe a given status of a language system, has much to do with the grammarian's decisions. The fewer instances a rule is meant to cover, the more elegant it can be. The higher its coverage, on the other hand, the more complicated a rule tends to become. It is the grammarian who decides where between these poles to settle a specific description of regularity in grammar.

In this spirit it is obvious that the definitions adopted for the present model are not meant to be better or truer than others in an absolute, objective sense. I only maintain that they are better than other definitions suited for the present purpose.

The word classification attained by reasoning along the lines of the six-step procedure will, if based on appropriate grammatical decisions, not depart too much from what a traditional description would be. That is, the classes the corpus words are allotted to will not differ much from the traditional ones **for most of the words**. This is due to the phenomenon captured by Tesnière (1959/1982: 53) in his distinction of "mots pleins" and "mots vides", or, as I prefer to call them, **content words** and **function words**. Tesnière's account for the distinction is clear-cut as always, but thereby also vague: "Les mots **pleins** sont ceux qui sont **chargés d'une fonction sémantique**". The distinction of content and function words is not uncommon in grammar. It comes down to labelling **verbs, adjectives, adverbs** and **nouns** as content words, and all the rest as function words. There is much to say about that distinction, but it may suffice here to mention just one objectively observeable feature of these word classes that motivates the distinction: Language development can most easily access those elements in the system of a language the speakers are conscious about. These are words (rather than endings, grammatical rules etc.), and in particular words with a clear meaning such as a process, a quality or a thing, rather than a relation between two semantic units. To put it differently, the words most open to change are "ceux qui sont chargés d'une fonction sémantique". Content words are therefore the **open word classes** into which newly created or borrowed words easily enter. New function words may emerge as well, but this is significantly less frequent and usually a new function word does not come from outside the language, as a content word may, but is by way of functionalisation taken from the stock of content words already present in the language. Tamis (1986: 8) points out that (French) interjections are an open class, too. In my opinion, this does not disprove what is said above, since interjections are a special case, because they usually do not fulfil syntactic functions in the way "normal" function words do. There are other criteria for distinguishing function and content words, e.g. frequency (cf. Zampolli 1977: 330ff.).

In the same way as traditional word classifications, the present one allows for words belonging to several word classes simultaneously. In very many languages the sketched word classification system will thus yield the four content word classes in much the same way as traditional approaches do. The function words, however, in many languages display so diverse combinability, that a different approach seems to be absolutely necessary. As their name suggests, the function words are crucial to the description of syntactic functions. They have a low type frequency, but an overwhelmingly high token frequency. A thorough account of their classification is therefore inevitable as a premise for the next steps towards translation syntax.

4.4. Dependency types

A system, for instance a syntactic system, can be described in terms of its elements and the relations among them (see 2.2.). The most basic elements of a syntactic system are at first hand words. In principle, all linguistic signs are elements of the system, but the most important of them are words. I take up other signs, such as morphemes etc., in 4.6. (see also 5.2.). Section 4.3. is dedicated to the task of classifying words, and the present section is about the relations among the words.

These relations make all the difference. The syntactic relations determine whether a long string of words is understood as a senseless list of words or as a sentence. Let me repeat: I maintain that **the syntactic relations make a sentence a sentence**. If only the words used in a sentence exist in the language and these words are arranged in accordance with the syntax of the language, then the sentence has a meaning and can be understood. Maybe the sentence does not seem "meaningful" or contains nonsense, but in order to arrive at this judgement one must first interpret it, and this implies that it has an interpretable content. Maybe its content is illogical or impossible or unlikely; maybe its message can only be imagined in a science fiction context or in a possible world, and maybe pragmatic implicature is needed to interpret violations of semantic combination restrictions - but all this does not alter the fact that the sentence has a content as soon as all its words are linked up by syntactic relations.

With this claim about the role of syntax I certainly do not intend to say that only sentences or texts that conform to a prescriptive or normative grammar are correct. Even ill-formed utterances can be understood and are (parts of) sentences in this sense. Language is a system of competing layers of rules, so hearers and readers are used to adapting their understanding to a speaker's or writer's "deviant" variety.

The choice of **dependency** the syntactic relation used in the present model has already been discussed and motivated. A more careful account of the syntactic structures of sentences requires not only the words, but also the dependency relations among them to be distinguished and classified. For this purpose, different dependency types are established. The following three subsections deal with the definition of **dependency types**, the distinction between **complements** and **adjuncts** and the problem of **valency**, respectively.

4.4.1. A definition of dependency types

The definitions of word classes and co-occurrence relations have been set up in such a way that they mutually determine each other (4.1.1. and 4.3.). The sixth step of this process (4.3.) yields not only word classes, but at the same time co-occurrence patterns. These patterns are made up of sets of words that co-occur with a given word in the corpus (third step) and, after generalisation (fifth step), they consist of sets of co-occurrents of a word class. The condition that was mentioned in the second step is still in force: A set of co-occurrents of a word class includes only words and syntagmata that are **paradigmatically** related to each other, and therefore a word class has not only one, but several sets of co-occurrents. From these distinguishable sets, a process of three steps leads towards a definition of dependency types. These three are:

- tidying up the network of co-occurrence relations by applying the idea of dependency,
- carefully comparing and sorting the sets that are left and
- labelling the sets.

The described process has brought about a network of co-occurrence relations. A first step to tidy it up has already been done: The grammatically insignificant co-occurrence relations, "mere co-occurrences", were sorted out (4.3. second step).

[27]

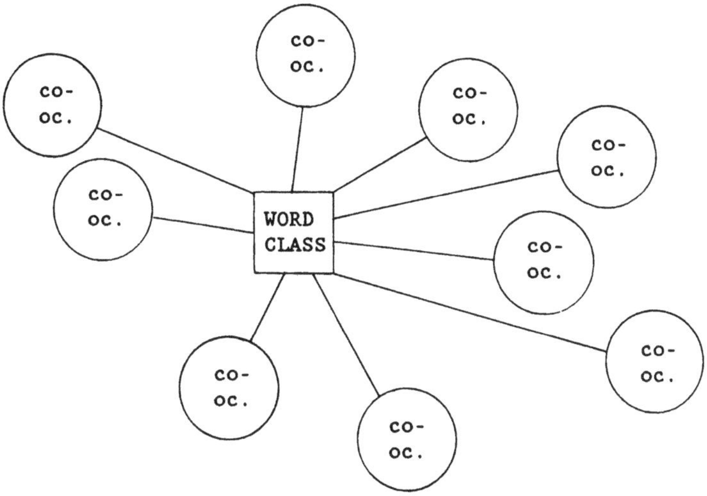

But still the relations list co-occurrences, not dependencies. The step from co-occurrence to dependency relations implies not only that the relations become directed in the way described in 4.1.2., but also that half of the relations can be abandoned. They are redundant, because each relation between any two words has been listed with each of the words. Having decided on the direction of the relation and thus having found in each pair of co-occurrent words a **governor** and a **dependent**, one can either note what the possible dependents of a given governor are or vice versa, but need no longer do both. The decisions made in 4.1.3. indicate which option to choose: The direction of the dependency relation has been established so that the relation is characteristic for the word class of the governor, but not necessarily for the dependent. Therefore, from now on the dependency syntax will from now on only state **what the possible dependents of a word class are**, but not what are its governors are. The latter information is in turn found with each of the governors in question.

[28]

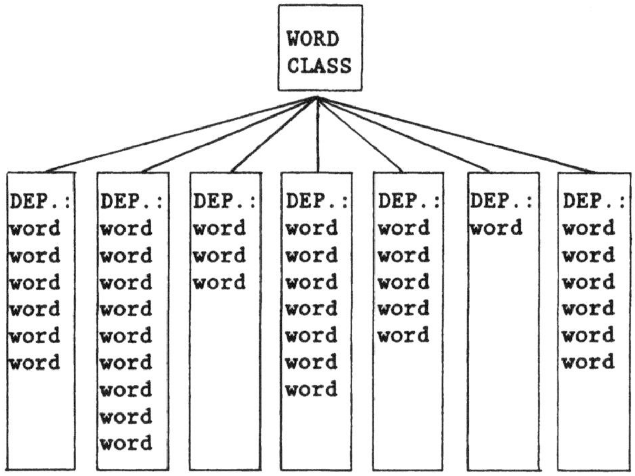

Suppose that thirteen word classes are left after the information about governors has been removed and that each of them has seven distinct sets of dependents. One might feel tempted to assign 91 labels to these sets.

[29]

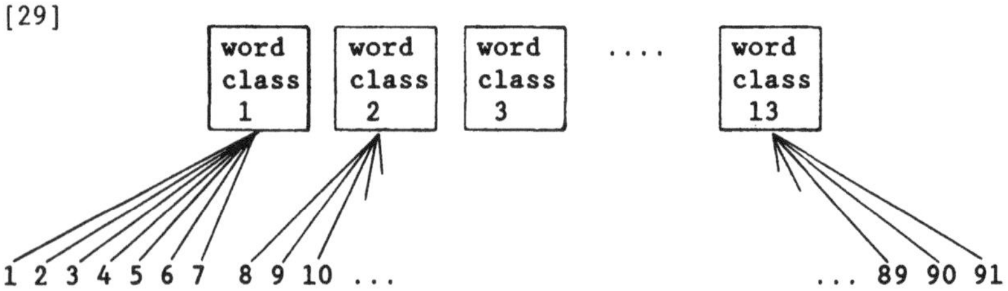

Such an approach, however, again fails to capture much of the regularity that can be found in the system. Many of the 91 sets will coincide except for the use of different governors. In the case of a large-scale corpus analysis yielding these 91 sets, in practice most likely none of the sets will literally coincide. In a similar way as in 4.3., fifth step, it must therefore now be made explicit in what features dependent sets should coincide in order to be merged into one dependency type.

The degree of abstraction adopted in 4.3. can help here as well. Let each word be a representative of its word class. The dependent sets then no longer contain words, but only word classes.

[30]

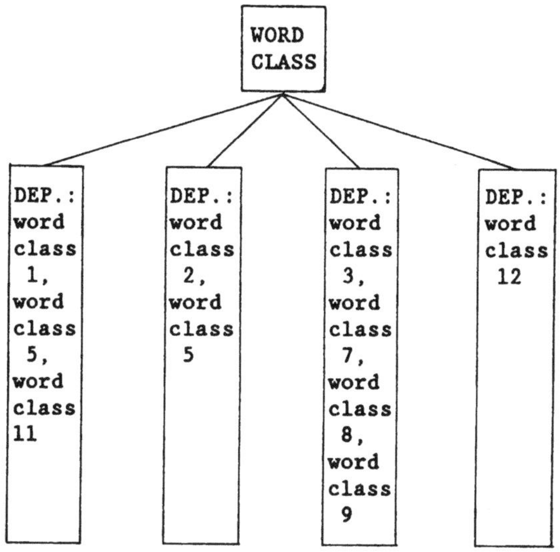

In many languages, however, such high abstraction goes one step too far. The aim of merging dependent sets is to find coincidences among the dependents of different word classes.

[31]

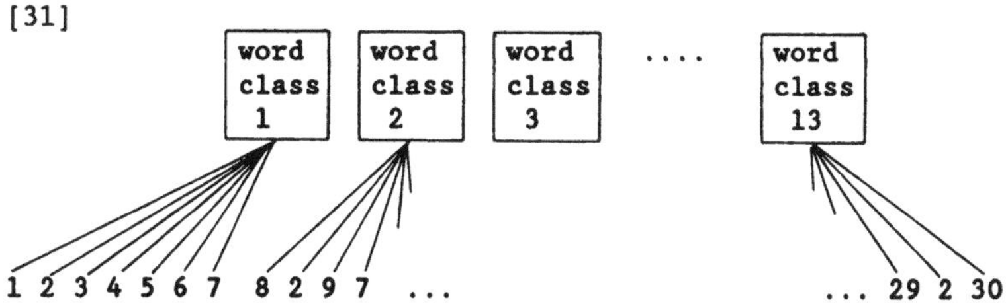

The abstraction required for this purpose does too much, in the same way as merging two dependent sets of the same governor does too much.

[32]

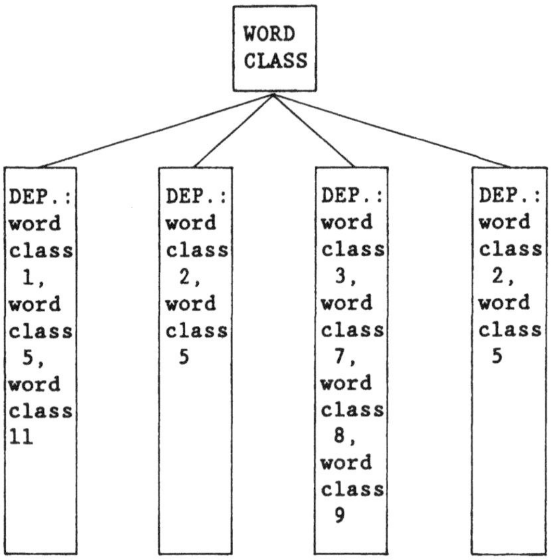

This must be avoided, because the requirement of **paradigmatic** relations among the members of a dependent set (dependency type), given a certain governor, is essential. But since word classes are defined by dependency patterns, how can it be that the word class level now turns out to be too abstract? The answer is hidden in the first step of the word class-defining process in 4.3.: If that analysis goes down to word level and groups different words with a common root as forms of one word (which makes sense especially in languages with morphological forms), words that are in complementary distribution have been grouped together in one word class and thereby are not paradigmatically interchangeable. Of course this is a very appropriate step in word classification, but it entails the need of distinguishing **syntactic forms** of words when paradigmatically defined dependency types are at issue.

Sets of dependents of different governors can thus be said to coincide when their elements coincide in **word class** and **syntactic form**. Dependents that meet this requirement are taken to belong to one **dependency type**.

This does not mean that the elements of a dependency type must all belong to one word class. But if dependent set A contains only nouns and adjectives of a certain case form, then dependent set B is considered to coincide with A, only if B also contains nouns and adjectives of the same case form and no other words.

What is **syntactic form**? Given the definition of syntax adopted for the present model, syntactic form includes both **morphological**

form (in part even word formation) and **word order**. Which one of the two plays what role depends on specific features of the language in question. Mel'čuk (1979a: 8) considers as a third form type prosody, but as I am in this study mainly interested in written language, I do not take up phonetic and phonemic phenomena, although they in principle very well may function in syntax. Which particular features of syntactic form should be considered in merging dependent sets into dependency types is determined by the requirement that the members of one dependency type, given a governor, must maintain their paradigmatic relationship with each other.

When the merging process has been pursued as far as possible without violating the paradigm requirement, **dependency types** are established and can be given names. These names describe the **syntactic function** of the words belonging to a particular dependency type. In this way, an intermediate level has been established between the syntactic form of a governor and the syntactic form of a dependent. It is a characteristic feature of dependency syntax (and of the present model) that this level of syntactic function is made very explicit. This is one of the arguments for choosing the dependency approach for machine translation: The structural transfer in translation, **metataxis**, is easiest described in terms of syntactic function, rather than syntactic form directly (see 5.6.).

The level of syntactic function between the syntactic form of the governor and the syntactic form of its dependents crucially contributes to keeping the system perspicuous and cross-linguistically applicable. In addition, it makes up the metataxis-directedness of this syntactic model. It is the lack of such an intermediate level that makes the form-to-form mappings in Gross's work (1975: 233ff.) so voluminous and, ultimately, so subjective. Gross's method is criticised among others by Busse and Dubost (1977: VIII), but their own French verb valency dictionary follows in many ways the lines of Gross's form-to-form approach.

It is quite expedient to use traditional names for dependency types, insofar as such names are available. "Subject", "object" etc. are such names for syntactic functions. The desire to model the regularity of the system in a syntactic description of a given language even at the expense of complete coverage of the rules leads to a distinction of dependency types that should be taken into consideration before dependency types are actually given their names. This distinction is taken up in the next subsection.

4.4.2. Complements and adjuncts

When defining word classes in a six-step process (4.3.), not only words with totally coincident dependency patterns are grouped together, but also words with similar patterns (fifth step). The decision about how far to go in this direction is determined by the desire to arrive at a word classification that should be similar to the traditional one, as far as content words are concerned, but should reclassify function words more exactly according to the needs of form-oriented dependency syntax. If this is the aim, the dependency patterns are confined to partial coincidence not only when they contain words, but stay so even when they have been abstracted to dependency types, thus contain only word classes with syntactic form features.

This means that, although word classes are defined in terms of dependency patterns, not each word of a class needs to have the full pattern that is characteristic for the class. The reason for this is the observation that in this way a good deal of the **regularity** in language can be captured. This regularity would be missed if precise coincidence of dependency patterns were required. This is, again, an instance of the general phenomenon that in syntax arbitrary but purposeful decisions are necessary.

Dependency patterns describe the capacity of words to **govern** other words, i.e. to have certain dependents. They state which dependency types can be governed by words from a given word class. But as is shown in the above paragraphs, a description of the government capacity of a word class does not imply that each individual word from the class has exactly that government capacity. So does one have to build up a **dictionary** with the government capacity of each word indicated? If this were so, the attempt to capture regularity would lead to exactly the result that was meant to be avoided (see 4.3. fourth step): a grammar about individual words instead of about general regularities. But fortunately the word class-defining process still guarantees a certain degree of coincidence among the governing capacities of words from the same word class. The individuality of words does not concern all dependency types the word class can govern, but only some of them.

For each word class, the dependency types that can possibly be governed can thus be divided up into two groups: Some of them are common to whole class, while others can be governed by only part of the word class.

This does not mean that the common dependents must always occur, neither that every word from the word class must have such a dependent in a corpus. All that is said here is about a syntactic **capacity** to govern.

Should there accordingly be a **dictionary** with the governing capacity of each individual word, at least as regards the latter group of dependency types? In principle yes. However, individuality is restricted also in this respect. It is not necessary to expect each word to have an individual governing capacity which is totally distinct from all other words' in the word class, but in fact there are within a word class **subclasses** with common governing capacities. In principle, a dictionary with information about governing capacity is necessary, but in practice most of that information can be formulated in **lexical redundancy rules**.

In the present model **subclass-specific dependency types are called complements**, whereas **dependency types, common to a whole word class, are called adjuncts**.

This distinction has its own history in dependency grammar. It is derived from Tesnière's distinction between **"actants"** and **"circonstants"**. Tesnière (1959/1982: 102) formulates the distinction only with respect to the dependents of a verb as the main governor of a sentence. His definition is semantic. He says that "actants" in some way or other participate in the event expressed in the verb, whereas the "circonstants" describe the circumstances, such as place, time, etc. In German, the main publication language of dependency grammar, the most frequently used terms are <u>Ergänzung</u> (Mannheim) or <u>Aktant</u> (Leipzig) on the one hand and <u>Angabe</u> on the other hand. In English <u>complement</u> and <u>adjunct</u> are common. Most authors use the distinction, whereas some have abandoned it (e.g. Hudson 1984: 77).

But although the distinction is widely used, there is no consensus about the definition (and thus about the exact function) of complements and adjuncts. Tesnière describes something that is felt by many grammarians, but seems extremely difficult to define precisely. Tesnière (1959/1982: 102ff.) proceeds directly from his semantic definition to the syntactic form of complements and adjuncts in French, but this definitely does not help when a cross-linguistic definition is sought. Quite a few authors (e.g. Nikula 1986: 17) try to work with the criterion of **structural necessity** in such a way that complements are said to be **obligatory** dependents, while adjuncts are **facultative**. A main problem in this approach is that necessity is difficult to judge, since it plays a role in competing rules systems on different levels such as syntax, semantics and the communicative function of texts (pragmatics).

Engel (1982: 113f.) points to the need for level distinctions in this context and Markku Moilanen (1985) has worked out the problem in more detail, unfortunately without including Engel's findings in the discussion. In any case, the necessity criterion does not divide dependents in the way grammarians feel they should be divided. Helbig and Schenkel (1969/1980: 33ff.) distinguish obligatory complements, facultative complements and free adjuncts, which means that adjuncts always are facultative and complements only in certain cases. This is also recognised by Nikula (cf. also Nikula 1976). The general idea of most grammarians seems to be something like the "central" or "most important" dependents, as opposed to "additional" or "supplementary" ones. This is also what Tesnière tries to capture.

According to Helbig (1982: 26), the essence of the distinction has to be sought in extralinguistic reality. But extralinguistic reality, if it exercises an influence on grammar, has to be dealt with at the pragmatic level of language theory and accordingly cannot, in my opinion, be detected except in concrete utterances in known situations, thus in texts. What is required for a dependency-syntactic model, however, is a description of the permanent, inherent properties words have before the possibilities of ellipsis and implicature on a pragmatic level possibly override the structural requirements. I therefore opt for the distributional definition of the complement-adjunct distinction I have given above. This follows as a self-evident consequence of the strictly form-reliant approach I have chosen for the present model. This definition is taken from Engel (1982: 112).

With the use of the single criterion of subclass-specific government capacity for the complement-adjunct distinction, I have implicitly decided not to follow the approaches of those scholars who establish either a scale or a hierarchy with more than two major classes of dependents (Vater 1978: 39; Somers 1984: 524; Heringer 1985: 97; cf. Eckert 1985), or allow for dependents that stand outside the complement-adjunct distinction (Tarvainen 1985a: 5; but cf. Tarvainen 1986: 186ff.).

Given this definition, the binary distinction between complements and adjuncts is closely related to the next concept: valency.

4.4.3. Valency

"**Valence**" is Tesnière's most famous term. He was neither the only nor the first scholar to use it in linguistics (see 3.5.), but it is certainly due to his work that the term has become so widely known and used. Tesnière's definition of valency is much more restricted than all that has later been made of it. Tesnière (1959/1982: 238) confines valency firstly to verbs as governors and secondly to the **number** of complements the verb can govern. In this spirit, many authors speak about avalent, monovalent, bivalent etc. verbs (e.g. Heger 1966: 143ff.). Kacnel'son (1948: 132) and de Groot (1949: 190ff.) represent in a way the other extreme. In their definitions valency is much broader and concerns not only verbs, but all words that can have syntactic relations to other words. It further describes not only the capacity to govern complements and not even only to govern dependents at all, but quite generally the capacity of having syntactic links. De Groot's syntax is not a dependency syntax, but if one wished to depict his system in dependency terms, one could say that de Groot's valency describes the relationship between a word and both its dependent(s) and governor(s). Kacnel'son uses the term in much the same way.

The definition of valency used in the present model takes elements from several authors. As far as the valency-bearing governor is concerned, I apply the concept of valency in principle to all words, but with respect to the dependents the valency information is about I restrict it to complements: **Valency is subclass-specific government capacity.**

When defined in this way, valency describes exactly that part of a word's government capacity which cannot be inferred from its word class membership. The dependency types a word can govern by virtue of its word class are the adjuncts. Those it can govern by virtue of its valency are the complements. When I in 4.4.1. recommend postponing the final decisions about dependency types until the complement-adjunct distinction has been made clear, I mean two things: Firstly, one might wish to choose the names of the dependency types in such a way that they can easily be identified as either complements or adjuncts. Secondly, it may be advisable not to proceed so far in merging dependent sets (4.4.1.) that one of two merged sets is a complement of its governor, while the other one is an adjunct of another governor. In principle such a pair of dependent sets could be merged if the other requirements are met, but such merger can bring about puzzling situations in practical work, when a single dependency type sometimes is valency-bound and sometimes not.

This is thus the connection point to a topic that is characteristic of this type of syntax: **the interaction of dependency syntax and dictionary**. A syntax of the present model must contain a dictionary with valency information. This information need not be given literally for every word, since a reference to a subclass of words is often sufficient. This subclassifying of words by means of valency patterns comes down to formulating **lexical redundancy rules on valency**.

Although the present model makes explicit use of the complement-adjunct distinction and thereby of a distributionally defined concept of valency, it is worth noting that there in theory is no principal difference between complements and adjuncts or between word class-specific and subclass-specific government. Their important role notwithstanding, these distinctions are brought about by the **arbitrary decisions** that make up the model. If the grammarian decides to have more and smaller word classes, the amount of valency information for each class decreases. If the grammatical decisions tend to lead in the other direction of creating fewer and bigger word classes, valency in consequence becomes more important. If there is only one word class, every information on government is valency, and if there are as many word classes as there are words, no valency is needed at all. Valency information can in many cases be expressed in lexical redundancy rules, but the non-valency government capacity, triggered by word class membership, can also be seen as a form of lexical redundancy rule. Again, the art consists in finding a good compromise between the extremes - one that captures as much of the grammatical regularity as possible. Different purposes may require different compromises.

4.5. Dependency trees

The four previous sections of this chapter describe the foundation of the present model of dependency syntax. 4.1. and 4.2. are about the definition of dependency and 4.3. and 4.4. in terms of that definition describe the elements and the relations, respectively, that make up the syntactic system of a language. The following sections take up some specific problems encountered in practical work on several languages in the framework of the present model.

In the previous sections I discuss mainly the dependency relations in word pairs, but I repeatedly mention that the rules about word pairs, recursively applied, link up the whole sentence to one dependency structure. This section gives a more complete account of what such structures look like (cf. Schubert 1986a: 20ff.).

Each word of a sentence has exactly one governor (see also 4.7.), with the main governor of the whole sentence as the only case of a word that is not governed on sentence level. As a result of the descriptions of the relations between each word and its governor, a structural description of the whole sentence is produced. This structure can now be graphically depicted. As only dependency relations are allowed and as dependency is a directed relation, the result is a directed graph, more precisely, a **tree structure** (see 4.7.). In contrast with the tree structures used in constituency-based grammars, a dependency tree does not contain abstract nodes. In a dependency tree every node carries a word or a morpheme. Consequently, a distinction between terminal and non-terminal nodes is not required. The branches of a dependency tree represent the relation "depends on" upwards or "governs" downwards. In 4.4., the possible dependency relations were classified and labelled, and these labels can now be included in the dependency trees as labels on the branches. If this is done, the syntactic relations that hold in a sentence need not stay implicit and need not be inferred, as Engel seems to think (1982: 31), but can be explicitly stated.

As the idea of contiguity is inherent to constituency grammar, much effort has been invested in accounting also for contiguity (and thereby for word order) in constituency trees. Although this to a large extent can be done successfully (at least for languages with a word order-bound syntax), it is in principle impossible to represent in one tree structure two different relationships among the same elements, e.g. constituency and word order. If this were possible, one of the two relationships would make the other redundant. Constituency grammar runs into serious problems (for which an elaborate apparatus of rules, filters and other tricks has been devised) as soon as the two relationships one wishes to depict simultaneously do not coincide. Typical examples are discontinuous elements, long-distance relations, gapping constructions etc. Dependency trees cannot either represent two relationships in a single tree, but in dependency trees word order does not have to play a role at all. Dependency syntax does not rely on the contiguity principle. Word order may well play a role in syntactic form (see 4.4.1.), but as soon as a word by means of its syntactic form has been assigned a dependency type label, syntactic form has fulfilled its function and need not be rendered in the tree. Dependency trees thus do not represent word order. They are not projective, at least not in the present model. There is a direction in dependency grammar that tries to make dependency trees projective (Ihm / Lecerf 1963; Hays 1964a; Kunze 1975), but for this purpose a complicated system of information on tree geometry is required which, in my view, is not necessary, at least not for the purpose of translation (but see 5.4.).

On the following pages, I give a few specimens of dependency trees that conform to the present model. They all presuppose a dependency syntax of the language in question. Where I do not have such a description at hand my labellings are tentative. The trees display some features that are explained and motivated in more detail in the following sections. The samples are from French, English, Esperanto, German, Swedish and Finnish.

[33] French:

Celui des deux époux qui, par l' effet de
'that of-the two spouses who by the effect of

l' hypothèque exercée sur l' immeuble à lui
the mortgage valid on the real-estate to her/his lot

échu en partage, se trouve poursuivi pour la
fallen [lot] her/himself finds followed for the

totalité d' une dette de communauté, a de droit son
sum of a debt common has the right to his

recours pour la moitié de cette dette contre
recourse for the half of this debt towards

l' autre époux ou ses héritiers.
the other spouse or her/his heirs'

This is an adapted version of an analysis by Luc Isaac (1986: 69f.)

[34]

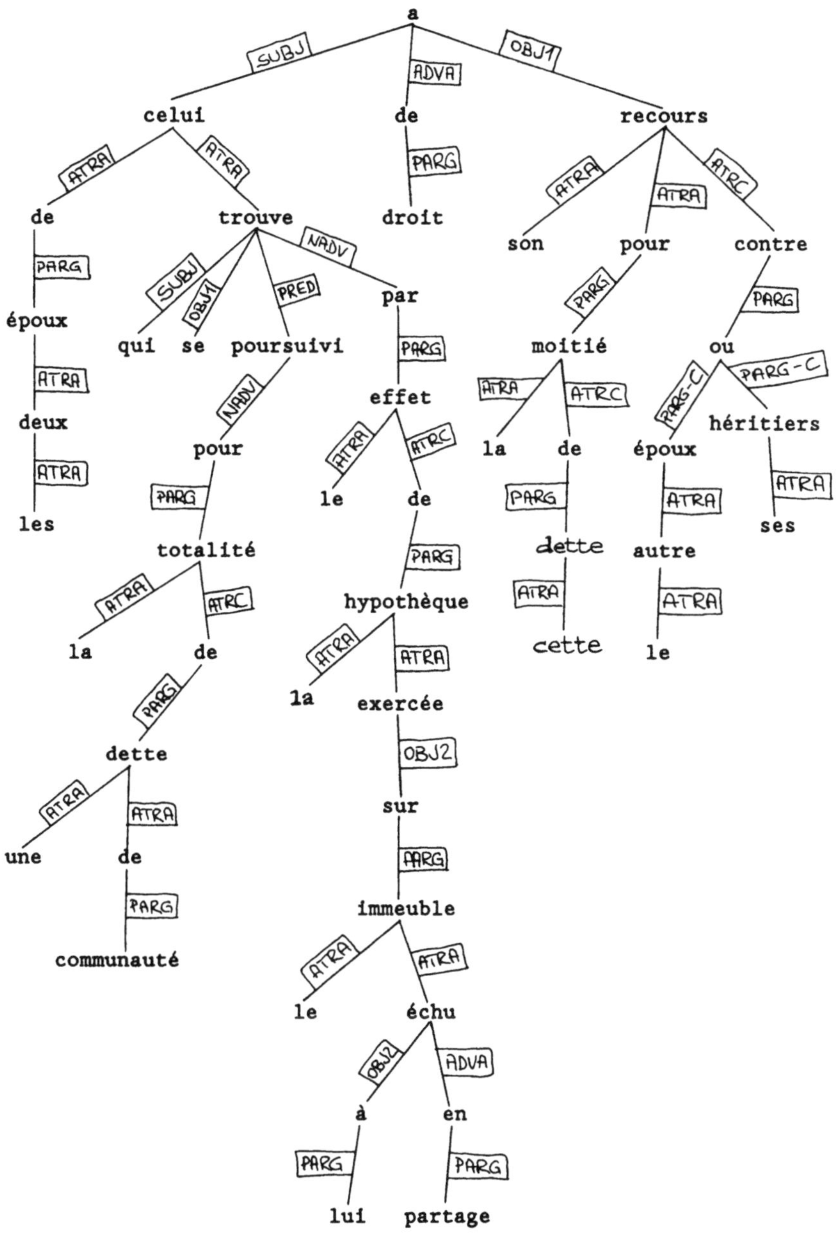
a
SUBJ
ADVA
OBJ1
celui
de
recours
ATRA
ATRA
PARG
ATRA
ATRA
ATRC
de
trouve
droit
son
pour
contre
NADV
PARG
SUBJ
OBJ1
PRED
PARG
PARG
époux
qui
se
poursuivi
par
moitié
ou
ATRA
NADV
PARG
ATRA
ATRC
PARG-C
PARG-C
deux
pour
effet
la
de
époux
héritiers
ATRA
PARG
ATRA
ATRC
PARG
ATRA
ATRA
les
le
de
dette
autre
ses
totalité
PARG
ATRA
ATRA
ATRA
ATRC
hypothèque
cette
le
la
de
ATRA
ATRA
PARG
la
exercée
dette
OBJ2
ATRA
ATRA
sur
une
de
PARG
PARG
immeuble
communauté
ATRA
ATRA
le
échu
OBJ2
ADVA
à
en
PARG
PARG
lui
partage

[35] English:
Scanning electronmicroscopy and related techniques such as X-ray analysis are a major feature of the laboratory activity.

The sentence is analysed in accordance with a unified version of the English dependency syntaxes by Maxwell (1986) and Korst (1986).

[36]

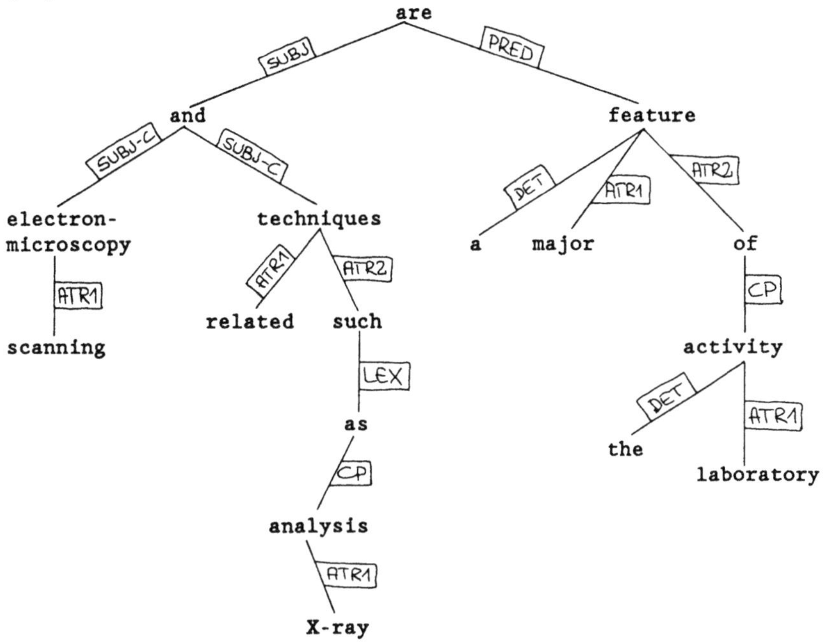
are
SUBJ
PRED
and
feature
SUBJ-C
SUBJ-C
DET
ATR1
ATR2
electron-
microscopy
techniques
a
major
of
ATR1
ATR1
ATR2
CP
related
such
scanning
activity
LEX
DET
ATR1
as
the
laboratory
CP
analysis
ATR1
X-ray

[37] Esperanto:

Nur tio gravas, ke la valoro de la informo
'only this is-important that the value of the information

mem estu multe pli malgranda ol la laboro necesa
itself be much less than tre effort necessary

por malĉifri ĝin, kaj pro tio, kvankam oni uzas
for decipher it and because-of this although one uses

la saman bazan algoritmon, ekzistas diversaj niveloj
the same basic algorithm there-exist various levels

kaj teknikoj de ĉifrado por la diversaj niveloj de
and techniques of deciphering for the various levels of

la informvaloro.
the information-value'

The sentence is analysed in accordance with the Esperanto dependency syntax (Schubert 1986a: 23ff.).

[38]

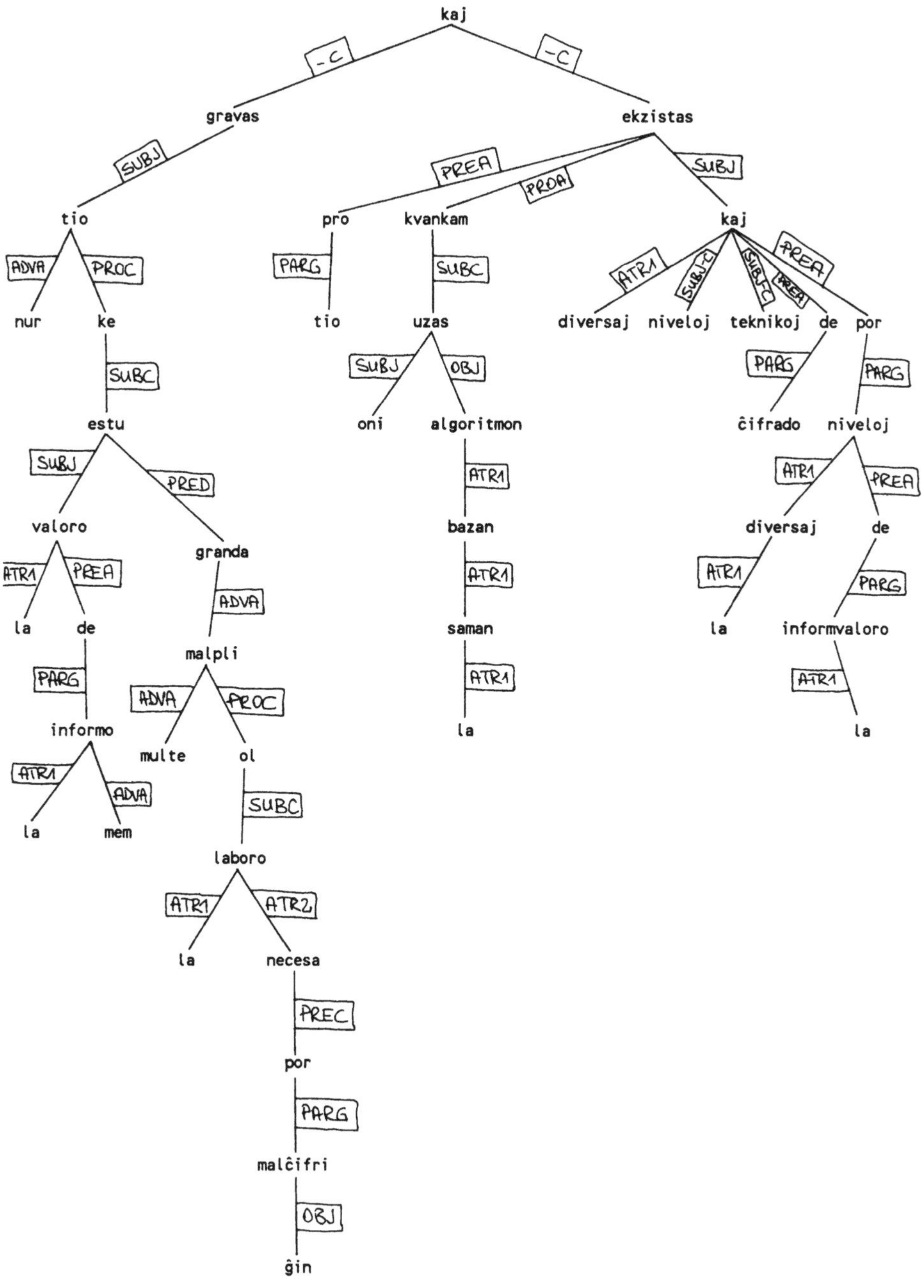
kaj
-C
-C
gravas
ekzistas
SUBJ
PREA
PROA
SUBJ
tio
pro
kvankam
kaj
ADVA
PROC
PARG
SUBC
ATR1
SUBJ-C
SUBJ-C
PREA
PREA
nur
ke
tio
uzas
diversaj
niveloj
teknikoj
de
por
SUBC
SUBJ
OBJ
PARG
PARG
estu
oni
algoritmon
ĉifrado
niveloj
SUBJ
PRED
ATR1
ATR1
PREA
valoro
bazan
diversaj
de
granda
ATR1
PREA
ADVA
ATR1
ATR1
PARG
la
de
saman
la
informvaloro
malpli
PARG
ADVA
PROC
ATR1
ATR1
informo
la
la
multe
ol
ATR1
ADVA
SUBC
la
mem
laboro
ATR1
ATR2
la
necesa
PREC
por
PARG
malĉifri
OBJ
ĝin

[39] German:

Die	**Durchführung**	**umfangreicherer**	**Wartungsarbeiten**
'the	execution	more-extensive	of-maintenance-works

an	**Rumpf**	**und**	**Tragflächen**	**sollte,**	**wenn**	**keine**	**schwerwiegenden**
on	trunk	and	wings	should	if	no	important

Gründe	**dagegensprechen,**	**grundsätzlich**	**nicht**	**über**	**den**
reasons	suggest-the-contrary	in-principle	not	beyond	the

im	**Wartungsplan**	**vorgesehenen**	**Termin**	**hinaus**
in-the	maintenance-plan	scheduled	date	[beyond]

aufgeschoben	**werden.**
put-off	be'

The sentence is analysed in accordance with the German dependency syntax by Lobin (1987).

[40]

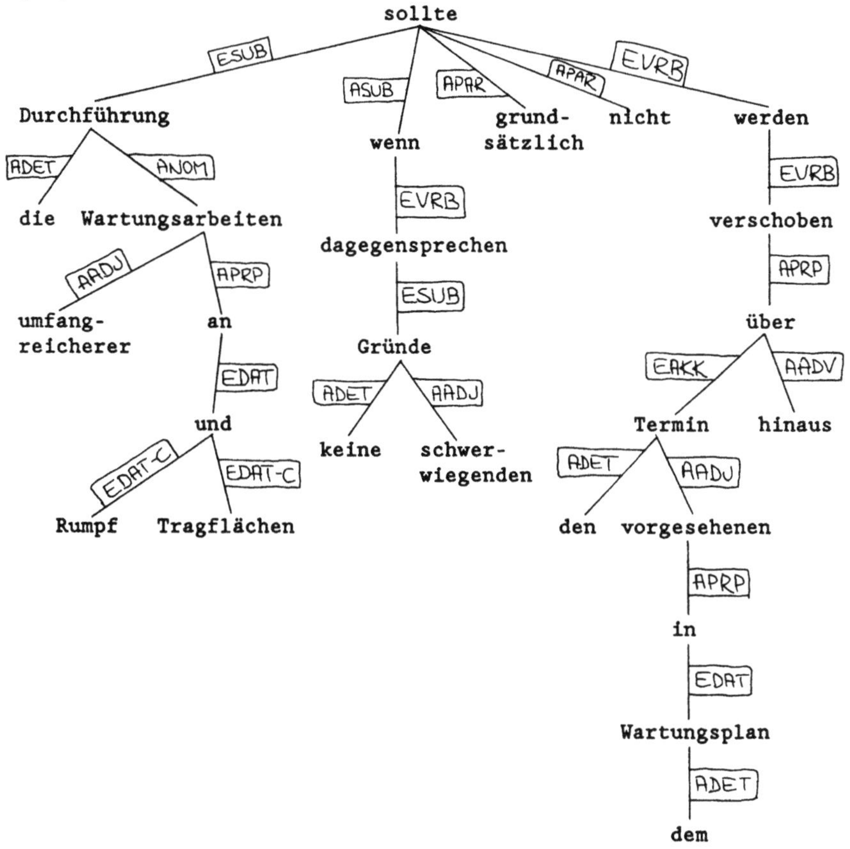
sollte
ESUB
ASUB
APAR
APAR
EVRB
Durchführung
wenn
grund-
sätzlich
nicht
werden
ADET
ANOM
EVRB
EVRB
die
Wartungsarbeiten
verschoben
dagegensprechen
AADJ
APRP
ESUB
APRP
umfang-
reicherer
an
über
Gründe
EDAT
EAKK
AADV
ADET
AADJ
und
Termin
hinaus
keine
schwer-
wiegenden
EDAT-C
EDAT-C
ADET
AADJ
Rumpf
Tragflächen
den
vorgesehenen
APRP
in
EDAT
Wartungsplan
ADET
dem

[41] Swedish:

När vi hittills har sagt att en kvadrat har
'when we hitherto have said that a square has

dimensionen två och en kub dimensionen tre, så
the-dimension two and a cube the-dimension three so

har det baserat sig på att en punkts läge i ett
has this based itself on that a of-point place in a

plan naturligt beskrivs av två tal medan
plane in-a-natural-way is-described by two figures while

läget i rymden fordrar tre tal.
the-place in the-space needs three figures'

The analysis is tentative.

[42]

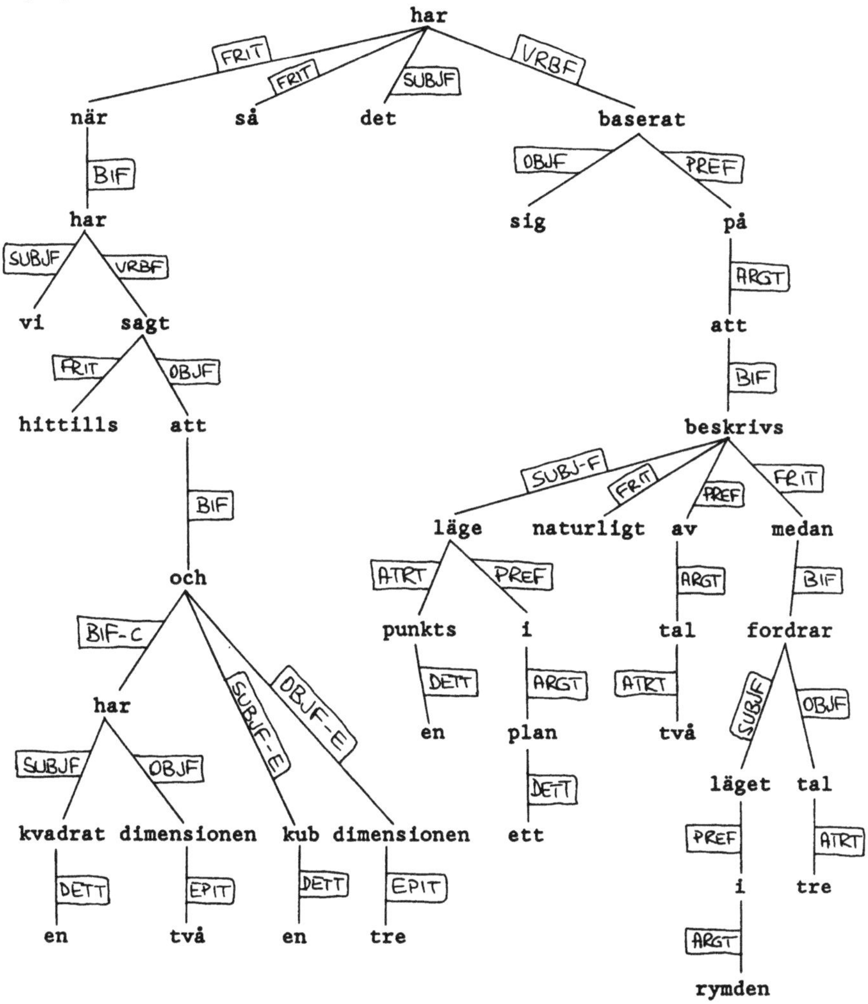
har
FRIT
FRIT
SUBJF
VRBF
när
så
det
baserat
BIF
OBJF
PREF
har
sig
på
SUBJF
VRBF
ARGT
vi
sagt
att
FRIT
OBJF
BIF
hittills
att
beskrivs
BIF
SUBJ-F
FRIT
PREF
FRIT
läge
naturligt
av
medan
och
ATRT
PREF
ARGT
BIF
BIF-C
SUBJF-E
OBJF-E
punkts
i
tal
fordrar
har
DETT
ARGT
ATRT
SUBJF
OBJF
en
plan
två
SUBJF
OBJF
läget
tal
DETT
kvadrat
dimensionen
kub
dimensionen
ett
PREF
ATRT
DETT
EPIT
DETT
EPIT
i
tre
en
två
en
tre
ARGT
rymden

[43] Finnish:

Kun Koivisto nyt on antanut sosiaalidemokraateille
'after Koivisto now has given the-social-democrats

myöntävän vastauksensa, minä pidän ehdotustani
positive his-answer I consider my-proposal

muodostaa sitoutumattomien porvarien vaaliliitto
to-form party-free citizens' election-union

entistä tärkeämpänä.
than-before more-important'

The sentence and its dependency tree are with minor adaptations taken from Tarvainen (1987: 123).

[44]

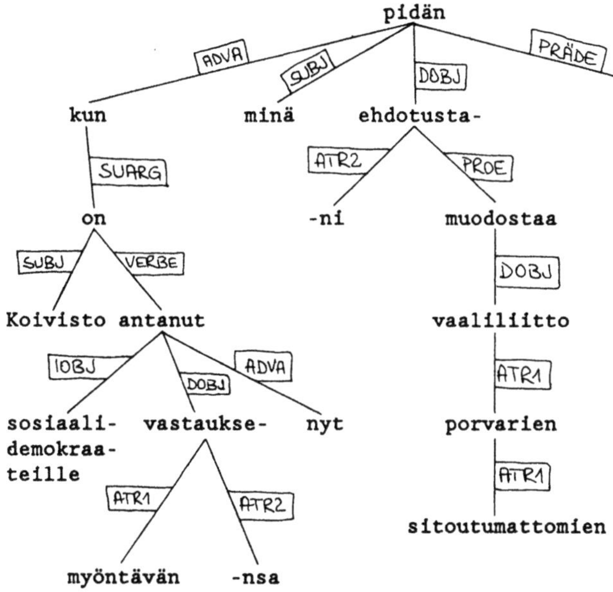
pidän
ADVA
SUBJ
DOBJ
PRÄDE
kun
minä
ehdotusta-
tärkeämpänä
SUARG
ATR2
PROE
KOMPE
on
-ni
muodostaa
entistä
SUBJ
VERBE
DOBJ
Koivisto
antanut
vaaliliitto
IOBJ
ADVA
DOBJ
ATR1
sosiaali-
demokraa-
teille
vastaukse-
nyt
porvarien
ATR1
ATR2
ATR1
sitoutumattomien
myöntävän
-nsa

4.6. The one-word principle

In the present model each word in a sentence (except the main governor) must be explicitly linked to a governor by means of a dependency relation (see also 4.7.). Speaking in terms of trees, this principle has two implications:

- There must not be empty nodes.

- There must not be more than one word on a node.

The first implication is somewhat weakened in the context of coordinated constructions (4.10.), but outside the constructions discussed there it should be maintained. In my opinion, refraining from empty nodes forces the grammarian to answer more precisely and more clearly the fundamental question of dependency grammar: "Which word does this word depend on?" If empty nodes are possible, one is too easily tempted to make descriptions not about the words found, but about abstract structures. This entails the danger of reasoning about "underlying" or "kernel" sentences, "implicit" predications or the like. I do not deny that it may be useful to think about such constructs and I acknowledge that they may have explanatory power, but form-oriented translation **syntax** has to go from a text as it is in one language (a "surface" text, so to speak) to that same type of text in another language. If this can be done straightforwardly without climbing down to an abstract deep structure and back to the surface, the solution seems safer to me. The easiest way to stay on the surface is to describe what is there and not what one could imagine in order to make the model work better.

This reluctancy in using abstract nodes implies also a specific view on ellipses which is discussed in 4.11.

The one-word principle also has the implication that there must not be more than one word on a node. In many languages there are fixed groups of words that occur together and seem to be a semantic unit. Such a group might be considered even syntactically to be a unit that only through the caprices of language development happens to have taken the shape of several words. If there are such units, it may seem desirable to describe the syntactic relations between the unit as a whole and the rest of the sentence and in consequence also to represent the unit on a single node of the dependency tree.

However reasonable such a procedure looks, in the present model I refrain from making use of this possibility. This decision is due mainly to the basic approach of this model, which relies on distributional co-occurrence without reference to meaning (4.4.1.). To see this, it should first be indicated what kinds of word strings might be candidates for multi-word units. One group contains fixed combinations of content words. They occur mainly in the realm of technical terms. Another group consists of function words, and especially groups of function words with content words that are in the process of developing from content words to function words. Examples are French à cause de 'because of', English as long as, German in bezug auf 'with regard to', ten tijde van 'in the times of'. In the German example the small b in bezug which in other contexts is spelled with an initial capital like all nouns in German, indicates that orthography standardisers feel that bezug is no longer a "real noun" here, thus no longer a real content word. In the Dutch example, the old case endings show that the expression has been fixed for quite some time. A third group of candidates are borrowed multi-word expressions, like in English a priori or ad hoc.

Content word units should be taken as several words, because they usually can be analysed as normal syntagmata. After all, a syntagma is not only a unit, but a structured one. The words in a noun syntagma (and most technical terms are noun syntagmata) in many languages, though not in English are open to morphological marking in exactly the same way as any syntagma. By taking the words of such a syntagma as a single unit one would make the words in the unit inaccessible to case, number and gender agreement or government. In addition, a fixed syntagma often allows for words to be inserted in the same way as does a normal syntagma. If one defines such a unit as being a single word, a word syntax has to be devised for accounting for these phenomena. It seems that content word units are usually sufficiently described in sentence level syntax, and there is accordingly no need to copy this description into an internal word syntax of multi-word units.

Function word units and units of function and content words in many cases do have a fixed **meaning**, but behave **syntactically** like a syntagma. The English example as long as does not have exactly the same distribution as as short as, as it can also introduce a subordinate clause, which is an argument in favour of a special status for this unit. But the special status, the difference between as long as and as short as, can be accounted for with normal sentence-syntactic means. This can be seen from the fact that the outside-link criterion applies: The subordinate clause can be said to depend on the second as in as long as in the same way as it depends on a single as. And the unit as long as depends on a governor in the higher-level sentence in the same way as a single as would. Thus, as long as is a syntagma which towards the outside is represented by its internal governor, the first as, and which has a dependent that depends on the second as:

[45] **Animals may be kept in the room as long as they do not damage the furniture.**

[46]

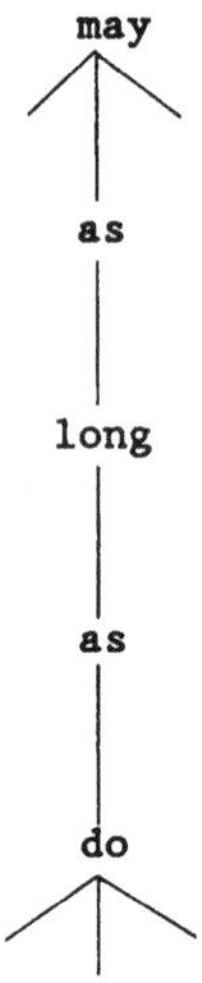

It would be an exaggeration to expect that a similar analysis can be given for each possible multi-word unit in every language. But for the practical reasons of translation (and machine translation with parsing and synthesis etc. involved) I choose to never analyze multi-word units as a single word in the present model.

This may cause problems in some cases. Foreign expressions like in English ad hoc are typical candidates for such problems. As the two words occur only together, neither of them has paradigmatic relations to any other word in English. The syntactic relation between the two can therefore not be analysed with the methods of the present model described so far. The practical solution adopted here is that the words in such a case are arranged in an arbitrarily chosen dependency relation, thus for example

[47]

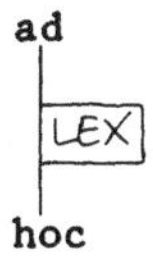

The relation among them is none of the dependency types a syntax of English in the present model contains. It is therefore assigned a special label that marks it as a **lexical** dependency. Units with lexical dependencies must be given in the dictionary. They as a unit belong to a word class. (This provision has been included thanks to an idea of Bieke van der Korst.)

While the above paragraphs deal mainly with practical decisions, still another question remains to be tackled, which is of more theoretical importance for the set-up of the syntactic system developed for a given language in accordance with the present model. This question is: **What is a word?**

The definition of the word as a unit of grammar is a wide field which I shall not enter in this study. As I am interested mainly in written language, I can apply a technical definition of the type "everything between two blanks is a word", however unsatisfactory such a definition is in language theory. In the above paragraphs I have emphasised the validity of this defintion by stating that in the present model a word (or word-like unit) never can be longer than from one blank to the next one.

But time has now come to acknowledge that the smallest linguistic sign and thus the smallest element of a syntactic system is not a word, but a **morpheme**. The internal structure of multi-morpheme words is a subject of grammar, and the formal side of this is a part of syntax (as defined in the present model). This study is concerned with translation-oriented syntax and stays on sentence level as far as possible. The boundary between sentence and word level is as arbitrary as the definition of a word, and therefore even sentence-level syntax sometimes can be made much easier when words are not taken as unanalysable units or as units with only variation of morphological form, but when they are divided up into several words. Technically speaking, the string between two blanks may thus contain more than a single word.

Three examples may illustrate the convenience of this decision. I borrow these examples from dependency syntaxes worked out within the framework of the present model. The authors (see the Foreword) did not work in contact, so that it is interesting to note that several of them decided independently that it is necessary to divide up words. Since only the Esperanto syntax

(Schubert 1986a) written within the present model has been published previous to this study, I cannot avoid quoting unpublished materials, with my apologies to the reader.

The first example stems from German dependency syntax (Lobin 1987). A certain subclass of German verbs have a verb particle that forms a single word with the root in some forms of the verb paradigm, but stands seperately (and not even adjacent) in others. When such a verb is combined with the subordinator _zu_ (similar to English _to_ [+ infinitive]), this word is incorporated in the verb between the particle and the root. In the following example, compare the particle+verb combination _stattfinden_ 'take place' and the particle-less verb _finden_ 'find'.

[48]					
	Die	**Boxveranstaltung**	**wird**	**woanders**	**stattfinden.**
			present		infinitive
	'the	boxing-match	will	elsewhere	take-place'

[49]									
	Die	**Studentin**	**wird**	**die**	**Bücher**	**in**	**der**	**Bibliothek**	**finden.**
			pres.						inf.
	'the	female- student	will	the	books	in	the	library	find'

[50]					
	Die	**Boxveranstaltung**	**findet**	**woanders**	**statt.**
			pres.		
	'the	boxing-match	takes	elsewhere	place'

[51]								
	Die	**Studentin**	**findet**	**die**	**Bücher**	**in**	**der**	**Bibliothek.**
			pres.					
	'the	female- student	finds	the	books	in	the	library'

[52]					
	Die	**Boxveranstaltung**	**hat**	**woanders**	**stattgefunden.**
			pres.		past participle
	'the	boxing-match	has	elsewhere	taken-place'

[53]									
	Die	**Studentin**	**hat**	**die**	**Bücher**	**in**	**der**	**Bibliothek**	**gefunden.**
			pres.						past ptc.
	'the	female- student	has	the	books	in	the	library	found'

[54]					
	Die	**Boxveranstaltung**	**scheint**	**woanders**	**stattzufinden.**
			pres.		inf.
	'the	boxing-match	seems	elsewhere	place-to-take'

[55]   **Die Studentin scheint die Bücher in der Bibliothek zu**
                        seems
        'the female-
            student   seems   the books   in the lib.   to

        finden.
        inf.
        find'

The tree structure of [54] with Lobin's dependency type labels looks like this:

[56]

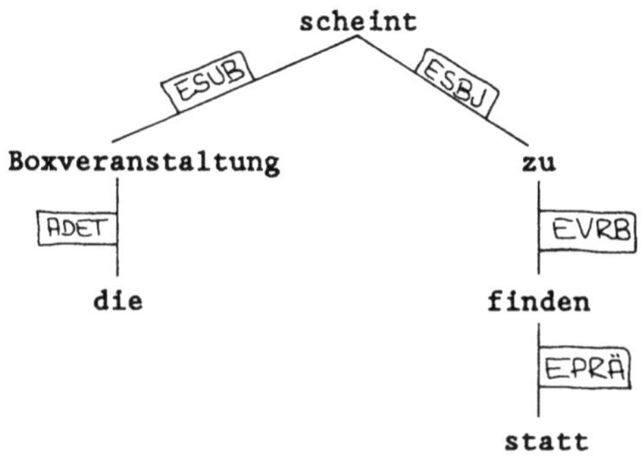

In a similar way, obvious contractions may be split up and reconstructed. This makes sense when the reconstructed forms are syntactically correct as well, so that they can be handled by general syntactic dependency descriptions that are included in the system anyway. German has a number of contractions of a preposition and an inflected article:

[57]   **am -> an dem**
[58]   **zur -> zu der**
[59]   **ins -> in das**

Similar cases exist in French (Isaac 1986: 11):

[60]   **du -> de le**
[61]   **des -> de les**

The French and English apostrophy contractions belong to this group as well:

[62] **j'ai -> je ai**
[63] **l'assassin -> le assassin**

[64] **I'm -> I am**
[65] **won't -> will not**

For French, Isaac (1986: 15) and Tamis (1986: 14 n. 2) also list more sophisticated cases. In [66] a word is split up into smaller words in a way that is impossible in normal spoken and written French.

[66] **auquel -> à le quel**

How far to go is again depends ulimately on the concept of purposeful arbitrariness.

These examples seem mainly to concern marginal orthographical peculiarities in German, French or English. But the idea of taking parts of an orthographical word as distinct units of sentence level syntax can also play a more functional role, especially in the case of enclitics. Dan Maxwell (1986: 1) divides up English nouns and what is traditionally called their genitive ending in two words and takes the 's or ' as a postposition. This yields an elegant account for those cases where the genitive mark is not attached to the internal governor of the syntagma, but to the last word in the string, as can be expected from a postposition:

[67] **the king of England's health**

Such a solution is not theoretically required, but is one of several possible options. Korst (1986: 15), working within the same framework, discusses the traditional analysis of nouns with a genitive case form.

Maxwell's idea for the English genitive can be said to have a structural function that is much more central to the analysis than the contraction examples above. In an agglutinative language, possibilities for assigning morphemes structural functions of this kind can be expected to abound. Indeed, Tarvainen (1987: 40) sets up three complete word classes of Finnish morphemes that by orthographic convention are not written separately. These are possessive suffixes, various modal and speaker attitude particles and the question particle (I use ' to denote morpheme boundaries):

[68] **kirja'ni**
'book-my'

[69]

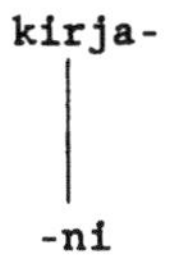

[70] **Hän'kin tuli.**
'he/she-also came'

[71]

[72] **Tuli'ko hän?**
'came-? he/she'

[73]

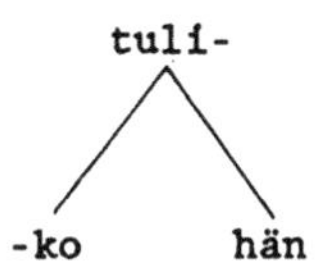

How far should this chopping up of words go? If certain affixes of Finnish are taken as words of their own, why not the inflectional morphemes of German or Dutch? Suppose a complete morphemic analysis of, say, German is possible. Would it then be meaningful to dissect the text until one gets a dependency tree with a single morpheme on each node? The one-morpheme principle? Theoretically such an approach seems possible and may yield interesting results if carried out with careful consequence. In an extreme version it would imply that the limit between the word and the sentence level is given up entirely. A sentence would be considered to be a set of syntactically arranged morphemes. The reason why I do not attempt at going this far in any of the examples shown in this chapter is, again, an arbitrary decision of model design. Its motivation is found in the purpose for which the present syntax model is devised: translation. Many of the morphemes that might be allotted their own nodes in the type of trees sketched in this paragraph cannot be translated directly. They are **function morphemes** which denote syntactic features of **content morphemes**. These features in turn have various functions: They may identify the government capacity of the word (e.g. a finite English verb, marked with a third-person morpheme, governs a third-person subject, whereas other finite and infinite forms do not). Features may also denote a meaning which is translatable on word level (e.g. number, in many cases) or on text level (e.g. tense). In short, the decision what to consider a word should be metataxis-oriented (on the function of features in metataxis, see especially 5.2.

To sum up the one-word principle, the following decisions can be noted:

- No empty nodes are allowed in a dependency tree, each node must carry a word.
- A "word" in a dependency tree must not be more than what is identified as a word by standard orthography in the language in question.
- A "word" in a dependency tree may well be less than what orthography takes as a unit.

These statements are restricted in two ways:

- In languages where there traditionally is no word limit in orthography, the problem of multi-word units is more open to decisions than in other languages.
- Asyndetic coordination may require empty nodes (see 4.10.).

4.7. The true-tree principle

Dependency trees are graphic representations of dependency relations established by virtue of the syntactic rules of a given language description. As such, they could be used just to depict syntactic structures. However, graphic structures are in many cases much more perspicuous than the precise formulations of grammatical rules. It can therefore at times be useful also to express decisions about the syntactic model in terms of trees.

Until now I have not really motivated my claim that the present model creates about **tree** structures. All that can be concluded so far is that co-occurrence relations yield **graphs** of sentences (or other pieces of text), which, by virtue of the definition of dependency, are **directed graphs**. The present section aims to motivate my decision to restrict these graphs to **true trees**.

The difference between an aribtrary graph and a tree is twofold. One difference is due to the graph being directed:

- There must not be undirected syntactic relations.

And the other difference is due to the directed graph being a tree:

- A node must not be governed by more than one governor. As a consequence, the descending branches of a tree can never meet again.

The following graphs are not trees:

[74]

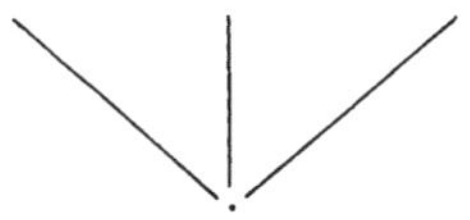

[75]

[76]

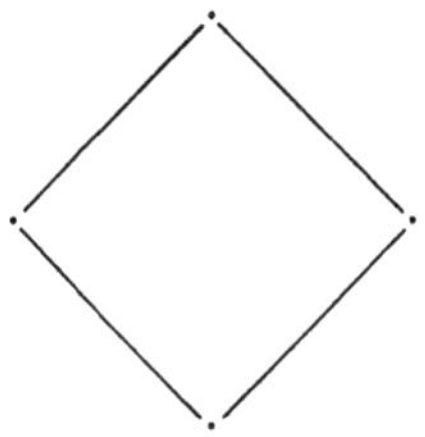

[77]

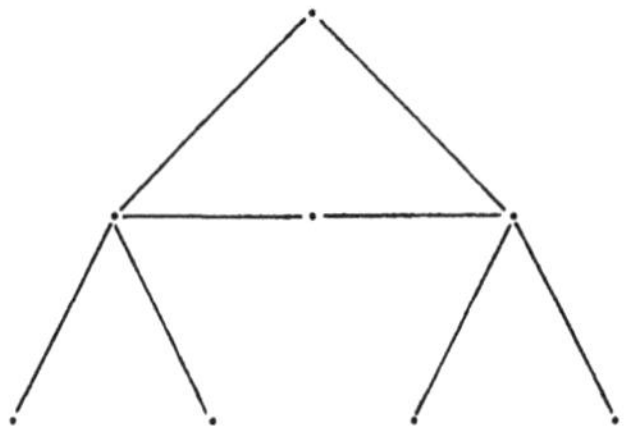

These strict provisions are not in general use in dependency grammar. Tesnière's stemmas (1959/1982: 15 n. 1) resemble true trees very much, but in coordinated structures he uses undirected relations between the conjunction and the coordinated words. These relations thus are not dependency relations (Tesnière 1959/1982: 327):

[78] **Alfred et Bernard tombent.**
'Alfred and Bernard fall'

[79]

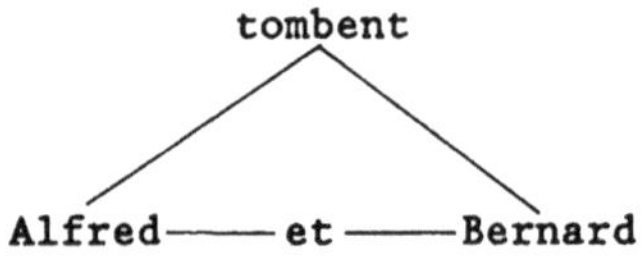

Hudson (1984: 85), who puts less emphasis on the arbitrariness of grammatical model design, acknowledges all the structures in [74] to [77] as dependency structures.

As most of the involved problems have to do with coordination, I return in the section on coordination (4.10.) to the solution I use in the present model.

4.8. Complex verb constructions

The above three sections (4.5. to 4.7.) deal with dependency trees and some particulars about their nodes and branches. In the light of the provisions in these three sections and of course of those in the four fundamental sections (4.1. to 4.4.) at the beginning of this chapter, this and the next three sections (4.8. to 4.11.) take up a few more general problems in syntax that are encountered in a number of different languages. The present section is about complex verb constructions.

Many languages have complex verb constructions. They usually consist of one finite and one or more infinite verbs. The infinite forms may be infinitives, participles, supina, gerunds etc. The verbs that can be finite in such constructions often belong to one of the subclasses of verbs called auxiliary and modal verbs. Combinations of the appropriate constructions are not uncommon, so that rather long chains of verb forms result. English examples are:

[80] **She has given him the book.**

[81] **She is giving him the book.**

[82] **She must give him the book.**

[83] **She has been giving him the book.**

[84] **She must have given him the book.**

[85] **She must be giving him the book.**

[86] **She must have been giving him the book.**

The analysis of [86] should obviously be something like

[87]

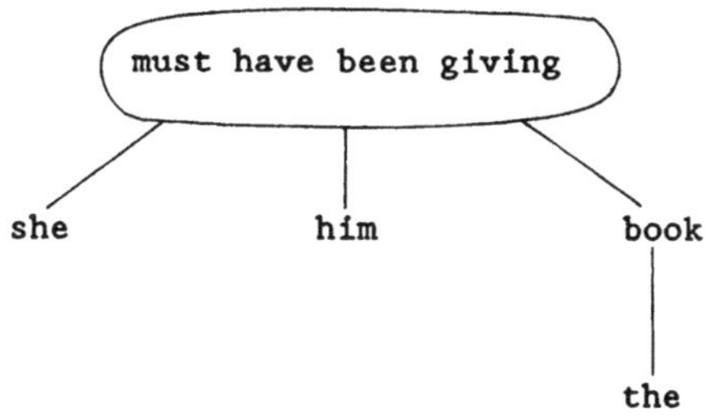

The question is now firstly how to analyse the verb complex and secondly where to hook up the dependents. There are authors who would not analyse the verb complex. Their motive may be the idea that such a complex verb form only through the imponderables of historical language development happens to appear in the shape of several words in one language, while its counterpart in another language well may be one synthetic form (cf. Latin imprimatur vs. English let it be printed). Such cross-linguistic translation equivalence is of course a semantic argument that has no value here. Tesnière is one of these authors, but he makes a distinction between modal and auxiliary verbs, and thereby between verb complexes and complex verb forms. In his analysis, [86] would become (Tesnière 1959/1982: 107, 110):

[88]

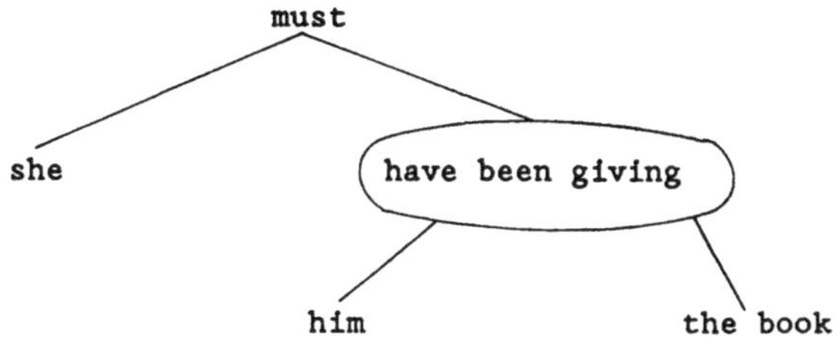

Engel, who applies a much more distributional approach than Tesnière, analyses the verb complex. His analysis of [86] would be (cf. Engel 1982: 163f.):

[89]

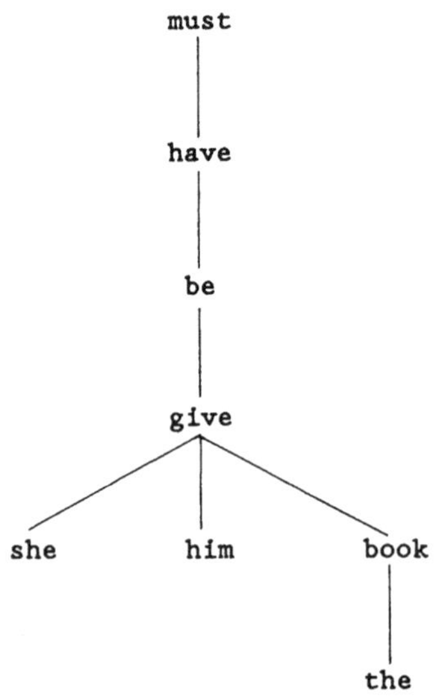

Tarvainen works with a semantic distinction of the finite verbs in complex constructions and gives in this respect a similar analysis to Tesnière's, but he depicts the relationships in a manner that is closer to Engel. Tarvainen uses blocks of nodes that fulfil a common syntactic function, although he normally gives each word a node of its own. One of these blocks is the predicate, and the whole verb construction lies within the predicate if it represents a single semantic unit (Tarvainen 1983a: 18, 1983b: 38, 1985b: 29, 60, 1986: 17f. for various languages). When working within the framework of the present model, however, Tarvainen (1987: 64ff.) does not use such blocks.

The strict distributional requirements of the present model (together with the one-word principle which is a consequence of them) makes it necessary to analyse the verb complex. The solution that follows from the principles of the present model looks like a compromise between Tesnière's, Engel's and Tarvainen's descriptions. I analyse the verb complex in a way which resembles Engel's analysis, but I follow Tesnière in my breakdown of the verb complex into individual dependents. I do not distinguish among the verbs concerned on semantic grounds and thus do not distinguish modal and auxiliary verbs:

[90]

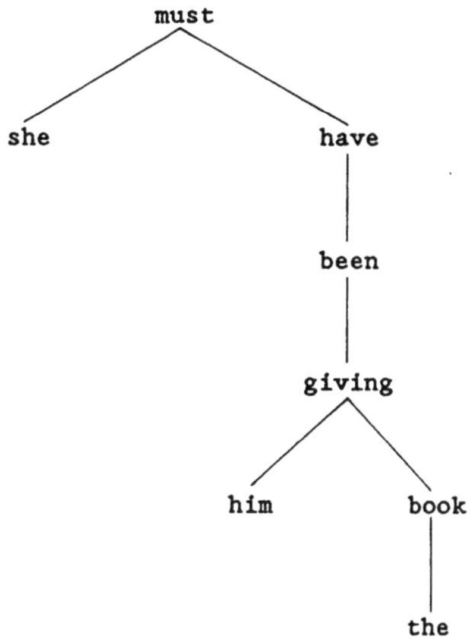

My guideline is the idea that the description becomes more elegant as it becomes simpler. By virtue of its word class a word has a dependency pattern. This pattern is determined by the possible dependency types the word can govern. For a specific word, the word class-specific dependency pattern is refined in two ways: by the **valency** of the word and by the word's **syntactic form**. This is a topic which I have not explicitly discussed before in this study. Indeed, when different words are grouped together as forms of one root (4.3. first step), these formally different word forms may have different dependency patterns. The change in government capacity that is brought about by a change in syntactic form (inflection etc.) normally concerns valency, i.e. the subclass-specific part of the dependency pattern, but it may also concern the word class-specific government capacity. For example a transitive Swedish verb loses its object valency when the passive morpheme -s is added. This is a change in the subclass-specific part.

How can this guideline be applied to complex verb forms? If the different finite and infinite forms a verb can have in a language with verb complexes are considered to belong to the same word class (this is a reasonable option), a change in valency can be observed among these different forms of the verb. Before analysing verb complexes, the "normal" combinatorial behaviour (outside verb complexes) of the different verb forms should be taken into consideration. In English, a tensed verb form must have a subject; an imperative may have one in certain cases, but normally does not; and participles and gerunds never have a subject. These are, with the example of one dependency type, changes in the valency pattern of the verb that are triggered by differences in its syntactic form. The most elegant solution now seems to me to be the one that maintains the same valency patterns when the forms in question have a role in verb complexes. This can be achieved for languages like French, German, English and Finnish, discussed by the authors I have referred to. For this purpose, the verb complex is analysed in such a way that the finite verb remains the main governor, while the nonfinite verbs depend on it or on other nonfinite verbs (Engel's solution), and the dependents are divided up in two groups: the subject remains an immediate dependent of the finite verb, whereas the rest of the substantival dependents are governed by the dependentially lowest of the verb forms (Tesnière's solution).

I have earlier used this solution in my analysis of Esperanto as the metataxis partner of all languages in the DLT machine translation system (Schubert 1986a: 97). That such an analysis is applicable for quite a number of languages is confirmed for instance by Nikula's account of Swedish (Nikula 1986: 38). The doubts Nikula (1986: 98) later expresses are not derived from syntactic considerations, but have to do with his attempt to find a Tesnière'ian parallelism between syntactic and semantic relationships.

Syntactic and semantic relations cannot always follow the same lines. This is most obvious when semantic relationships suggest more than one government relationship to a single dependent. There is a complex verb construction with this sort of phenomenon: "accusativus cum infinitivo" (AcI) that is possible with perception verbs in a number of languages.

[91] **I yesterday saw him give her the books.**

The complication lies in the fact that a semantic analysis (and often also semantically inspired syntax) considers him to be governed by both verbs. It denotes the patient of saw and the agent of give. In the present model, however, him can only have a single (syntactic) governor, and the two verbs are obviously the candidates. But which analysis is closer to the principles of the model?

[92]

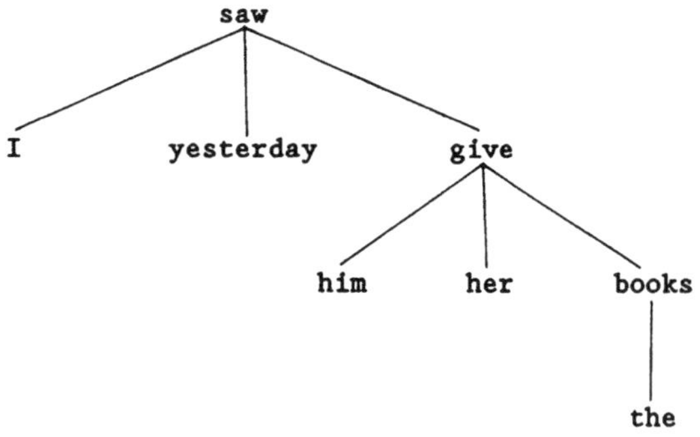

[93]

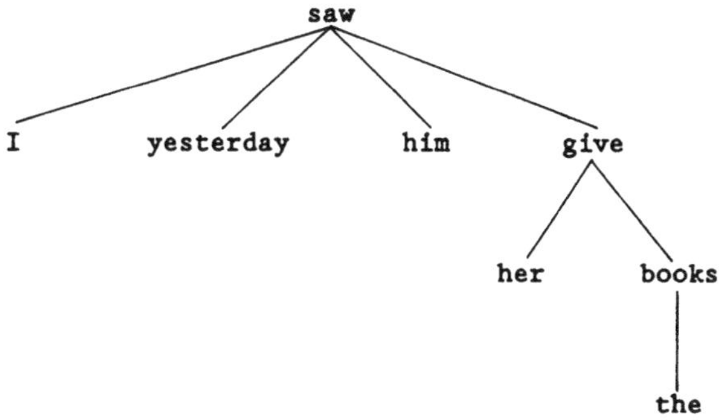

In any case, the construction contains a peculiarity that is not found in other constructions. which solution allows this peculiarity to be more easily described. If one opts for [92], one has to account for the uncommon subject valency of the infinitive and for the syntactic form of him as the subject of give have to be accounted for. Normally infinitives have no subjects and subjects are normally in the nominative case, but here it is accusative. The explanation is not found in the immediate governor, give, but in the fact that give in turn is governed by a word from a special subclass of verbs. The problem cannot be removed by giving him another label. The dependency type that normally takes the accusative form of a pronoun, the object, is present as well. Choosing this option, one would have to explain a valency for an additional object brought about not by the immediate governor of that object, but by a governor higher up. If, on the other hand, one opts for [93], one has to account for the fact that saw has besides its object him has another dependent with an infinitive as its internal governor, It cannot have this second dependent when the object is absent. I opt for the second analysis for two reasons. Firstly, the peculiarities of the AcI construction are in this analysis a consequence of the valency of the governing verb, and secondly, the infinitive need not be assigned any government capacity that it has not got in other infinitive constructions as well.

By applying the principles of the present model, a solution can be found that confines the scope of a special construction to a word and its immediate dependents without influencing words farther away in the tree.

4.9. Subordinate clauses

In the present model, a sentence is a main governor with its dependents. In many languages, by far the most frequent main governor is the finite verb. Its dependents, if any, are syntagmata that may in turn consist of words with dependent syntagmata (The recursiveness of this description is dealt with in 4.12.). The same structure, a finite verb with dependents, may, however, occur several times in a single sentence. Due to the principles of the present model, there can be only a single main governor. Two sorts of construction are possible in sentences with more than one finite verb. Either the finite verbs are coordinated (see 4.10.), or one of them is the main governor and the others are subordinated, forming with all their dependents a **subordinate clause**. This section is about the latter case.

It is not necessary at a cross-linguistic level to discuss how the main governor and the governors of subordinate clauses are identified in specific languages. The argument here proceeds in the same way as in normal cases of governor-dependent relations. What is interesting here is the question which dependency structure the present model assigns to subordinate clauses and how the link to the main governor is established.

In many cases a subordinate clause is identified by special words occurring in it. These words may in word classification (4.3.) be grouped under the heading of subordinators, subordinating conjunctions, subjunctions or the like. English examples are _if_ and _that_. In an analysis of English, such a word can be said to be an adjunct (see 4.4.) of a verb and a governor of another finite verb:

[94] **The trains are late, if it snows in the mountains.**

[95]

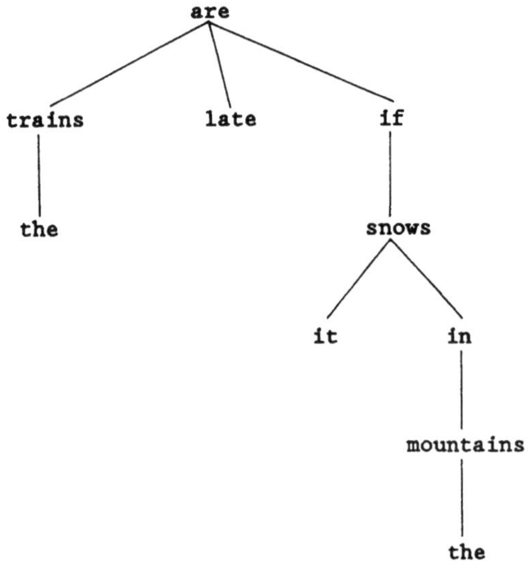

But perhaps this is not the only possible analysis. Not all subordinate clauses are governed by a subordinator. In that case the internal governor of the subordinate clause may be taken as an immediate dependent of the main governor:

[96] **They said the trains would be late.**

[97]

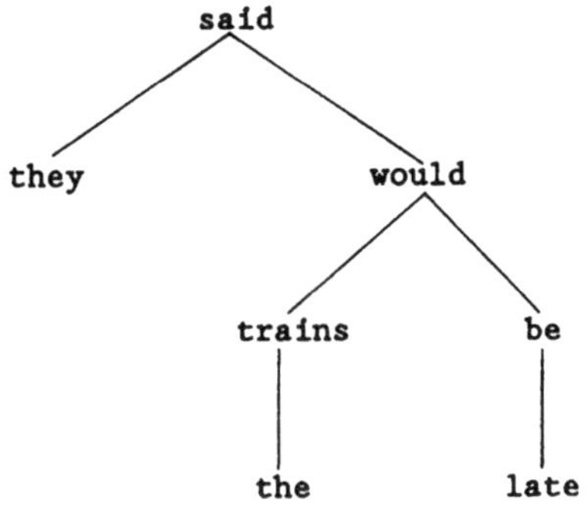

It is possible to insert a subordinator in [96], but as it is optional, the analysis might be that the subordinator depends on the subordinated verb rather than governs it:

[98] **They said that the trains would be late.**

[99]

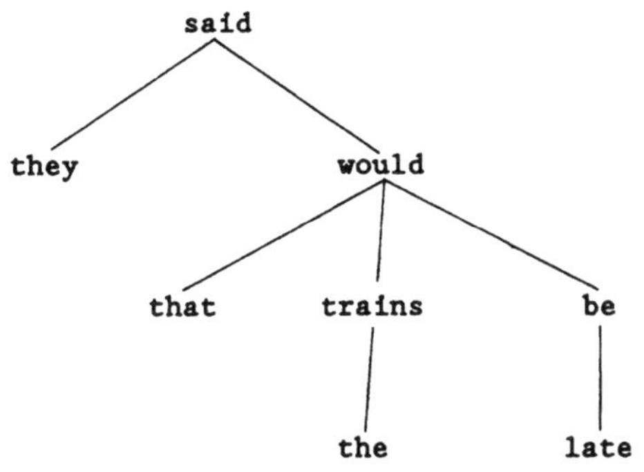

If [98] is analysed in this way, it seems more consistent to assign the same structure to [94]:

[100]

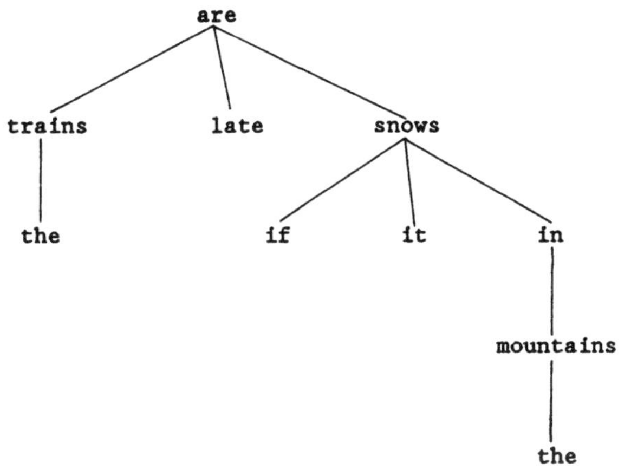

The subordinator can now be seen as an adjunct to finite verbs. But not all words that typically introduce or accompany subordinate clauses are subordinators. They may fulfil another syntactic function in the subordinate clause as well. Relative pronouns provide a good example of this.

[101] **Nehmen Sie den Strauß, der Ihnen am besten gefällt.**
'take the bouquet which you best pleases'

In [101] the subordinate clause does not depend directly on the main governor (nehmen), but on its object (Strauß). This is due to the fact that a relative clause with the masculine pronoun der can occur only by virtue of a masculine noun (Strauß). This is not arguing with form determination (see 4.2.), but with a dependency relation. It is noteworthy, however, that the dependency is not established directly between Strauß and der, but between Strauß and the clause in which der occurs. This one of the decisions that must be made in describing a language within the framework of the present model. There are good reasons to let Strauß govern der immediately, and also good reasons to take gefällt as the governor. In order to keep the description simple, the preference goes to a description that accounts for a word and its government capacity with as little reference to words higher up in the tree as possible. If the verb of the relative clause governs the relative pronoun, it behaves exactly like any other finite verb: It governs a subject and an object etc. in accordance with its valency. If Strauß were taken as the governor of der, der would in turn have to govern gefällt. One would have to account for a finite verb that has no subject when governed by a certain word that fulfils the requirements concerning the morphological form of subjects:

[102]

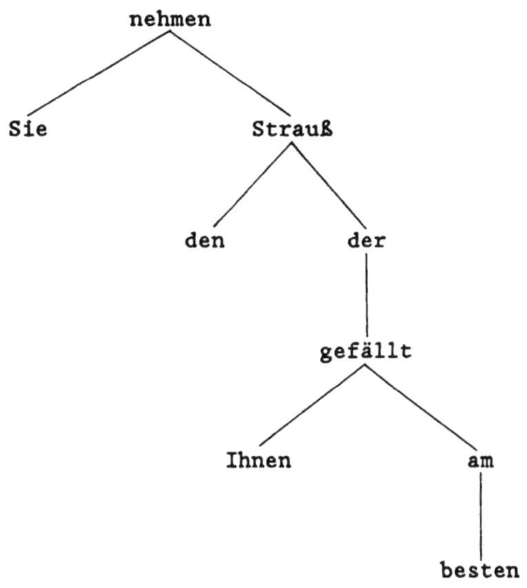

Now the discussion is reduced to the question of whether the subject should govern the verb or vice versa (See 4.1.1). The description becomes simpler if the verb is the governor in all cases. But isn't this also true for an analysis in which the subject always governs the verb? The answer is no, because in this case the same argument would allow for an object-like governor of relative clauses:

[103] **Nehmen Sie den Strauß, den Sie am liebsten mögen.**
'take the bouquet which you best like'

[104]

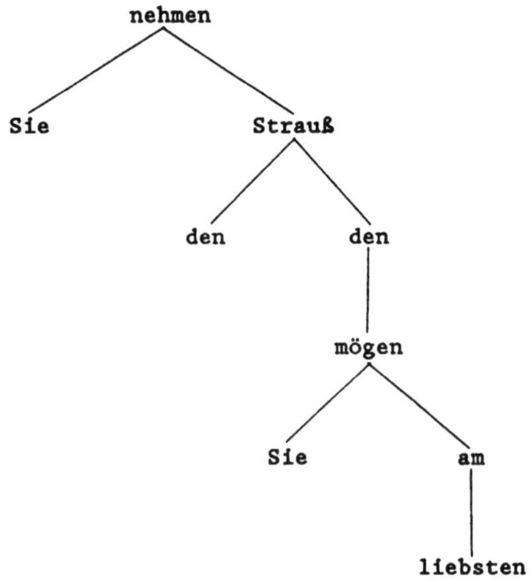

This is an additional argument for the decision taken in 4.1.3.: The finite verb is the main governor of the sentence. I therefore analyse relative clauses as in [105]:

[105]

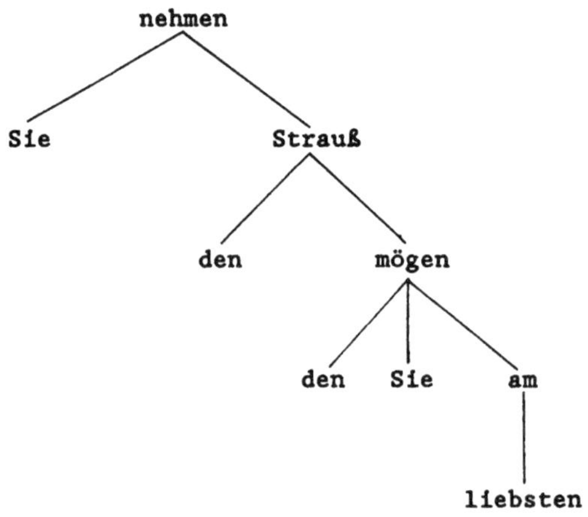

In the context of relative clauses it is interesting to note that the famous problem of discontinuous constructions etc. does not exist in dependency syntax. In other words, as dependency syntax is not bound to the contiguity principle and does not attempt to represent word order together with dependency in a single tree, the constructions in question can be dealt with without creating the problems found in constituency trees (cf. also Hellwig 1986: 197):

[106] **Whom did you say it was given to?**

[107]

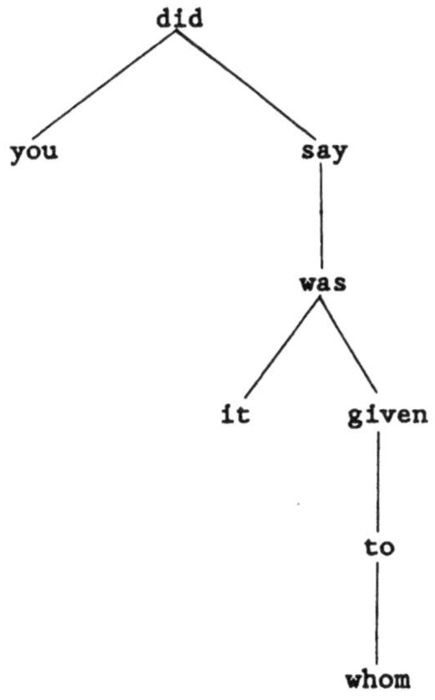

4.10. Coordination

Coordination is a tricky problem in all approaches to syntax. In the present model it is first noticed when in the analysis of co-occurrence relations (4.1.1.) certain words turn out to co-occur with almost everything. These words are then called conjunctions. The group that is traditionally labelled conjunctions in English grammar and in works written in English is syntactically significantly less coherent than other word classes. It contains words of very different syntactic behaviour. A word classification in the present model may thus well arrive at a number of distinct classes for what are traditionally called conjunctions. As is shown in 4.3., this is one of the main objectives of redefining word classes: a distributionally motivated account of function words. To put it differently: a neat description of how the function words function. In this section I speak only about coordinating conjunctions such as English _and_ or _or_. In many languages there are differences among conjunctions with respect to what they can coordinate: syntagmata, clauses or sentences. But in the general considerations of this section, these particulars do not yet play a role and can be neglected for the time being.

A **coordinated construction** is a construction where two or more corresponding syntagmata together have paradigmatic relations with other syntagmata, thus syntactically function as a unit. Normally, such coordinated syntagmata occur next to each other. If there is a coordinating conjunction that links the syntagmata, the construction is syndetic, if not, it is asyndetic. Syndetically coordinated constructions are easy to identify by the presence of the conjunction, but in the case of asyndetic coordination a more careful analysis is required in order to distinguish two coordinated dependents from two dependents of the same dependency type that occur in parallel. The role of the comma and other punctuation marks in syndetic and asyndetic coordination is taken up at the end of this section.

Further investigation into specific languages is required for defining what **corresponding syntagmata** are. For German Engel (1982: 261) speaks of "gleichartige Elemente", but what exactly has to be considered to be 'of the same kind' may be defined on a variety of different levels, Engel adds.

How can coordinated constructions be described in dependency syntax? In the rest of this section I take up six solutions that are first sketched in graphs to give an overview. I illustrate them all with a Tesnière-like sentence:

[108] **Alfred, Bernard et Charles travaillent.**
'Alfred, Bernard and Charles work'

Solution 1:

[109]

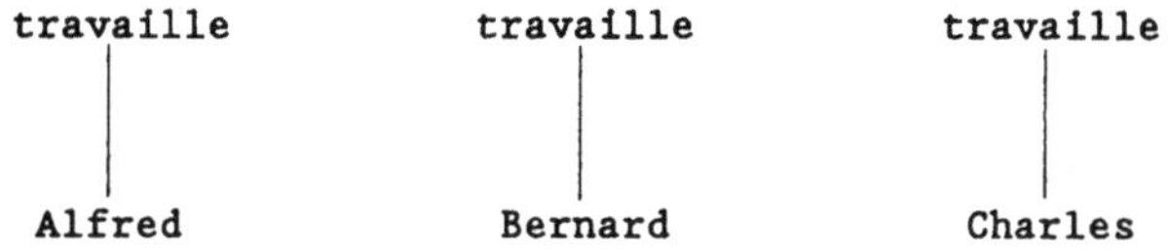

Solution 2:

[110]

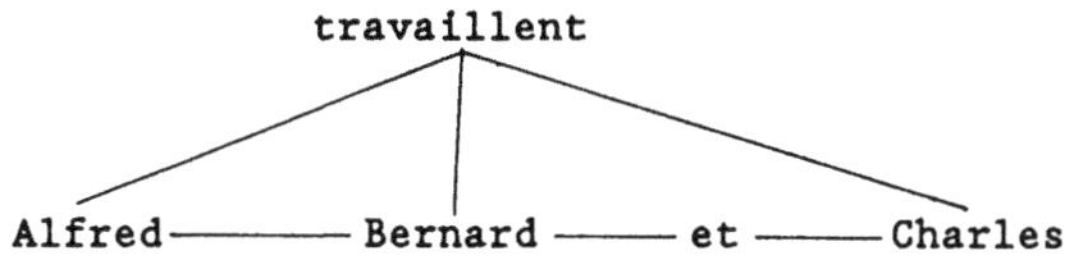

Solution 3:

[111]

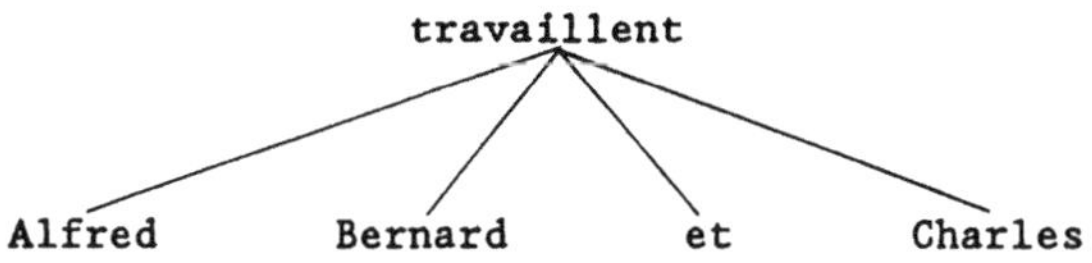

Solution 4:

For the sentence

[112] **Alfred et Bernard travaillent.**

See the exaplantions below.

[113]

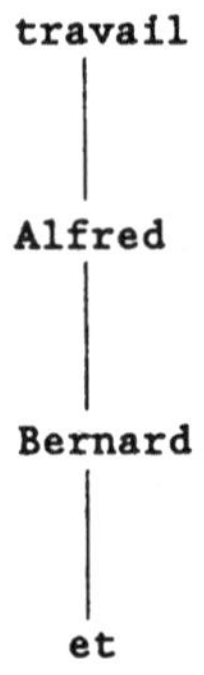

Solution 5:

This and the next solution are again for [108].

[114]

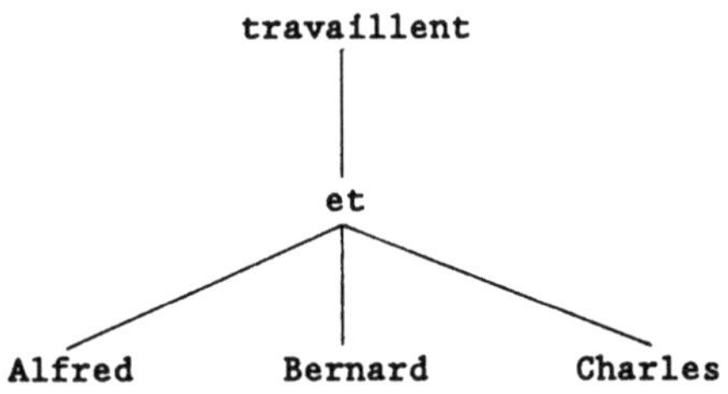

Solution 6:

[115]

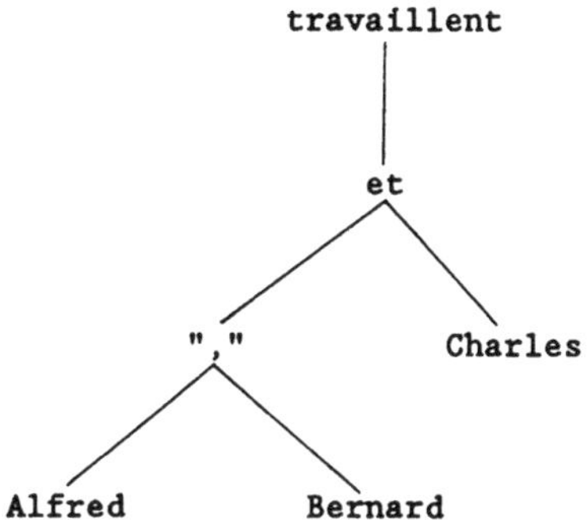

Solution 1: This solution comes down to **restoring** words of non-coordinated sentences that are held to have been merged. This sort of solution is discussed by Hans Jürgen Heringer, Bruno Strecker and Rainer Wimmer (1980: 150) as sort of a transformational augmentation of Tesnière's system (but not suggested as their own solution).

As far as words are concerned, the present model is intended to describe what there is and not what the grammarian would like to have. (This is no contradiction to the arbitrariness that is inevitable and useful at the level of syntactic categories and their units. It admittedly is a minor contradiction to the restoration of contractions, see 4.6., that is used for instance in [131] below.) This principle implies that any solution which would resolve the coordinated constructions by restoring "underlying" simple sentences, is discarded. Moreover, it has been shown that not all coordinated constructions can be split up in a meaningful way. This, however, is a semantic restriction that concerns sentences like:

[116] **The house and the garden cost one million guilders.**

which (semantically) is not the same as

[117] **The house costs one million guilders and the garden costs one million guilders.**

A further complication in coordinated structures is the problem of how to account for dependents that syntactically seem to depend on several of the coordinated syntagmata. Some authors discuss the possibility of including a given word several times in a single dependency tree, so that the structure remains a true tree, still letting each of the governors govern an instance of the common dependent. For Tesnière's sentence [118] (Tesnière 1959/1982: 340) this would yield:

[118]	**Alfred**	**achète**	**des**	**livres**	**et**	**des**	**cahiers**	**neufs.**
				plural			plural	plural
	'Alfred	buys		books	and		notebooks	new'

[119]

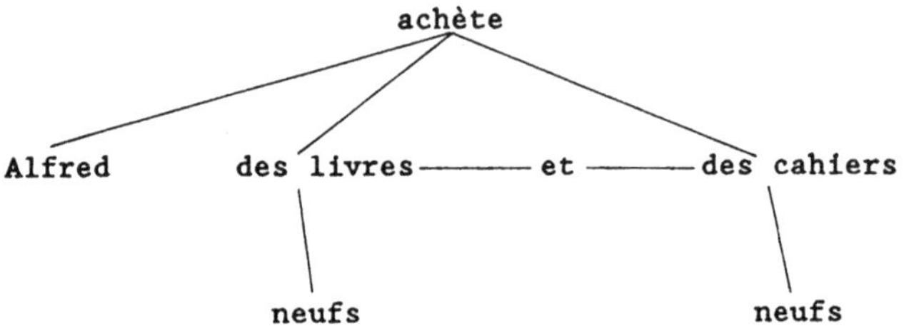

Heringer, Strecker and Wimmer (1980: 150) discuss such a possibility within their assessment of Tesnière's account of coordination, but do not find it convincing. In their opinion, no satisfactory solution can be found within Tesnière's system.

Solution 2: This is Tesnière's solution (1959/1982: 327), but it also cannot be accepted for the purposes aimed at here, since the principles of the present model allow only dependency relations to be be used. In Tesnière's analysis, each of the coordinated syntagmata is directly linked to the common governor, while there are horizontal (undirected) lines between the internal governors of these syntagmata. The conjunction is, where appropriate, placed on one of these horizontal non-dependency lines:

[120] **Alfred et Bernard tombent.**
'Alfred and Bernard fall'

[121]

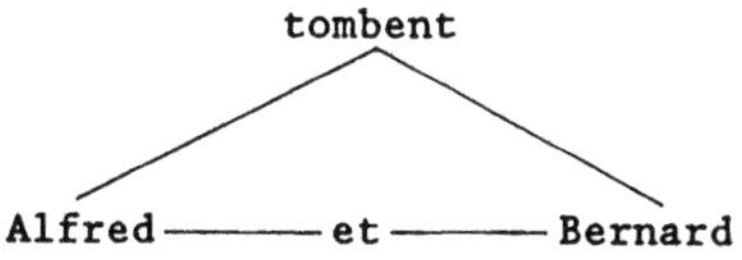

In order to show the enormous number of sentences that would be created by splitting up coordinated structures in simple sentences (solution 1), Tesnière (1959/1982: 344f.) formulates a somewhat extreme example which yields 81 underlying sentences:

[122] **Les maîtres, les pédagogues et les éducateurs**
'the masters the pedagogues and the educators

donnent, répètent et ressassent des avis,
give repeat and scrutinise some opinions

des conseils et des avertissements aux
some advice and some warnings to-the

écoliers, aux collégiens et
grade-school-students to-the high-school-students and

aux lycéens.
to-the grammar-school-students'

Tesnière analyses coordinated sentences as a unit, so that [122] becomes:

[123]

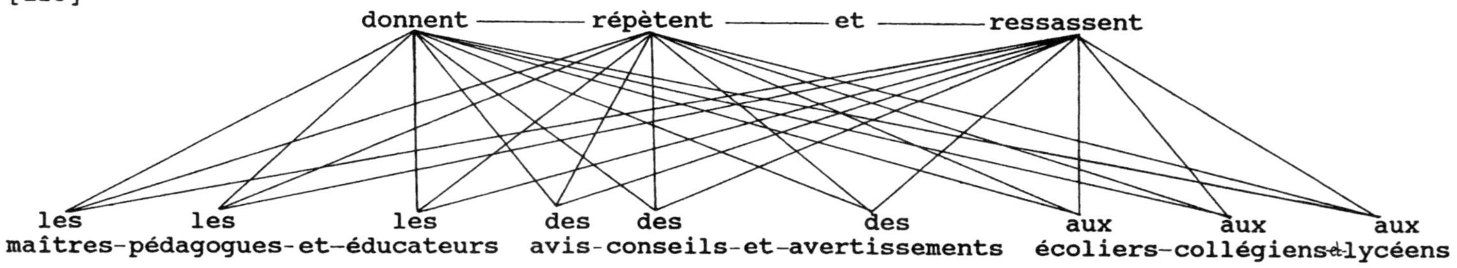
donnent
répètent
et
ressassent
les
les
les
des
des
des
aux
aux
aux
maîtres-pédagogues-et-éducateurs
avis-conseils-et-avertissements
écoliers-collégiens-et-lycéens

Even if splitting up coordinated constructions is rejected, there still remains the problem of dependents that syntactically (and even semantically, although that is no argument in the present model) can be said to depend on several elements of a coordinated construction at the same time. Tesnière (1959/1982: 340) in such cases allows a word to have several governors:

[118]	**Alfred**	**achète**	**des**	**livres**	**et**	**des**	**cahiers**	**neufs.**
				plural			plural	plural
	'Alfred	buys		books	and		notebooks	new'

[124]

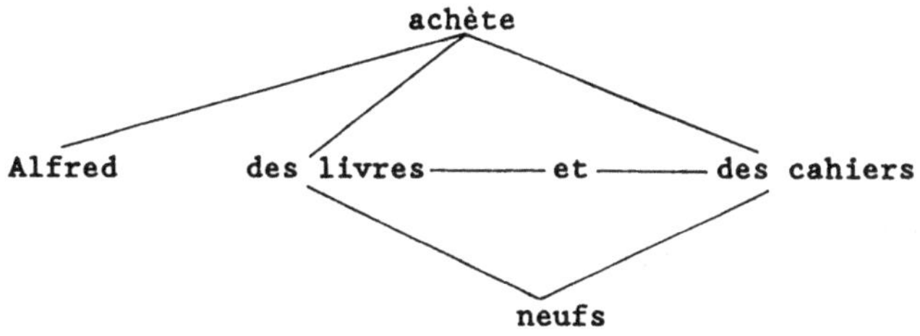

Solution 3: In this solution the conjunction and the coordinated syntagmata are all immediately governed by a common governor. This solution is advocated by Kunze (1972 [quoted from Heringer / Strecker / Wimmer 1980: 250]; cf. Kunze 1975: 106; Reimann 1985: 131) and discussed also by Heringer, Strecker and Wimmer (1980: 144). It appears also to be the solution adopted in Kirschner's (1982: 10) computational application.

There are two disadvantages to this solution: the common governor may have more dependents that are not part of the coordinated structure. Therefore a way to indicate the scope of the conjunction would have to be found. Although this is noted as a major shortcoming by Heringer, Strecker and Wimmer, the problem could be easily remedied by giving the coordinated dependents a special label, or, if one prefers to avoid increasing the number of labels beyond the one which is already present (dependency type), a special label suffix (see solution 6). However, this does not remove the second disadvantage: What to do with common dependents?

This solution nevertheless has an advantage that seems interesting for models other than the present one: In solutions 5 and 6 an inserted conjunction makes the distance in the tree longer between (in this example) the verb and its subjects. In solution 4 the distance is still less recoverable. There are, however, models that use this distance as a syntactic category. Johannes Erben (1958/1972: 266) distinguishes Satzglieder 'parts of a sentence' of first, second, third etc. degree. This degree indicates the distance from the finite verb in terms of the number of branches that establish the direct link. With this method Erben accentuates the difference between the dependents of a finite verb and those of other governors, relating them all to the verb. Tarvainen (1985b: 26) argues in a similar way. In the present model this distinction does not play a role and no measuring of distances is required. However, if this is desirable in another application for a specific purpose, Heringer, Strecker and Wimmer (1980: 144) themselves say how the problem can be remedied, at least for solutions 5 and 6 (but not so easily in 4): The conjunction is passed by in counting degrees. However, they reject this simple solution because of supposed difficulties in sentence generation, which they unfortunately do not specify.

Solution 4: This is Engel's solution (1982: 263f.). It is much closer than solutions 1 to 3 to the principles of the present model. Engel's reasoning is distributional. He argues that the second coordinated syntagma (in my example [112] this is Bernard) occurs by virtue of the first (Alfred) and the conjunction (et) by virtue of the second (Bernard). The linking element may also be a comma. I have had to reduce my example sentence [108] to [112], because Engel does not say how to go on for more than two coordinated syntagmata. It is noteworthy that Engel himself is not satisfied with this account and finds it inconsistent (Engel 1982: 263). Unfortunately he does not tell us why.

Engel (1982: 32) is the author who perhaps most explicitly emphasises the arbitrariness of decisions about the direction of dependency relations. It may therefore be allowed to turn around the relation between the conjunction and the second syntagma. This would make Engel's solution extendable for more than two coordinated syntagmata. [108] would then become:

[125]

```
travail
   |
Alfred
   |
  ","
   |
Bernard
   |
  et
   |
Charles
```

Engel's solution is closer to the present model not only because it is based on distributional arguments for the internal structure of the coordinated construction. Engel's account also gives a description of the construction that fits in with the idea that there are paradigmatic relations between other words (e.g. ils in [108]) and the coordinated construction **as a whole**. In view of these relations, it is required in the present model to let the whole construction depend on a single internal word. This word is in Engel's account the internal governor of the first coordinated syntagma.

There are, however, still two arguments against the adoption of Engel's solution here. Firstly, inheritance of syntactic features is important for form government and agreement with regard to syntactic form. The plural form of the verb travaillent is determined by its subject being either plural or coordinated. In Engel's account, however, the immediate dependent of the verb is a singular noun, and the information as to whether there is a coordinated construction must be looked for deeper in the tree. This is not impossible, but if a simpler solution can be found, it should be preferred. Simplicity in this respect is crucial to metataxis.

The second argument against Engel's solution is the same as before: There is no consistent way of analysing common dependents of coordinated syntagmata.

Solution 5: This solution is suggested by Nikula (1986: 93ff.). As it is very close to the solution I propose for the present model (solution 6), I discuss its advantages and disadvantages together with that solution. Nikula's account allows for a number of augmentations that I use in the present model, but as Nikula himself does not work it out in so much detail, it is difficult to argue about the ideas he might have about the topics. But as far as I can see, my solutions for the prescribed number of certain dependency types and also (partially) my common-dependents solution are compatible with Nikula's system.

Solution 6: This solution, finally, is the one I adopt for the present model.

The principles formulated above (4.6. and 4.7.) already point out the direction in which a solution within the present model ought to be sought. There should be

- dependency relations only (this excludes constructs like Tesnière's horizontal lines),
- one place for one word and
- no copying or restoring of words.

A coordinated construction as a whole has paradigmatic relations with other words and should accordingly be rendered as **a single syntagma**. In contrast to Engel's solution (4), the internal governor of the syntagma here is the conjunction and the coordinated syntagmata are its immediate dependents. [108] thus becomes:

[115]

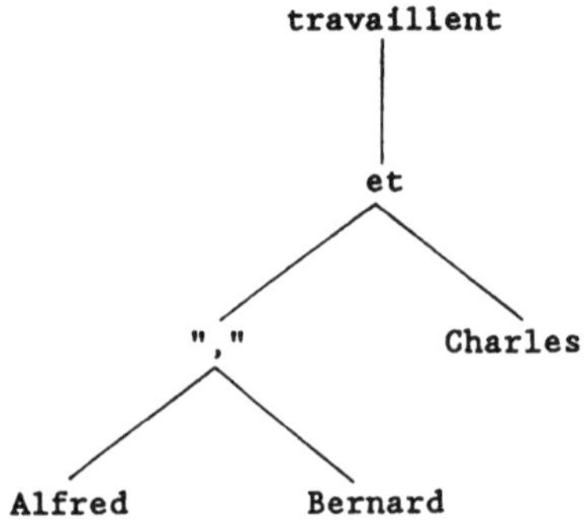

The coordinating conjunction _et_ governs the three subjects in [108] not by virtue of its own valency, but through the verb it depends on. The special multiplying effect of coordination can thus be described straightforwardly: The coordinating conjunction can occupy one place in the government pattern of its governor and thereby acquires the government capacity of its governor for this place (i.e. for this dependency type). The government patterns of certain words in many languages contain provisions about the possible or required number of certain dependency types. A French verb, for instance, can have only one subject, but a virtually indefinite number of adverbial adjuncts. One of the advantages of the description of coordinated structures adopted for the present model is that these statements about the number of dependents can be formulated without taking coordinated structures as exceptions. It is not necessary to specify everywhere in the description of government patterns that, for instance, "a finite verb governs one subject (or more, provided that the subjects are coordinated)" or "a finite verb governs any number of adverbial adjuncts (which may or may not be coordinated)" etc. Given the present solution, coordination of syntagmata is a phenomenon that stays within the syntagma. Words that are not directly involved in a given coordinate structure are not afflicted by its peculiarities. With respect to these words, which make up the rest of the sentence, the complex syntagma is as usual represented by a single word.

When this one-syntagma solution is adopted, a number of questions remains to be treated:

- How many elements can a conjunction coordinate?
- What about common dependents?
- What about asyndetic coordination?
- How to distinguish asyndetic coordination and parallel dependents?

Coordination is not confined to pairs of syntagmata. [122] contains several examples for three coordinated syntagmata, and higher numbers can easily be imagined. The number of coordinated elements is virtually unlimited. In my view, the grammarian has to decide between two possible ways of handling such structures. The first option is just to let the conjunction govern all the syntagmata on the same level as Nikula does (solution 5).

The second option takes the comma as sort of an auxiliary "word" (as Engel does, see solution 4) and uses the definition that a coordinating conjunction (to which class thereby also the comma is allotted) governs exactly two coordinated syntagmata. In my account of Esperanto (Schubert 1986a: 59ff.) I have adopted the latter solution. My decision has to do with the problem of common dependents.

Heringer, Strecker and Wimmer (1980: 145ff.) discard the coordinator-governed structures because they find them ad hoc, but also because they do not know where to place common dependents in such a tree. In my opinion, however, the present solution is well suited for this purpose. The coordinating conjunction represents the coordinated syntagmata towards the rest of the sentence. Until now, in this study "the rest of the sentence" has always been a vague description of the governor of the syntagma in question, and possibly of words higher up in the tree, by which that immediate governor in turn is governed. But why not also common dependents? Dependents that in a syntactic analysis seem to be governed by both or all the elements of a coordinated construction can easily be rendered as governed by the word that represents the coordinated construction as a whole: the conjunction. In this way the two possible syntactic interpretations of the following well-known example can be rendered (cf. Mel'čuk 1979b: 143 n. 1). In order to distinguish the coordinated syntagmata from common dependents, I introduce a label suffix "-C" for the former.

[126] Russian: **bystrye protony i nejtrony**
'fast protons and neutrons'

[127]

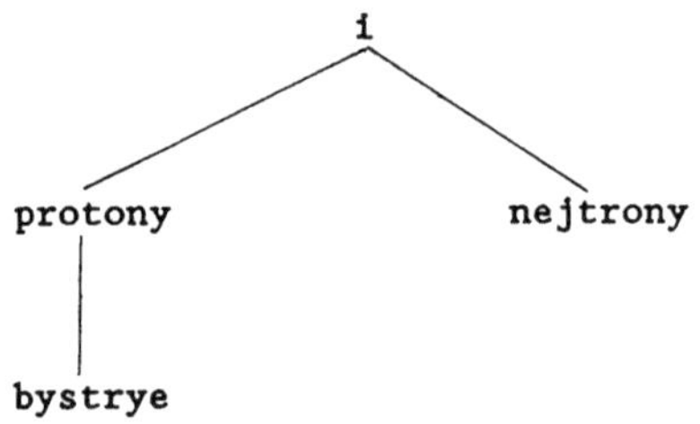

[128]

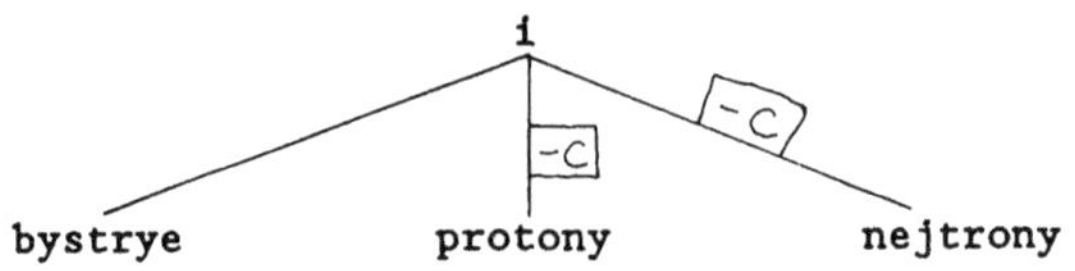

The above decision to let conjunctions coordinate exactly two dependants divides up the construction into pairs and can now be used for expressing the possibility, if necessary, that a common dependant may be common not to all, but only to some of the coordinated syntagmata:

[129] Russian: **bystrye protony i nejtrony, i èlektrony**
'fast protons and neutrons, and electrons'

[130]

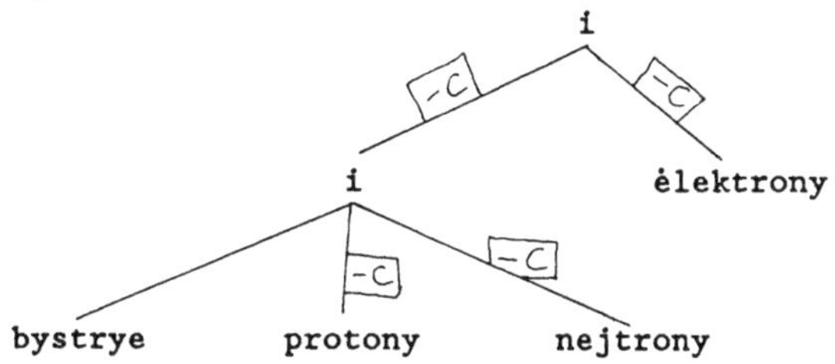

Possibilities for easily rendering the scope of common dependants are also the reason why solution 3 is not adopted here.

Given these decisions, **asyndetic coordination** may force the grammarian to violate the one-word principle (4.6.). If syndetically coordinated syntagmata have a common representative, the conjunction, asyndetic coordination requires a similar means. Using the comma as a word, I have already introduced an auxiliary symbol. In the case of asyndetic coordination one might use the comma as well, but if there is no such punctuation mark in a certain language, an arbitrary auxiliary symbol seems to be the most practical solution. In a way, this is nothing but an empty node.

Although this option in a certain way violates an earlier formulated principle, the one-syntagma solution for coordination is so advantageous especially for metataxis that I prefer to use it in the present model.

In the beginning of this section a question was raised which now can be answered: What is the difference between asyndetically coordinated and unrelated parallel dependents? In Engel's chapter "Häufung" (1982: 261) they are not clearly distinguished. In the present model, coordination means that a number of syntagmata function as a unit with respect to the rest of the sentence. If in a language several parallel dependants are possible under the governor in question and if there is no other indication that would require a group of dependants to be taken as a unit, there is no reason to do so. In other words, syntagmata whose number is not restricted by the government pattern of the governor and which do not have common dependents, should be taken as parallel dependents. If one of the conditions is not met, they are coordinated. I admit that this is a rough definition that may be refined by the particular requirements of the structure of one or language or another.

Applying the decisions of this section, one can draw a tree for Tesnière's sentence [122]:

[131]

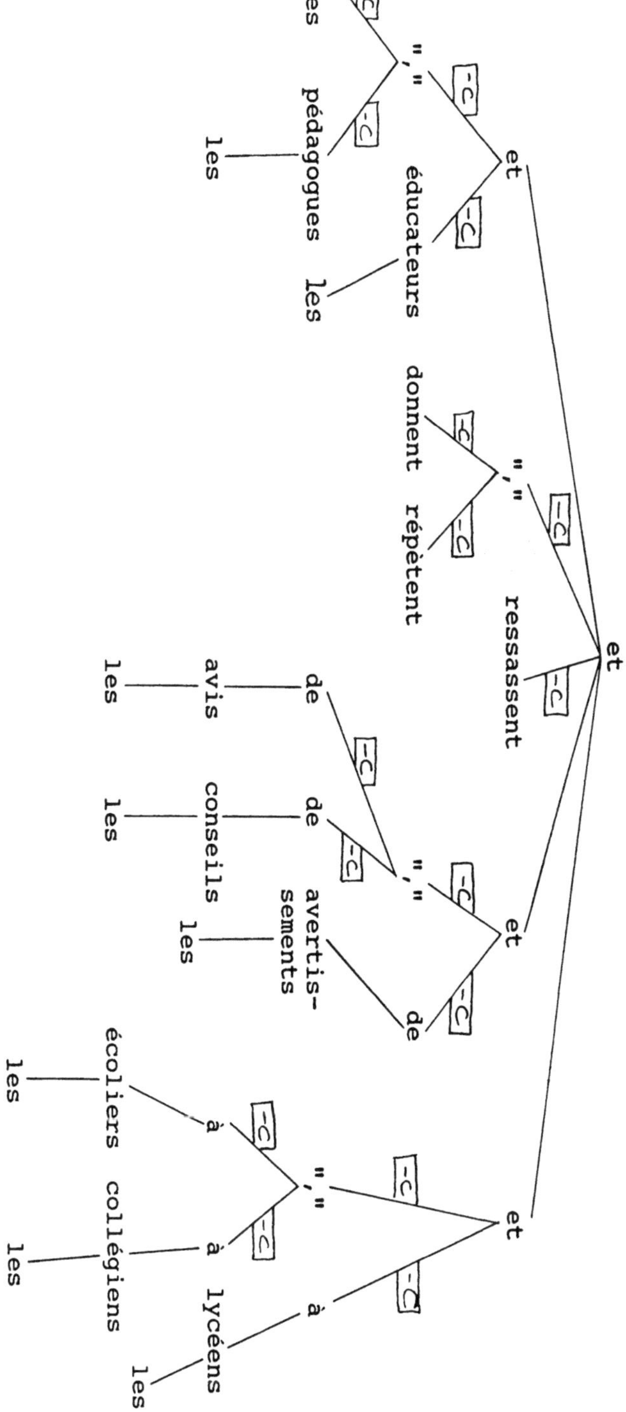
et
et
","
-c
maîtres
les
pédagogues
les
éducateurs
les
donnent
répètent
ressassent
de
avis
les
de
conseils
les
de
avertis-
sements
les
à
écoliers
les
à
collégiens
les
à
lycéens
les

4.11. Ellipsis

Ellipsis is another notorious problem of syntactic theory. Before addressing ellipsis, it is worthwhile to make sure that one is aware of its essence. Etymology tells us that ellipsis derives from a word meaning 'omission'. Elliptic sentences are sentences where something has been left out. In my view one fact is crucial to the understanding of ellipsis: Ellipsis is a **construct** of grammarians. It is senseless to ask whether or not ellipsis in reality exists. The assumption of ellipsis in a grammatical model is one of the grammarian's arbitrary decisions. There may be very good reasons for doing making this assumption, but one should remain aware that it is not part of observable reality, but of the grammarian-made model.

In accordance with the principles used hitherto in the present model, the first attempt to cope with ellipsis should aim at describing the dependency relations between the words that really are there. Only if this does not lead to acceptable results, the analysis may move somewhat further from the text by restoring "omitted" words etc. I hereafter refer to such a procedure as "restoration"

A dependency syntax for German would have to account for the following sentences:

[132] **In der Tür standen zwei Männer. Der größere trug**
'in the door stood two men the taller carried

eine Leiter und der kleinere trug einen Werkzeugkasten.
a ladder and the smaller carried a toolbox'

Restoring "omitted" words would yield

[133] **Der größere [Mann] trug eine Leiter und der kleinere**
'the taller man carried a ladder and the smaller

[Mann] trug einen Werkzeugkasten.
man carried a toolbox'

Restoration has the advantage of making the possible government patterns simpler. Normally, a subject can be a nominative noun (and a pronoun etc.), but not an adjective. If words are not restored, this rule has to be augmented by a provision that allows also for adjectives and certain determiners in the function of a subject, and, in a similar way, in the function of other dependency types. Restoring has the disadvantage that it is a complicated problem on text-semantic level. It seems very easy in the given example, but examples are always in some respects simpler than reality. Given the emphasis on form in the present model, I prefer a solution that somewhat extends the descriptions of possible syntactic forms of dependency types and avoids the text-semantic restoration problem. The second sentence in [132] can be syntactically analysed without reference to the preceding sentence, and yields this tree (labels from Lobin 1987):

[134]

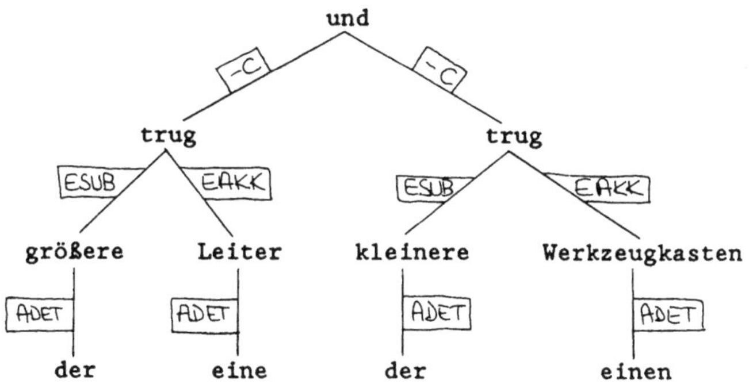

Ellipsis has influence not only on the description of the syntactic form of dependency types. It is important both for analysis and for synthesis to have the ellipsis problem in mind when formulating rules about **obligatory dependents** (see 4.4.2.). What is obligatory in "normal" cases, may not be so in ellipsis.

The most complicated cases of ellipsis occur when ellipsis and coordination interfere. It seems worth mentioning that the solution adopted in 4.10. for **common dependents** of coordinated syntagmata has been tailored to describe in a non-elliptic way many cases that otherwise might be subsumed under ellipsis. In [118]:

[118]	**Alfred**	**achète**	**des**	**livres**	**et**	**des**	**cahiers**	**neufs.**
				plural			plural	plural
	'Alfred buys			books	and		notebooks	new'

there is no need to restore another neufs, since an elegant way of letting the common dependent depend on the coordinated structure as a whole has been devised. The same method applies on sentence level (example from Tesnière 1959/1982: 340, labels from Tamis 1986):

[135] **Les enfants rient et chantent.**
'the children laugh and sing'

[136]

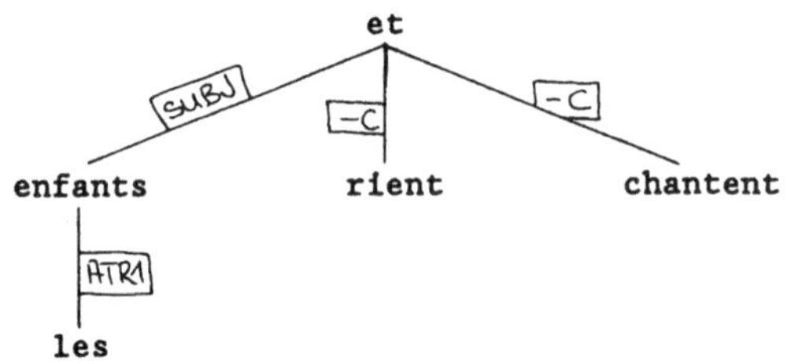

These possibilities can easily be combined, as was shown in [131] (4.10.).

The analysis of [132] does not entail too many problems, since the "omitted" words have only one dependent each. But there are more problematic cases:

[137] **Der größere Mann trug eine Leiter und der kleinere**
'the taller man carried a ladder and the smaller

Mann einen Werkzeugkasten.
man a tollbox'

What could be restored here is a second instance of the verb trug which would have two dependents, a subject and an object.

[138] **Der größere Mann trug eine Leiter und der kleinere**
'the taller man carried a ladder and the smaller

Mann [trug] einen Werkzeugkasten.
man carried a toolbox'

[139]

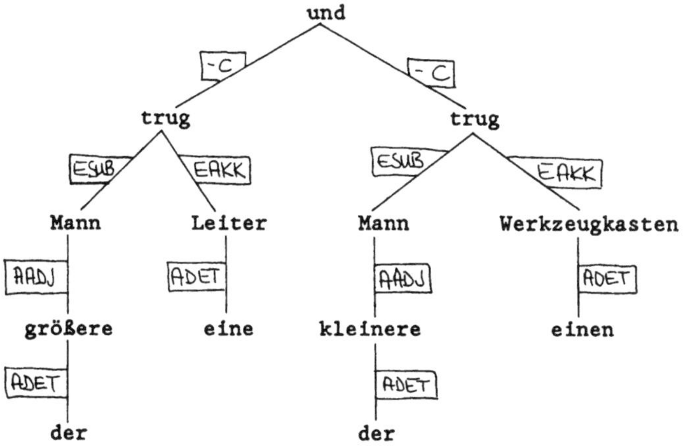

If restoration of words is still rejected, a possible solution would be to acknowledge that nevertheless a node should be inserted in the structure. This would mean introducing an empty node (see 4.6. and 4.10.).

[140]

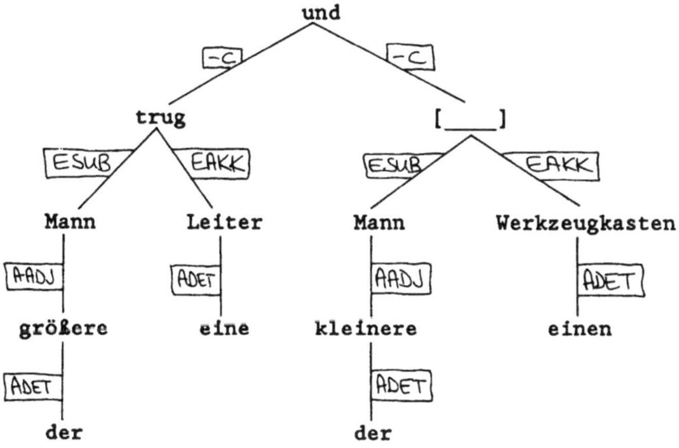

Another solution is to consider the two dependents to depend directly on the conjunction:

[141]

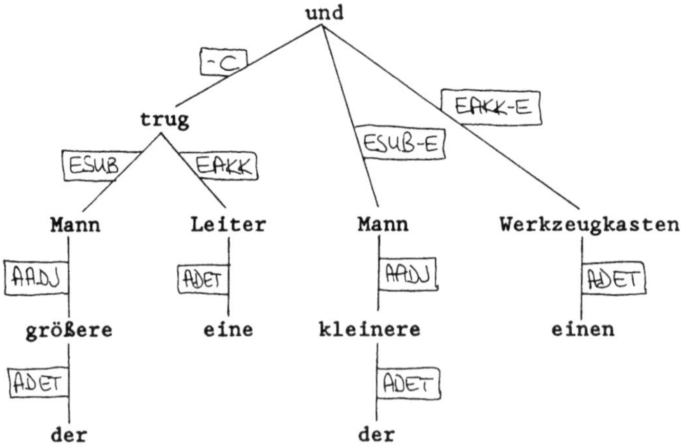

The second solution seems to be preferable within the framework of the present model. Strictly speaking, however, a certain degree of restoration cannot be avoided even in that case. The conjunction has to be equipped with the appropriate government capacity. This must be taken from somewhere and this ultimately also involves restoration. In the example, the conjunction can take that government information from its first dependent. If it is always possible so doubtless to find the source of government information, it is obviously as easy to restore the word. Yet, there is still another argument for taking the conjunction as the immediate governor of the dependents. In this way it is more clearly acknowledged that the occurrence of the special construction (whether termed ellipsis or not) is due to coordination. It may be advisable in some way to mark dependents that are found under a governor only by virtue of restored government capacity. Similar to normal coordination, these constructions could be identified by a label suffix. I have chosen an "-E" (Ellipsis) in appropriate cases.

But although one of the solutions seems to be preferable, it is not the only possible way out. Which solution to adopt is ultimately again an arbitrary decision. If the syntactic properties of the language in question do not suggest anything else, I prefer this solution, which is in harmony with the conjunction-governed structures used in other coordination cases. But I am aware of the fact that further investigation is required as to the possible depth of elliptic constructions. The solution preferred here is only feasible, when the "omitted" word is immediately governed by the conjunction. If other words can occur between the conjunction and the omitted word, then a different solution may be needed.

4.12. The generative productivity of dependency syntax

A dependency syntax is part of the grammar of a specific language, and a grammar describes the regularities of a language in a static way, rather than providing an algorithm for analysing or synthesising sentences or texts. Nevertheless I have in the preceding sections, when illustrating the present model, quite often spoken about analysis of corpus texts and similar exercises. This appears to be a suitable way of presenting the model, but I should like not to create the impression that the present model is analysis syntax only. Analysis syntax is only a restricted subset of what is aimed at with the present model, and in addition, it is in practice insufficient for the application I have in mind. Machine translation requires analysis and synthesis. Metataxis, in particular, is a process which starts with syntactically analysed source language texts as the input and results in synthesis of syntactically correct texts in a target language. Metataxis thus presupposes both **analysis** and **synthesis**. Let therefore a few words be said about the **generative productivity** of the present model of dependency syntax.

Generative power is a term that in generative grammar is used neutrally with respect to analysis and synthesis. What I have in mind here is the capacity to generate sentences and texts by translating from one language into another. I term this capacity **generative productivity**.

Metataxis has to provide the rules for finding the syntactically **correct** translations of a given sentence. Dependency syntax must provide the framework for the metataxis process: It has to describe the syntactically possible sentences in the target language. Seen from this conceptual viewpoint, generative productivity nevertheless is not so different from generative power.

What can dependency syntax tell us about the syntactically possible sentences of a given language? In the present model, the answer to this question is implicit in the answer to another, relatively simple question: Which are the possible main governors of a sentence? **Given the possible main governors of sentences, all syntactically possible sentences can be inferred.**

Maybe this needs some illustration. I take Danish as an example. A dependency syntax for Danish within the framework of the present model has been devised by Ingrid Schubert (1987). In her analysis, there are twelve word classes. The possible governor of a sentence is in Danish a finite verb (or a conjunction that coordinates finite verbs). There are other, marginal possibilities which I ignore for the moment. If the governor is known, its possible dependents are specified by the government capacity of its word class, in this case of verbs. The dependency types specified in this way are the complements and adjuncts (see 4.4.2. about this distinction) shown in [142]:

[142]

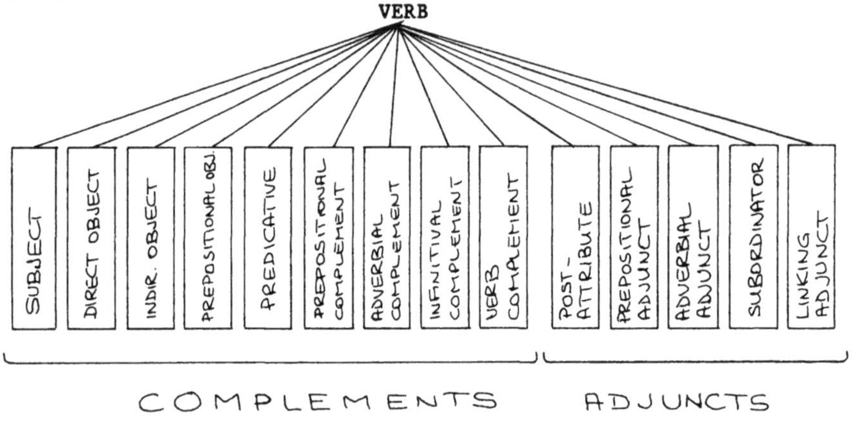

Most of the complements may be represented in a sentence by one instance only, each of the adjuncts several times. Now the syntactic functions of possible dependents are specified, and their syntactic form can be found in the description of dependency types. A subject, for example, may be any member of the following list: noun, pronoun (nominative), placeholder (which may occur together with a second subject out of the other word classes), finite verb (internal governor of a subordinate clause), infinitive (normally with a dependent infinitive marker <u>at</u>), numeral, conjunction that coordinates two instances of these word classes. One of the possible forms of a subject is a noun. Now the process is repeated recursively: The government pattern of nouns specifies the possible dependents of a noun.

[143]

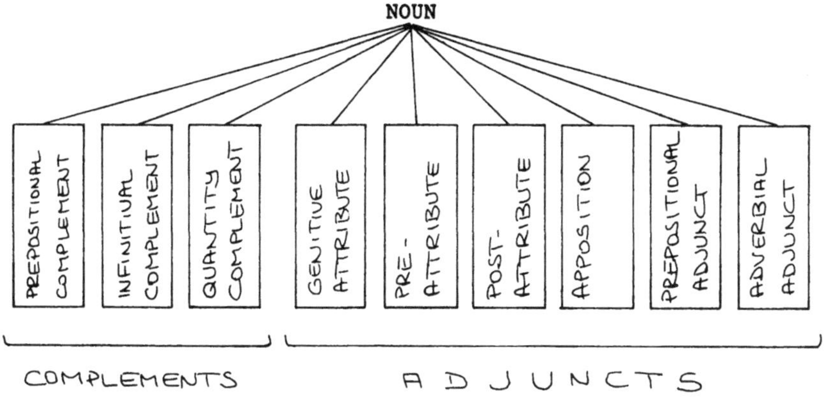

The form descriptions of each dependency type specify which word classes these dependents may belong to and what syntactic features they should have.

This recursive process is not expanding as in a top-down constituency syntax, but rather slot filling. In the general form I outline above, it over-generates. If only word classes and dependency types are taken into consideration, the results are only applicable for words with the maximum government capacity of their word class.

[144]

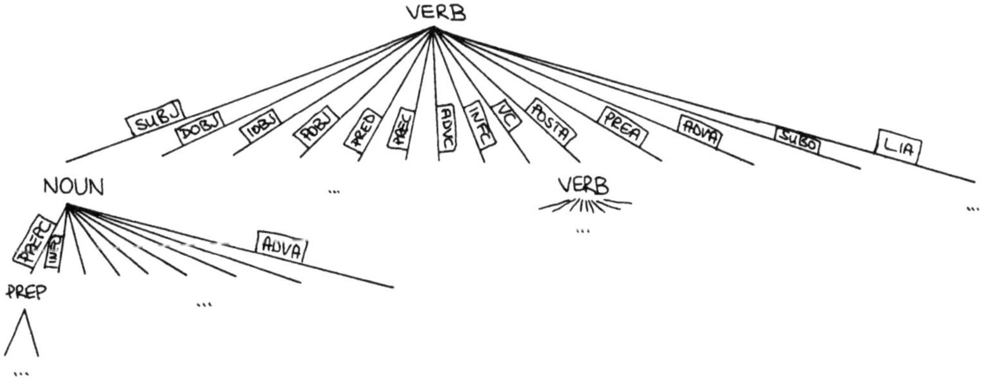

The general trees, built up in this way, can be reduced to actually possible structures as soon as concrete words are inserted. Now the government capacity of the nodes is restricted by the individual **valency** of the given word.

[145]

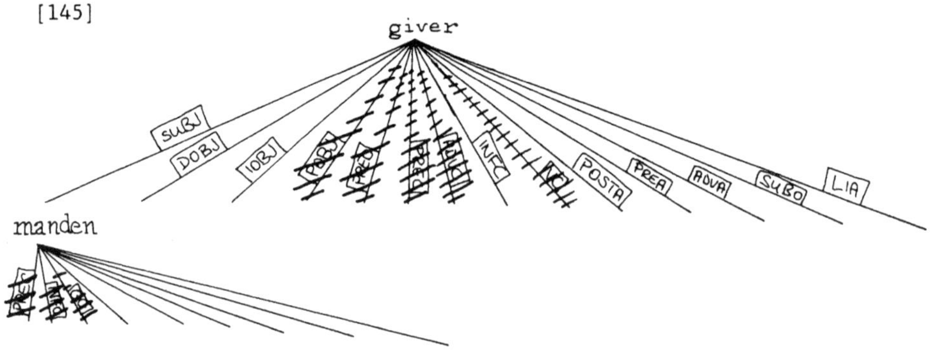

In this way the syntax generates **the syntactically possible sentences of the language**. Of course no semantic or pragmatic restrictions are applied here.

If I understand recent publications (Vijay-Shanker / Weir / Joshi 1986; Joshi 1987) on tree adjoining grammars correctly, they achieve a similar productivity in a constituency syntax - with much more effort.

I return to a method of applying in metataxis this knowledge about the syntactic possibilities (5.1.1.).

4.13. **Principles of dependency syntax: A summary**

To summarise this chapter, I here formulate a number of principles which are valid for the present model of dependency syntax. Details are found in the twelve sections above.

1. Syntax is concerned with the **form** of the linguistic sign.

2. Syntax is concerned with form on all levels from **morpheme** to **text**.

3. Words in sentences are related to each other by **dependency** relations.

4. **Dependency** is directed co-occurrence.

5. The **syntactic form** of words is their shape as described by morphology, word formation and word order.

6. The **syntactic function** of words with respect to other words is described in terms of dependency types.

7. A word group that as a whole is **paradigmatically** related to other words or word groups is a unit. Its elements are syntactically related and form a **syntagma**.

8. A syntagma has a single **internal governor** which represents the syntagma to the rest of the sentence.

9. With the exception of the main governor of a sentence, each word in a sentence has exactly **one governor**.

10. Each word is represented exactly **once** in a dependency structure (dependency tree).

11. Dependency structures are true **trees**.

12. **Empty nodes** in dependency structures should be avoided.

Chapter 5

Metataxis

To translate means to express a given meaning in another language. If a whole text is taken as a single **linguistic sign**, then to translate is to exchange the **form** of the sign, preserving its **content**. With more or less conscious reference to this idea, many efforts were (and are still being) made to handle translation as manipulation of form. The designs for mechanical translation that turned up every now and then during the last centuries heavily relied on the tacit assumption that form would do. Early computational translation also began with this presupposition, but later experience has shown that in order to handle form properly, a high degree of understanding of the content of the text being translated is indispensable.

Language has different means for expressing meaning. Roughly speaking, these are **morphemes** and **relations**. Related morphemes make up higher-level units, such as **words**, **syntagmata**, **clauses**, **sentences** and **texts**. All these must be handled by translation. The replacement of form, which can be considered the essence of translation, should accordingly treat both morphemes and relations, and thereby work at all the levels built up by them. Translating morphemes, and often groups of related morphemes such as words, is the main function of a **bilingual dictionary**. Translating the relations is **metataxis**.

"**Métataxe**" is a term coined by Tesnière (1959/1982: 283). His chapter on metataxis begins with the following definition:

> 1. Bien que l'analyse structurale de la phrase simple soit toujours fondée sur les mêmes principes généraux, quelle que soit la structure qu'adopte telle ou telle langue pour y couler un exprimende sémantique donné, il n'en résulte pas que les différentes langues fassent toujours appel à des structures identiques pour exprimer des idées qui pourtant se correspondent exactement sur le plan sémantique.
>
> 2. En pareil cas, la traduction d'une langue à l'autre oblige à faire appel à une structure différente. Nous donnerons à ce **changement structural** le nom de **métataxe**.

To date, Tesnière's metataxis is by far not as widely known as valency or other concepts from his works. Indeed, there are only a handful of authors who seem at least to have noticed the concise 37 pages on metataxis in Tesnière's 675-page chef-d'oeuvre. Heringer, Strecker and Wimmer (1980: 162) mention metataxis in passing, but do not investigate it profoundly. In their view, metataxis has to do with foreign-language teaching which many linguist without justification categorically consider to be unscientific and not worth any serious attention. In a discussion of semantic valency and the language-specificness of deep cases Engel (1980: 11) mentions metataxis as an interesting approach that has not found followers. The most positive judgements come from the translator and translation theoretician Peter Newmark (1981: 32) who sees in translation theory a link between text grammar on the one hand and valency, dependency and case grammar on the other hand. In this connection, he calls Tesnière's metataxis chapter "forty pages of valuable translation theory". In a recent statement, Newmark (1987: 174) distinguishes contrastive linguistics and translation theory, viewing the former as static (describing the differences between two languages) and the latter as dynamic (describing the translation process). He attributes Tesnière's metataxis in part to the one and in part to the other discipline.

Tesnière (1959/1982: 283) says that metataxis, the structural rearrangement of a sentence being translated, forces the translator not just to translate mechanically, but to **rethink** the sentence as a whole. In machine translation, this rethinking is then again realised by algorithms, thus brought back, so to speak, to "mechanical" procedures on a higher level. The option for dependency syntax in (machine) translation is an option for metataxis. When proposing dependency syntax for the DLT machine translation system (see 1.2. and 7.5.), I also dedicated a chapter to metataxis (Schubert 1986a: 166ff.). Brief accounts have also been included in other studies (Schubert 1986c: 131ff.; 1987: 114f.).

Metataxis is the structural side of translation. Of course many scholars have dealt with the phenomena involved, without terming them metataxis. An abundance of interesting works is found in the realm of contrastive linguistics and translation theory. Reviewing their achievements and their import for language theory or for machine translation is far beyond the scope of this study. A few works should nevertheless be mentioned that are more closely related to metataxis, although they also do not use the term. These are works in contrastive dependency syntax. Metataxis translates relations and a dictionary translates words. A bilingual **valency** dictionary, however, does both (see 5.1.). In this way, a bilingual valency dictionary can be said to be related to metataxis. There are many studies on selected problems of contrastive dependency syntax. (A list of studies concerning

Scandinavian languages, including Finnish, as compared with German and English is given in Schubert, forthc. b.). To the best of my knowledge, however, there are only two dependency studies that attempt to cover the complete syntax of two languages. These two studies are both written by Kalevi Tarvainen and illustrate the fact that he does not view contrastive grammar as static, but as dynamic, and therefore has written both a German-Finnish and a Finnish-German contrastive dependency syntax (Tarvainen 1985a,b).

The model of dependency syntax described in chapter 4. is strictly **form**-oriented. In a less obvious way, it is also translation-oriented, or, to put it differently, **metataxis**-oriented. A metataxis description for a specific language pair is a set of rules that transform texts and sentences from one language into the other. In a first approach, these rules are bound to a single translation direction taking one language as the source language and the other one as the target language. On a more theoretical level the question of **reversibility** of metataxis rules is certainly worth discussing (see 8.). The starting point for a set of metataxis rules is a text, syntactically analysed in accordance with a metataxis-oriented model of dependency syntax. A metataxis rule system thus establishes a link between the dependency syntaxes of two languages. So, a metataxis rule system is **specific for a language pair** and a translation direction, in other words, specific for a couple of a source and a target language. It should be emphasised that the two dependency syntaxes that are linked by a metataxis rule system are **autonomous**. This means that they should be oriented towards metataxis as such, but not specifically towards another language, nor towards a specific translation direction. Only one dependency syntax is needed for a single language, regardless of the languages into or from which it is to be translated. In this way, the theoretical system built up in this study is kept **modular**. A consequence of this modularity is that so-called "attuning" of syntaxes for structural transfer (Appelo 1986: 41), which would essentially diminish the cross-linguistic applicability of a metataxis system, can be avoided.

Translation concerns morphemes and relations, and metataxis deals with the relations part. Structural transfer, however, is so closely interwoven with lexical transfer that both have to be seen as cooperating when metataxis is at issue. Lexical transfer, the translation of morphemes, words etc., is so essential to translation that even in a structural account it cannot be passed by as just an additional phenomenon. The close relationship between the two sides of transfer plays a central role throughout this entire chapter.

The close link between structural and lexical transfer notwithstanding, the semantic and pragmatic difficulties of lexical transfer are kept outside the metataxis model as presented here (and as being implemented for the DLT system). A basic assumption of this chapter is that the entire metataxis process is free from these problems, or rather, that it only prepares their solution, which then is accomplished by other subprocedures of the translation process. If the bilingual dictionary contains two possible translations for one source language word, metataxis will deliver two translations of the sentence, and if there are three words in the sentence with three equivalents each, metataxis will deliver nine translations. The objective of the metataxis process is to let these alternative translations be syntactically correct as such, and to let them be possible syntactic equivalents of the source language sentence. A choice can then be made in a separate subprocedure on purely content-related (semantic and pragmatic) grounds (cf. the word expert system described by Papegaaij, Sadler and Witkam, 1986, and by Papegaaij, 1986). The strict dividing line between structural transfer (metataxis) that multiplies its results with the options of the bilingual dictionary on the one hand, and lexical transfer as an interpretation and selection process on the other hand, ought to be seen as a conceptual image which clarifies the appropriate design ideas in a system like DLT. In an implementation for machine translation, the two subprocedures may be intertwined in a more sophisticated way so that they can influence each other.

For the sake of the discussion I in the above paragraphs speak about structural versus lexical transfer. It ought, however, to be pointed out that the dividing line between what metataxis can deal with and what it should leave to other subprocedures of the overall translation process essentially is not exactly between structure and lexical choices, but rather between form and content. The syntactically possible translation alternatives metataxis delivers thus may differ not only in word choice but also in syntactic structure. This is possible exactly when the difference between two syntactic structures conveys meaning. The notorious cases of ambiguity as to the governor of prepositions very often are examples of this phenomenon. So if the syntactic analysis of the source language text (the parsing) delivers alternative analyses of a sentence, the choice among which cannot be made on purely syntactic grounds, metataxis has to handle all the alternative source language trees and to deliver the syntactically possible target language alternatives for all of them.

In the following sections I present a model for metataxis that is directly linked to the dependency syntax model of chapter 4. In 5.1. sentence level metataxis rules are shown to be lexical redundancy rules about the words in a bilingual dependency dictionary. In 5.2., word level phenomena concerned with syntactic form, such as morphemes and syntactic features, are taken up. These two facets of the metataxis system are put into a structured order in 5.3. where the step-by-step procedure of handling dependency trees in metataxis is explained. 5.4. examines the prospects for text level investigations and some preliminary solutions, while 5.5. discusses the synthesis steps that follow metataxis proper in order to attain a plain text as the final result of translation. The final section, 5.6., motivates the choice of dependency syntax, and thereby of metataxis, for machine translation, answering the question left open in 2.3.

5.1. Metataxis as contrastive lexical redundancy rules

A metataxis system for a specific language pair is a system of rules which carry out the structural change that makes up the relations part of translation. The process that is devised in these rules has a clearly defined starting point: A text or sentence syntactically analysed in accordance with the dependency-syntactic model of chapter 4. The input to metataxis is a source language dependency tree and the output is the set of its target language equivalents. Put differently: **Metataxis transforms dependency trees.**

Part of the function of metataxis is thus **generating texts** and sentences in accordance with the dependency syntax of the target language. In the discussion of the generative productivity of dependency syntax (4.12.) the basic unit for indicating what is a possible sentence in a given language turned out to be the word. The whole description of all syntactically correct sentences is implicit in the description of a certain set of words, namely the possible main governors. The word, in addition, is the basic unit of lexical transfer. It therefore seems sound also to base the description of the metataxis system on the word. Units smaller or larger than the word will be taken up in later sections.

The three subsections which follow take up the role of metataxis in the overall translation process (5.1.1.), the way the design of dictionary entries and metataxis rules enable their interaction (5.1.2.), and the possibility of arranging metataxis rules in a system of layers that allows the grammarian to formulate these rules in a comfortable way (5.1.3.).

5.1.1. The scope of metataxis

Metataxis means structural change. The linguistic sign that is translated is first of all a text (and only secondarily smaller units of a text, such as a sentence or a word). Metataxis accordingly has access to all levels of structure. It is syntactic transfer within the entire realm of syntax, in the larger sense of the definition of syntax in this study (2.1.).

To put it in more concrete terms: Metataxis rules may change the syntactic form (4.4.1.) of a word, its morphological markings, its word-formational structure, its word class. They may change the syntactic function of a word, assigning it a certain dependency type. They may change the configuration of dependency relations, drawing lines of dependency to a new governor or reversing the direction of a dependency relation. They may add or remove words or morphemes. Metataxis rules are effective on all levels of syntax (see 2.1.): word, sentence and text level. They may add or remove word, clause and sentence limits. They may merge or split up dependency trees.

This means that at a cross-linguistic level there is virtually no limitation to the kind and scope of the structural changes that are allowed in metataxis.

For a given language pair, however, there may well be syntactically motivated limitations. The ultimate limitation is the requirement that input of a given form be transformed into output of another well-defined form. These form definitions are the dependency syntaxes of the source and the target language. Given these definitions, metataxis is not as unrestricted as it may seem at first sight from the above paragraphs.

In the introduction to this chapter I point out that metataxis is the structural side of the translation process, while lexical transfer and disambiguation - at least from a conceptual viewpoint - is seen as a mechanism that selects the semantically best-fitting translation from alternatives submitted by metataxis. The output of the metataxis process is a large number of **alternative** translations. Since metataxis is **syntactic** transfer and since syntax in this study is strictly **form**-oriented, neither in the syntactic analysis that precedes metataxis, nor in metataxis itself can any **content**-based decisions be made. These are dealt with by semantic and pragmatic rule systems. The important point of the discussion here is the consequence that **a metataxis rule system must not leave anything untransformed** that conforms with the dependency syntax of the source language. Metataxis must not reject any sentences.

There is another, related provision that should be borne in mind as well: Since metataxis is concerned with the form of the linguistic sign, everything it deals with is ultimately **language-specific**. Nothing can "stay the same" in translation. There may be good reasons for giving a word class or a dependency type in German the same name as in Dutch (for instance "verb" or "subject"), but by virtue of their being form units from two different grammars, they are nevertheless by definition different. There must be an explicit metataxis rule that transforms a German subject into a Dutch subject, if such a mapping is desired. If the structures of a text in a source and a target language coincide, this is not the consequence of having left the same what "is the same" in these languages, but rather of applying the transformation rules of metataxis.

Metataxis should thus handle everything in the input text and must neither leave out, nor reject anything. Metataxis is not just a rule system for coping with some residual differences between two languages, but rather carries out all formal changes in translation.

5.1.2. Tree-structured dictionary entries

In transforming a dependency tree from a source language into a dependency tree in a target language, one basically has to perform two functions: transforming words and transforming dependency type labels. I have earlier called these functions word translation and dependency transfer (Schubert 1986c: 130).

One might suppose that metataxis now is simple. Word translation is easily accomplished by taking equivalents from the bilingual dictionary (the appropriate semantic choices are beside the point for the moment), and all one has to do is to devise transfer rules for the labels.

Is metataxis really so simple? In principle, yes. But unfortunately neither words, nor dependency labels can be transformed correctly without taking into account the neighbouring words and labels. The farther in the tree one has to look, the more complex a metataxis rule system becomes. It is thus a general aim to restrict the need of context sensitivity in this respect as far as possible.

Although metataxis is not that simple, it is still a good approach to begin with translating words. As the concise ideas on generative productivity (4.12.) already show, a word, once chosen, makes a good deal of information inferable about its combinatoric behaviour. This is the main idea about the step-by-step process of applying metataxis rules: Take a word in the source language tree, replace it by its equivalent from the bilingual dictionary and try further to adapt the **hybrid tree** that results from this operation to the target language syntax. I do not motivate here this way of handling trees, but work it out in more detail in 5.3. What is important now is the idea that, while a source language tree is gradually transformed into a target language tree, it always remains a tree. Until the hybrid tree has been completely translated, it obviously does not conform to either of the two syntaxes involved, but it always is a tree structure in accordance with the general principles of metataxis-oriented dependency syntax.

Here another problem disturbs the simplicity one might initially hope to achieve. It is a well-known fact that word-by-word translation is impossible. This is due to two facts. Firstly, it may be virtually impossible to translate certain words unless their context is taken into consideration. This is especially valid for function words. One can hardly translate off separately without knowing that it, for instance, occurs in put off the decision. And secondly, one source language word may translate as several target language words and vice versa, or a word group may as a whole translate as another word group. The second phenomenon has a consequence which at first sight seems to be a pure formality, but which nevertheless is decisive for the set-up of the whole metataxis rule system: What the bilingual dictionary should deliver is not just words or word groups, but syntactically related words. This is necessary in order to put the translation equivalent in the tree where the original word was. So, if a dictionary entry in a single translation alternative contains a group of more than one word on the target language side, this word group should not appear there just as a string, but with the syntactic relations among the words indicated. Dependency syntax tells us how to indicate these relations. In other words, **the bilingual dictionary contains dependency trees**.

The explanation given in the above paragraph does not really motivate such a general statement as this. But nevertheless the statement is purposeful. What is motivated above is at first hand that word groups on the target side of the dictionary should be entered in the form of labelled tree structures. There are reasons to extend this provision to include single-word entries on the target side as well, and also the entire source language side of the bilingual dictionary. The latter will be discussed in 5.3., but the former can be motivated here: Even a single word can be treated as a tree structure, albeit a very small tree with only one node and no branch or label.

Tree-structured dictionary entries are a powerful instrument of contrastive translation syntax. The rest of this subsection is dedicated to an outline of their main functions.

In the present approach, tree-structured entries are needed in an especially obvious way as soon as a word group, rather than a single word, occurs on at least one of the two sides of the bilingual dictionary. This is the case in two sorts of constructions: constructions where a group of content words together form a semantic ensemble that as a whole translates to a certain equivalent, and constructions where a function word is semantically so vague or ambiguous that it hardly can be translated without reference to neighbouring words.

Examples of the first case are:

[146] English: **board of management** -> German: **Vorstand**

[147]

[148] German: **Leistungsbewertung** -> French: **appréciation de la valeur professionnelle**

[149]

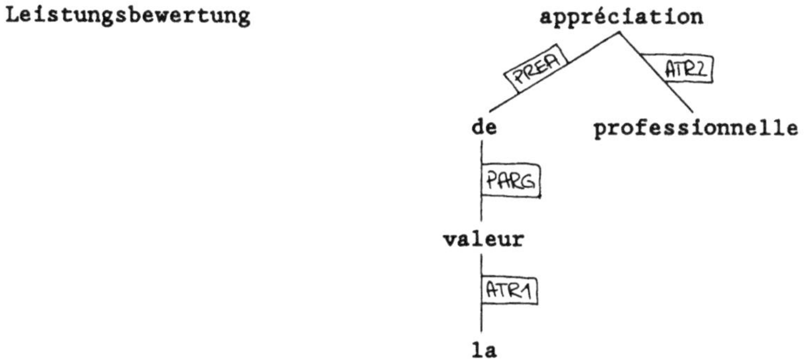

Examples with word groups on both sides occur frequently in terminology:

[150] Swedish: **rörliga kostnader** -> Spanish: **gastos variables**

[151]

[152] Dutch: dadelijk opvraagbaar -> Portuguese: de levantamento à ordem

[153]

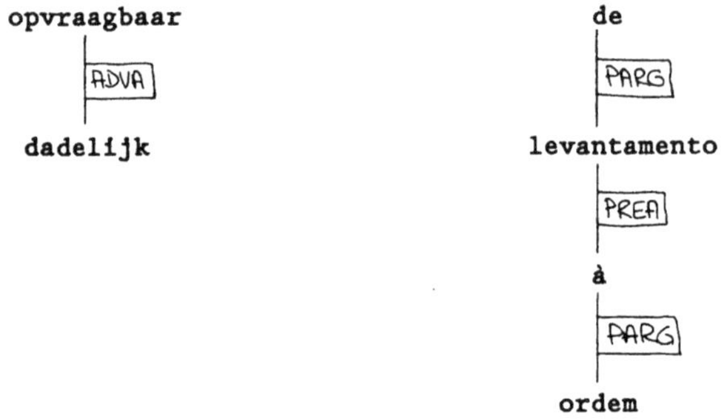

[154] Italian: politica di moneta a buon prezzo -> German: Politik des billigen Geldes

[155]

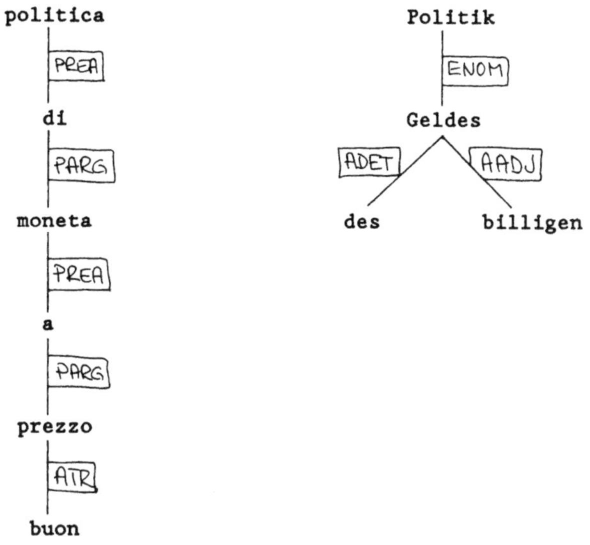

The terms in examples [146] to [154] are taken from Munniksma et al. (1975); the trees are my own tentative analyses.

Although common bilingual dictionaries usually give translations for function words as well, it is hardly possible to enumerate all words that might be considered equivalents of a certain function word in various constructions. Some function words rather require a syntactic explanation in a dictionary than a translation, e.g. French *y*, German *es*, Russian *li*. If the choice of a certain equivalent has semantic consequences, bringing about a difference in the meaning of alternative translations, the decision cannot be taken in metataxis. But in many other cases the decision for a certain equivalent is syntactic. The choice is often very much, or totally, restricted by the government capacity of the immediate (or an indirect) governor of the word in question. An example are various Dutch translation equivalents for English *to* in [156] and [158]:

[156]	English:	Dutch:
	go to [somebody]	**naar [...] gaan**

[157]

[158] English:
sell to [somebody]

Dutch:
aan [...] verkopen

[159]

In the last examples a word was indicated in brackets, which is not part of the bit of text translated by the current entry, but is needed to describe the construction completely. This possibility quite naturally follows from common practice in dictionaries. Tree-structured entries should be expanded systematically, because their expressiveness is thereby increased in an important way. The function of these positions for related words is to determine **dependency relations** in the target language. This function is two-fold. First, governor-dependent relations are established, and secondly, the particulars of these relations are determined.

I first discuss the establishment of governor-dependent relations. Replacing a node or a subtree of the source language dependency tree by a node or subtree of the target language amounts to a structural change in the tree. If the piece to be replaced has dependents, information must be given somehow as to where these dependents must be hooked up in the new, hybrid tree. One may use a default rule that, if nothing else is stated, the dependents of the replaced subtree become dependents of the new subtree, but this is not unambiguous. As soon as the new subtree contains more than one node, the question arises which of the words in the new subtree should govern the dependents in question. More precisely, which of the words should govern which of the dependents. In other words, a tree-structured entry should provide **connection points** for all possible dependents.

[160] English; German:
He does not see her. -> **Er sieht sie nicht.**

[161]

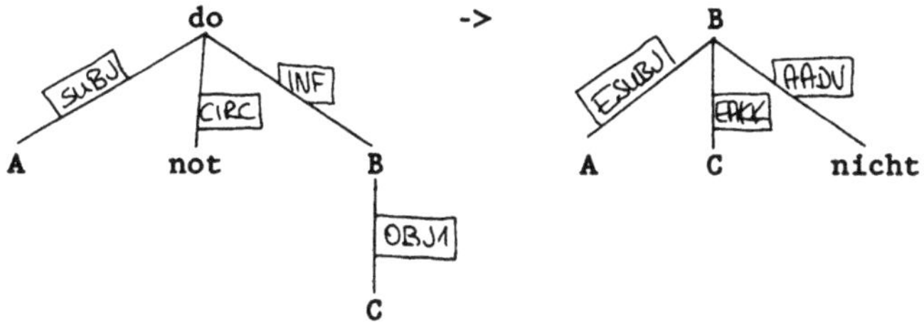

It is not enough just to establish these dependency lines. They should also be labelled. A tree-structured entry thus should contain all the information needed for correctly installing the new subtree in the dependency tree being transformed. If target language dependency types are given, this makes also the syntactic form of the words inferable, which in a later step are linked to the connection points.

[162] English: German:
He gives it to her. -> **Er gibt es ihr.**

[163]

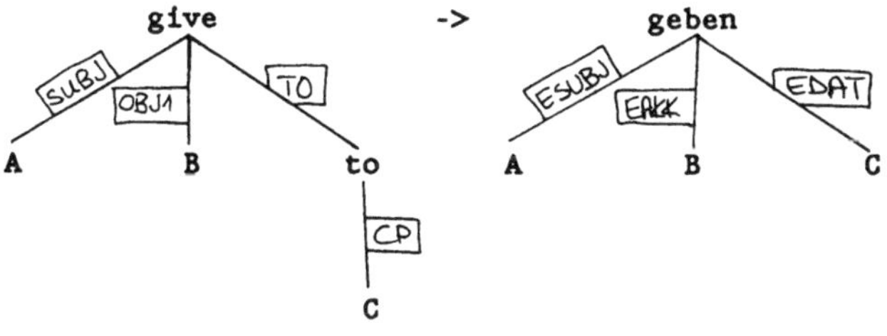

[164] German: French:
Er durchschwimmt den Fluß. -> **Il passe la rivière à la nage.**

[165]

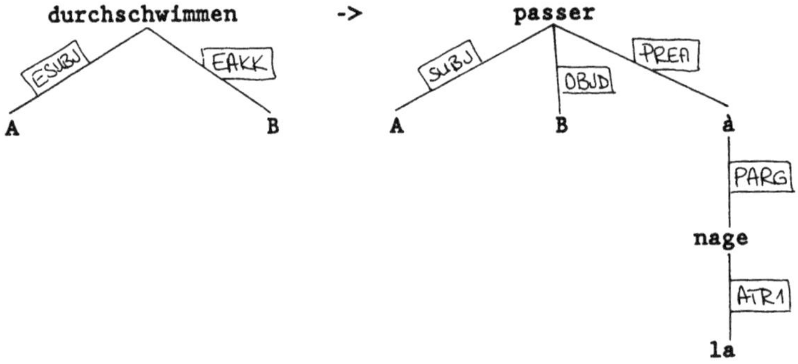

[166] English: French:
I like him. -> Il me plaît.

[167]

[168] Swedish: German:
Han serveras kaffe. -> Ihm wird Kaffee serviert.

[169]

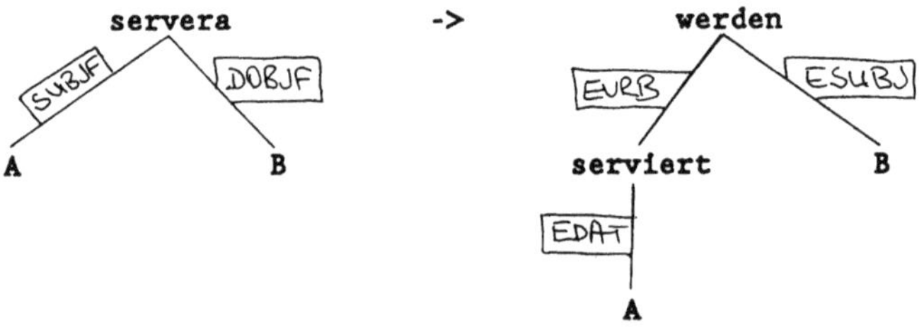

[170] English: German:
I need help. -> Ich brauche Hilfe.

[171]

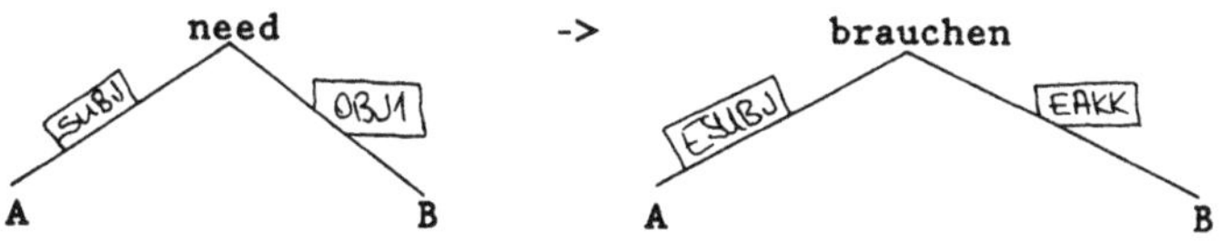

[172] English: German:
I need help. -> Ich bedarf der Hilfe.

[173]

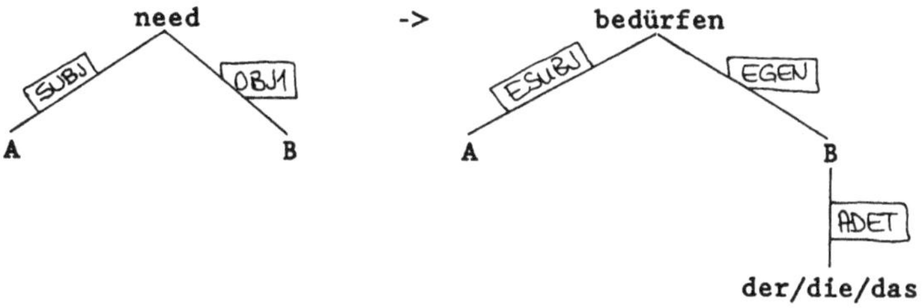

What was said above contains a crucial idea: If an entry in the bilingual dictionary contains all the information about how to install it in a tree, this can be recursively applied for building up the whole tree. Accordingly, **the complete translation syntax is contained in the bilingual dictionary**.

Is metataxis thus superfluous? No, it is not. But since a bilingual dictionary with tree-structured entries is a **dependency dictionary**, it provides for translating both morphemes and relations. Metataxis is thus entirely contained in the dictionary. Or to put it more precisely, metataxis can at a conceptual level be looked upon as entirely contained in the bilingual dictionary.

This said, one can start removing metataxis information as much as possible from the dictionary. Of course it would be senseless to enter for each syntagma in the bilingual dictionary complete metataxis information. This would not only mean wasting time and effort, but it would again mean failing to account for **regularity** in language (see 4.3.). Indeed, much of the metataxis information that in principle might be found in dictionary entries, is redundant for smaller or larger groups of entries.

Metataxis is therefore in the next subsection described as a set of **contrastive lexical redundancy rules**.

5.1.3. Levels of redundancy

The function of metataxis information in tree-structured bilingual dictionary entries is shown in 5.1.2. to be twofold: Starting from the idea of hybrid dependency trees being transformed from source into target language step by step, the metataxis information indicates both the place to attach a dependency branch with a word not translated in the current step (the connection point) and the dependency type assigned to a word on such a branch. As far as this information applies to groups of entries, rather than to a single one, it can be formulated in redundancy rules. This subsection tells how to do this in an efficient way.

Grammatical rules for human languages normally either are very complicated or have a lot of exceptions. When two languages are linked as in translation, the irregularities in one language are added to those in the other. In this situation, a flexible way ought to be sought to let rules and exceptions co-exist and override each other in a desirable manner.

As a first step in this direction, it should be acknowledged that, not surprisingly, the decision about what is regular and what is an exception is up to the grammarian. It depends on the coverage of the rules the grammarian devises. As a second step, it can be noted that there are not only rules and exceptions, marked off by purposeful arbitrary grammatical decisions, but that one may also formulate rules with different scope. There may be a rule that is valid throughout the language pair, another one that is valid for a certain word class, say, verbs, another one that is valid for most of the verbs, still another one for some twenty special verbs, and a single exception. If the description of how to handle the exception also is recognised as a rule, there are only rules and no exceptions.

The point of this quickly drawn sketch is the idea that metataxis can best be described as a set of rules with different levels of scope. The result will be a system of **layered rules**. In order to let these rules interact in a purposeful way they are organised in a **hierarchy**. Details about this hierarchy are elaborated in 5.3.3., so that it may now suffice to say that the narrower the scope of a rule is, the higher its position in the hierarchy. Thus, a more specific rule overrides a more general one. Given this provision, metataxis redundancy rules can be formulated without at the same time accounting for the exceptions to the rule.

It is necessary to ensure that a metataxis system for a specific language pair handles everything encountered in correct input (5.1.1.). Since metataxis is responsible only for the translation of relations, not of morphemes, metataxis must presuppose that the words in the input text are found in the dictionary and provided with translation equivalents. (Specific word forms may of course, through morphological redundancy rules, be reduced to the basic forms entered in the dictionary, such as infinitives, nominatives, singulars etc.; see 5.2.) If this presupposition is met, metataxis has to provide transformation rules for all possible relations. In accordance with the aim of ensuring that nothing remains untranslated, it is useful to begin with the lowest level in the rule hierarchy, thus with the rule with the widest possible scope.

Returning to the question put at the beginning of 5.1.2., it is not difficult to determine what these widest-scope rules should deal with: As words are translated by the dictionary, these metataxis rules translate the labels. The most general metataxis rules possible are rules which, without any further context information, translate a given source language dependency label into precisely one dependency label of the target language. These one-to-one transformations have of course many shortcomings. It is therefore the task of the grammarian to devise more specific rules for the cases that are not properly treated by these most general rules. In addition to the label-transforming rules, there would, theoretically, also have to be a set of rules that transform word classes into word classes. Normally, however, these rules are implicit in the dictionary, because the translation equivalent of a given word is also a word (or a syntagma with a corresponding head word) that belongs to a word class. The most general metataxis rules are called the **unmarked metataxis rules**. If a metataxis rule system contains only the unmarked rules, it can already transform all correct input, although the translations will not be of acceptable quality.

When formulating more specific rules, the unmarked rules - and all other rules that are more general than the one being formulated - make up sort of a background: A more specific rule obviously needs only to account for transformations that are not dealt with satisfactorily by the more general rules. An expedient working procedure is thus the following: Having formulated the unmarked label-transforming rules, take the labels (dependency types) one by one and look for cases where the unmarked rule does not yield the desired result. Find as many of these cases as possible and formulate a rule for transforming them correctly. The new rule need not account for all specific cases, just the most general of those that are left. Another group will be treated by a still more specific rule, and so on. At the end, there will be some rules that concern just a single entry in the bilingual dictionary. There is no redundancy in such a rule; it remains directly entered in the dictionary. This means that metataxis information is not totally removed from the dictionary, but only the **redundant** part.

After this abstract description, the discussion should return to a level somewhat closer to common grammatical argumentation. The unmarked rules can be said to be generally valid for the language pair. They are **language pair-specific**. Such a rule is for example this: "A source language subject becomes a target language subject." This is a necessary rule, however trivial it may seem. As metataxis rules are tree transformations, they can be depicted as a pair of an input and an output tree. (I use the label prefixes "S-" for source and "T-" for target language. Prefixes are needed to distinguish elements of the two languages in hybrid trees, see 5.3.)

[174]

One step higher in the hierarchy, thus one degree more specific, are "context-sensitive" rules that transform words only when they are governed by a word from a certain word class. These are **word class-specific** metataxis rules.

[175]

[176]

These rules can be used for the pair Russian-English, for example, since Russian (deverbal) nouns may have an object which translates into English as a prepositional complement (usually with <u>of</u>).

[177] **pol'zovat'sja slovarëm**
infinitive instrumental case
'use dictionary'

[178] **pol'zovanie slovarëm**
noun instrumental case
'usage of-dictionary'

In a similar way rules may be **subclass-specific** and, finally, **word-specific**.

The context sensitivity of metataxis rules need not be confined to the governor as in the examples above. Any number of nodes and labels from the tree may be involved in a single rule. A pair of somewhat rough German-Finnish metataxis rules which I have set up with reference to Tarvainen's more careful description (Tarvainen 1985a: 113) takes into account three nodes and two labels:

[179] German: Finnish:
Kalle bittet mich um das Buch. -> **Kalle pyytää minulta kirjan.**

[180]

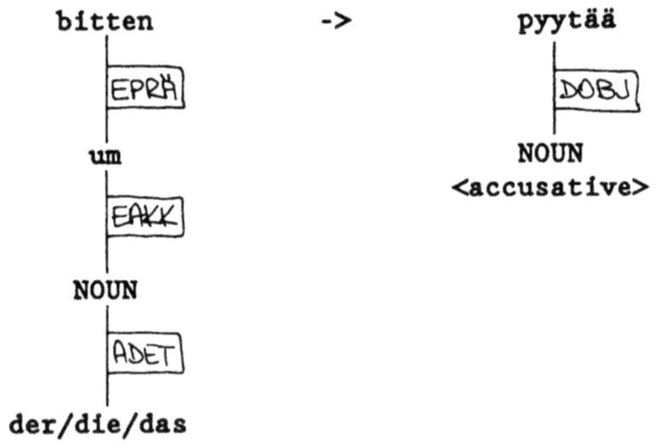

[181] German: Finnish:
Kalle bittet mich um -> **Kalle pyytää minulta kirjaa.**

[182]

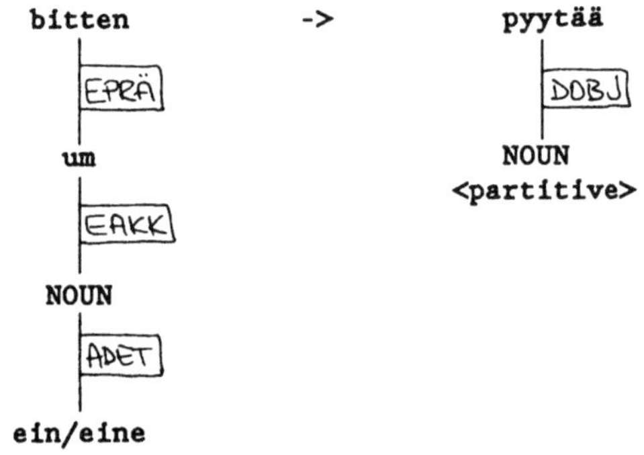

A Russian-German rule treats the transformation from a Russian participle construction to a subordinate clause in German:

[183] Russian: German:

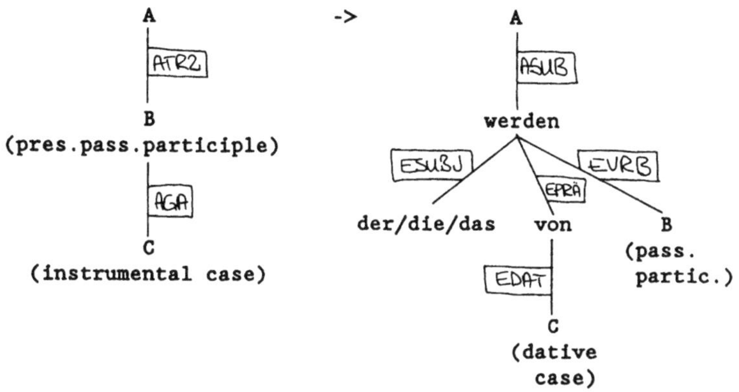

[184] Russian:

problema	**izučaemaja**	**učёnymi**
noun	adjective	noun
	present pass.partic.	
nom.	nom.	instrumental

'problem being-studied by-scholars'

[185] German:

das	**Problem,**	**das**	**von**	**den**	**Wissenschaftlern**	**erforscht**
	nom.				dative	pass.ptc.
'the	problem	which	by	the	scholars	studied

wird,

is'

(The assignment of articles in German is dealt with by other rules.)

The illustrations given here can only give an incomplete impression of the possibilities of a powerful metataxis system. More types of metataxis rules are taken up and illustrated in connection with a more precise account of the organisation of the rule hierarchy and the process of tree transformation in 5.3.

5.2. Word level metataxis: features and signs

What is said in 5.1. is mainly concerned with words and their relations, although the basic units of translation were previously said to be **morphemes** and **relations** (5.). Indeed, words are more obviously units than morphemes and suggest themselves for introducing the idea of metataxis - all the difficulties with a cross-linguistic word definition notwithstanding. But it is now necessary to investigate the role of morphemes in metataxis more carefully. This discussion of course makes sense only for languages where there are multi-morpheme words. For an ideal isolating language this section is superfluous.

When words consist of morphemes, a distinction of function and content morphemes is possible in a way similar to the corresponding distinction for words (see 4.3.). Roughly speaking, the mutual combination of content morphemes is the concern of **word formation** and the combination of content and function morphemes of **morphology**. Function morphemes often have paradigmatic relations with each other (forming what is traditionally called the paradigm of a word), and the actual morpheme constellation a specific word displays indicates its **syntactic form**, as opposed to its syntactic function (there are other indicators of syntactic form; see 4.4.1.).

In the grammatical study of many languages, it is common to describe under the heading of syntactic form not only those characteristics of words that are explicitly expressed by means of certain morphemes, but also others that can be traced in a certain dependency or in form determination, such as form government and agreement. It is for example common to consider gender a syntactic property of nouns both in Russian and in German, in spite of the important difference that in Russian gender can be read from the form of the root morpheme, whereas in German it must be stated explicitly in the dictionary. The function of gender in the syntax of these languages is to trigger in the word itself and in related words a specific shape of certain elements of syntactic form, although this does not influence the syntactic functioning of these elements. For instance, German gender influences the shape of case morphemes in the noun and in dependent adjectives. These features can thus be related to both syntactic form and syntactic relations. In the following discussion, I subsume both these characteristics and morphologically expressed syntactic form under **syntactic features**.

In 4., syntactic features were used for detecting dependency relations and for assigning words dependency type labels with respect to their governors. Is the role of syntactic features finished when that is done? Or do syntactic features play a role in metataxis? In other words: Are syntactic features relevant to translation? The answer is not simply yes or no. In fact, the question can be better formulated as follows: **Which syntactic features are translation-relevant in what way?**

As an illustration, a few grammatical features will be reviewed with the following three questions in mind: (i) Are they syntactic? (ii) If so, are they relevant to translation? (iii) If so, in which way? Such features are found in a variety of languages:

in verbs:

- tense
- aspect
- voice
- mood
- number
- person
- conjugation type
- phonematic regularities
- ...

in nouns:

- gender
- case
- number
- definiteness
- declension type
- phonematic regularities
- ...

in adjectives:

- gender
- case
- number
- degree
- phonematic regularities
- ...

etc.

These are features in a couple of word classes mainly from European languages. There are other features in these and in other languages, and there are alternative terms for these features. All the list is meant to suggest is the fact that very diverse phenomena are candidates for translation-relevant syntactic features. A careful examination of these features is therefore called for.

All these features have a form and a function. In the source language, translation-oriented syntactic analysis is primarily concerned not with the form of the features, but with their function. Form is interesting only inasmuch as it makes recognition of the feature possible. Rules about regularities involving sound pattern, such as assimilation, sound harmony and the like, may therefore be useful tools for syntactic analysis, but their task is to detect other features. They are not features in themselves. The same is valid for conjugation and declension type.

Features have form and function, but they do not necessarily have form and content. That is, not all features are **linguistic signs**. And to make the matter seem still more complicated, those features that are signs are not necessarily translation-relevant in all their occurrences.

Among the features that are signs and accordingly carry meaning are tense, mood and aspect. Noun gender, on the other hand, is not a sign. Person and number, as features of the verb in languages like German, Russian or Finnish, are signs. However, there is a difference in translation relevance: In German a finite verb must have a subject (with a few exceptions). The information concerning person and number is triggered by the subject and may be said to be redundant when again expressed in the verb. So, it is perhaps sufficient to translate these features from the German subject and then arrange the syntactic form of the target language verb according to the rules of that language. In Russian and Finnish, on the other hand, a subject is not obligatory, and the number and person information in the verb may be the only source of information for a subject-inserting Finnish-German or Russian-German metataxis rule.

When the same feature occurs redundantly in several syntactically related words, this is because of form government and agreement. In form government and agreement, there is a determining and a determined word (or several determined words). The determining word is the one in which the feature in question is inherent (such as noun gender) or brought about by its syntactic function (case in nouns). A feature may also occur as a free semantic choice, that is, because the speaker or writer wants to express the meaning it carries (number in nouns; see 4.1.1. sentence [6]).

The features of a determined word are in principle redundant. They contribute to the recognition task of syntactic analysis, but once the dependency structure is established they do not add anything to the translation. Metataxis becomes simpler when redundant features are filtered away before the tree is submitted to the metatactic transformation process. In practice, however, one has to be careful about the details of such a filtering process. A word that normally carries a certain feature redundantly, may in special constructions have a form-determining function. This can be seen, for example, in number agreement between Russian nouns and adjectives. Number is normally a redundant feature in an attributive adjective. The noun is the determining word:

[186]	**My**	**kupili**	**krasivuju**	**novuju**	**mašinu.**
			sg.	sg.	sg.
	'we	bought	pretty	new	car'

[187]	**My**	**kupili**	**krasivye**	**novye**	**mašiny.**
			pl.	pl.	pl.
	'we	bought	pretty	new	cars'

In view of examples like [186] and [187], number appears to be redundant in adjectives. But in [188], though not in [189], adjective number is nevertheless translation-relevant:

[188]	**My**	**kupili**	**novuju**	**i**	**staruju**	**mašiny.**
			sg.		sg.	pl.
	'we	bought	new	and	old	cars'

[189]	**My**	**kupili**	**novye**	**i**	**starye**	**mašiny.**
			pl.		pl.	pl.
	'we	bought	new	and	old	cars'

Metataxis must have access to these features in order to translate [188] as [190] and [189] as [191], respectively:

[190] **We bought a new and an old car.**

[191] **We bought new and old cars.**

This is only one possible complication that should be taken into account before filtering away too much. Another notorious "disturbance" in the systems of syntactic features is the fact that seemingly redundant features may be charged with pragmatic functions and may by virtue of pragmatics disobey the normal rules of form government and agreement. This is the case, for example, in the politeness function of the plural and other features in many languages (cf. Schubert 1985a).

The examples show the following: Although form government and agreement concern features that under appropriate circumstances are redundant, it is not always advisable to throw the redundant information away, since the direction of form determination may differ between source and target language. For this same reason, one cannot expect all syntactically required redundant features in the target language to be installed in their appropriate places by metataxis rules. Further synthesis steps are therefore required after metataxis proper. I return to these questions in 5.5.

5.3. The metataxis process

A metataxis system for a language pair contains contrastive lexical redundancy rules that transform source language dependency trees into target language dependency trees. As this system is built up with the bilingual dictionary as a starting point (see 5.1.), it is basically word-based. This fits in well with the fact that the nodes of dependency trees carry words. These words are characterised by a number of translation-relevant syntactic features (see 5.2.).

It is a bit vague to say that the words in a dependency tree "are characterised" by features. Are these features made explicit or kept implicit? In practice, it is expedient to equip the words on the nodes of dependency trees with explicit **feature lists**. In the feature list, the translation-relevant categories with their actual values can be included (e.g. "number: plural", "case: accusative"). Does this destroy the alleged elegance of dependency trees? The elegant simplicity of dependency trees is above all a theoretical advantage. And **in theory**, no feature lists are required. The syntactic features can be inferred from the tree of words and labels. But since this recognising procedure has to be carried out in any case in order to build up the dependency tree, it is **in practice** more efficient to carry along explicit feature information instead of repeating in metataxis the same feature-recognising process.

Whether or not in a particular application this measure is taken, dependency trees carry words and labels, and syntactic features are accessible.

I describe the metataxis process from three viewpoints: Firstly, how does the interaction between metataxis and dictionary work (5.3.1.)? Secondly, how is an applicable metataxis rule selected with respect to the input pattern (5.3.2.)? And thirdly, how is a rule chosen out of several applicable rules (5.3.3.)? These considerations lead towards a more structured set-up of different types of rules, which is dealt with in 5.3.4. Subsection 5.3.5. finally sums up the metataxis process in a ten-step procedure.

5.3.1. Metataxis rules and dictionary entries

Metataxis rules are lexical redundancy rules. They contain transformation presciptions that apply to all or to many entries in the bilingual dictionary. Accordingly, the input and the output pattern that make up a metataxis rule, do not have explicitly given words on all their nodes, but **variables** which can be filled in by various words that fulfil certain conditions. Some of the rules shown in 5.1.2., for example, contain word class variables. Other metataxis rules may have variables that refer to specific features. It is, however, possible to have words on some of the nodes in a metataxis rule. Often these are function words, but also content words can occur.

Most rules with variables contain at least one variable that stands for a word to be translated, and some other variables that represent words that will be translated in a later step of the process. The latter are the connection points mentioned in 5.1.2. By means of the connection points or rather by means of labelled or unlabelled connection branches, the metataxis rule prescribes how to transform the dependents of the word being translated. Such a rule can look like this (see [169] in 5.1.2.):

[192] Swedish: German:

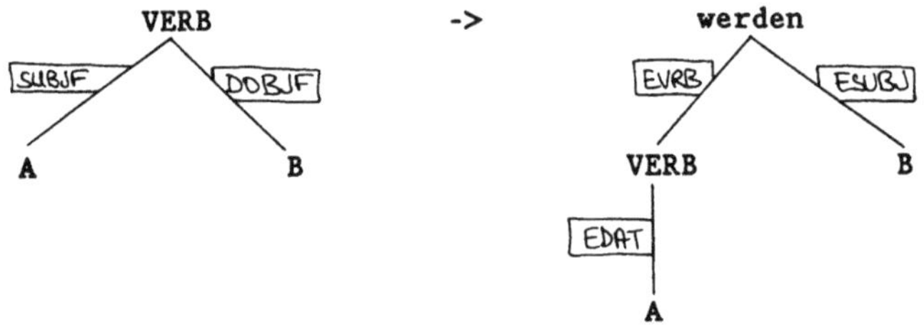

The next subsection will, among other things, explain what to do about the dependents. But before tackling them, the current word must be translated. For this purpose, the metataxis rule uses the bilingual dictionary. The translation equivalent of the given source language word is installed in the tree in place of the original, and the dependents are arranged in accordance with the prescriptions of the rule. If more than one translation equivalent is found in the bilingual dictionary, a corresponding number of copies of the hybrid tree are produced and further handled separately.

5.3.2. Selecting applicable metataxis rules

A metataxis rule consists of an input and an output pattern. The input pattern is a source language dependency tree and the output pattern is a target language one. If the input pattern coincides with the tree to be translated, the rule can be applied and the translation (a syntactically possible translation) is the one given as the output pattern of the rule. But in view of the infinite productivity of language, of course there cannot be a seperate rule for every possible source language sentence. There cannot even be a separate rule for every possible sentence structure, since their number is also virtually indefinite.

Metataxis rules should therefore be devised in such a way that they can transform a sentence step by step. Here again, the design of the translation process can profit from one of the fundamental ideas of dependency syntax: The idea that a sentence of whatever length and complexity consists of nothing but a single word with a handful of dependent syntagmata, and that these syntagmata in turn have an internal governor with dependent syntagmata. The **recursiveness** in linking elementary trees (tree adjoining, so to say; see 4.12.) can be taken as the guiding principle in metataxis as well.

For translating step by step, the structure of dependency trees is especially suitable. Two types of **symbols** are to be transformed: dependency labels and words, possibly with features. The basic idea now is to scan the source language dependency tree symbol by symbol, trying to find a metataxis rule that transforms the symbol. Due to the complexity of metataxis rules, in many cases several symbols will be transformed at the same time, but a single symbol is nevertheless the object of the search.
With this aim, the source language tree is scanned beginning from the main governor. Then an applicable rule is looked for.

- A rule is **applicable**, if it matches with the tree to be translated.

- A rule matches with a tree, if its input pattern matches with the tree to be translated.

- The input pattern matches, if its internal governor (the highest symbol in the input pattern, which may be either a label or a word, or a variable for a label or a word) matches with the current symbol to be transformed and the dependent symbols in the input pattern match with dependent symbols in the tree.

- A symbol in an input pattern of a rule and a symbol in a tree match, if either they coincide, or the input pattern of the rule is a variable of which the symbol in the tree is a valid instance.

For example, the metataxis rule [193] matches with the dependency tree [194].

[193] English: German:

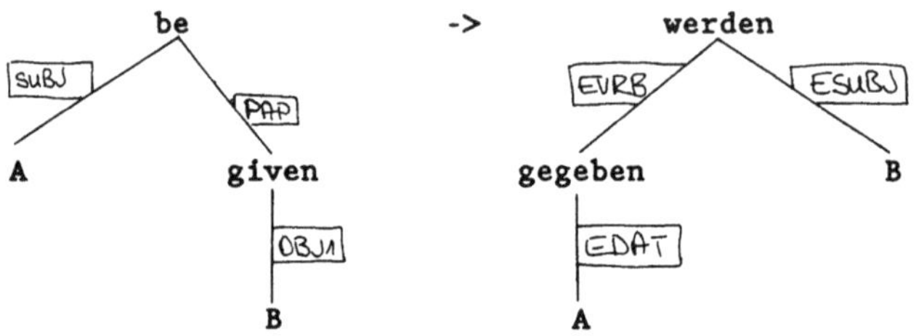

[194]

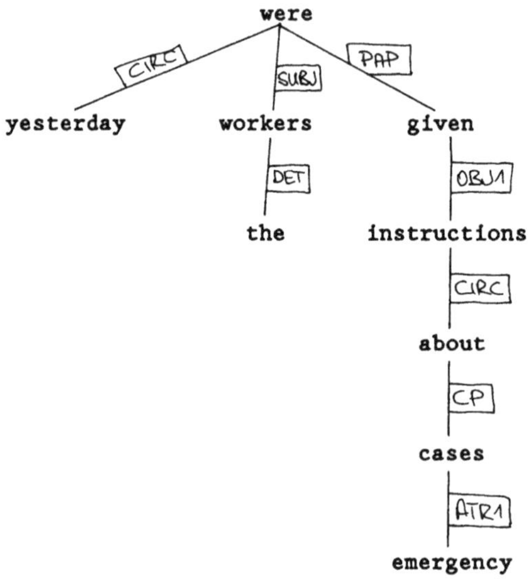

A metataxis rule may contain a complex dependency tree as its input pattern. What was said above implies that there may be additional symbols in the tree being translated. Their presence does not prevent the rule from matching. However, it is possible to devise metataxis rules with the explicit condition that a certain symbol (word or dependency type) **not** be present. For this aim an **emptiness symbol** is introduced. If the metataxis rule [193] is changed to [195], it no longer matches with [194].

[195] English: German:

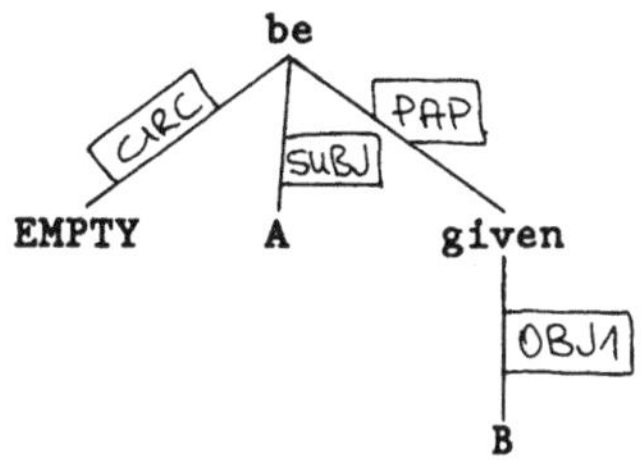

-> ...

The next subsection deals with the question what to do when several alternative rules match with the current symbol. Now I first describe how to go on after having applied one metataxis rule.

The result of the first application of a metataxis rule to a source language tree is a **hybrid tree**, that is, a tree containing some source language symbols and some target language symbols.

One might find it cleaner not to work with a hybrid tree, but rather with an untransformed source language tree which is, as it were, only read, while beside it a pure target language tree is being built up by metataxis rules. In theory, the two procedures may be equivalent, but in practice the hybrid-tree method has the valuable advantage that no bookkeeping whatsoever is required to determine which parts of the two trees correspond at each stage of the transformation process and which part of the target language tree is to be built on. Indeed, dependency trees of the metataxis-oriented type devised in this study are well-suited for a hybrid-tree procedure.

In a hybrid tree, there is a **borderline** between source and target language symbols. The general tree scanning procedure makes it likely that the borderline in the course of metataxis application will procede from top to bottom of the tree being translated, but one cannot expect that there will always be a straight and uninterrupted line. The freedom in formulating metataxis rules is (for good reasons) so large that at a specific moment a hybrid tree may contain for instance a target language word that governs a source language word that governs a target language word.

In spite of this possibility one may suppose that there is a single borderline between the elements of the two languages. The borderline then gives an indication where to continue. The aim is to transform the whole tree into target language. Thus the first source language symbol encountered immediately under the borderline is a reason to take action. As there normally simultaneously will be several source symbols under the borderline, one has to choose one. Let the **next symbol** to be transformed be the leftmost one that is found immediately under the borderline. When the next symbol has been identified, the same procedure as above is applied to it. An applicable rule is sought and applied. Given the unmarked rules (5.1.3.), there is always an applicable rule.

In this way the tree is transformed step by step, top-down and left to right.

5.3.3. A hierarchy of metataxis rules

The above subsection describes how to find an applicable rule, and 5.3.1. how to apply it. But in many cases one finds not a single applicable rule, but many. Should all the applicable rules be applied in parallel, yielding alternative translations? Or is there a preference order that would allow the selection of a single rule? As a consequence of the design principles for metataxis rules on different levels of redundancy and of specificity (see 5.1.3.), there must obviously be rules that override other rules. So, not all applicable rules should actually be applied. A twofold question must now be investigated: What criteria is the priority ranking of metataxis rules based on? And is there always exactly one rule that has absolute priority, or may alternatives nevertheless result from metataxis rule application?

The guiding principle in the **hierarchy of priority** that is needed for metataxis rules is the idea that **a more specific rule prevails over a more general rule**.

The selection of applicable rules (5.3.2.) is entirely based on the input pattern of the rule. In the same way, the hierarchy of priority is built exclusively on characteristics of the input patters of different rules. With the specificity criterion as a guideline, the input patterns of two applicable rules can be compared. These patterns are dependency trees, and the structure of dependency trees suggests the the comparison should proceed top-down. First the internal governors of the two input patterns are compared. If one of them is more specific than the other, the corresponding rule prevails over the less specific one. What does "more specific" mean? On a word node, a variable is the more specific, the narrower its scope is: A variable for all possible words is less specific than a variable for a word class, which in turn is less specific than a subclass variable. Any variable is less specific than a literally given word.

The question whether the internal governor of the input pattern is a word or a variable distinguishes what can be called word-specific and general metataxis rules. The distinction of these two types of rules has a practical consequence: It determines for a concrete application, where to place a certain rule. General rules are part of the metataxis rule system which in the form of redundancy rules is removed from the bilingual dictionary, whereas word-specific rules are entered in the dictionary under their governing word. This is only a practical distinction, but it again emphasises the fact that **the bilingual dictionary is a set of metataxis rules**.

The distinction of word-specific versus general rules is relatively rough and may still leave quite a number of candidate rules among which to choose. Within a group of rules governed by equally specific symbols the priority hierarchy is established by the provision that **the more complex rule is more specific and prevails over the less complex rule**. Complexity is measured by the number of nodes in an input pattern.

Within a group of equally complex rules, a further ranking is yielded by a comparison of dependent symbols, beginning from the top of the input pattern. Dependent symbols are compared in the same way as the internal governors.

As long as there are deeper levels of labels or word nodes in the input patterns compared, the hierarchy can be still more refined. But the distinctions given here already yield a fairly sophisticated set of criteria for ranking metataxis rules. In practice, this many criteria may be sufficient. What should be noted is the fact that the whole hierarchy is based on the source language side of the rules only. This seems to be well-motivated, since the need for a priority ordering arises when the metataxis rules are compared with the source language tree to be translated.

What still demands some clarification is the reasoning on which this hierarchy is based. Essentially, there is only a single criterion that appears in a number of slightly different shapes. This is the **criterion of specificity**: The more specific rule prevails over the more general one. This is, of course, a much too general regularity to be a peculiarity of syntax or of grammar. Because of its broad scope in areas outside of language science, it would indeed need motivation on a much more abstract level than can be taken up in this study. I therefore take it within this study ultimately as an axiom. Other scholars of language science find it self-evident and trace it back as far as Pāṇini (Hudson 1984: 16).

To sum up, metataxis rules are hierarchically ranked by means of a specificity comparison of the following elements of their input patterns:

- the internal governor,
- the complexity of the entire input pattern, and
- symbols immediately depending on the internal governor.

If necessary, the last step can be repeated recursively on progessively lower levels.

Having established the priority hierarchy of metataxis rules, I can now illustrate how the hierarchy is used for selecting a correct translation equivalent out of several possibilities when this can be done on syntactic grounds. A good example is the translation of English verbs that may be used both transitively and intransitively. A normal bilingual dictionary gives alternative translations for such verbs, when the target language has to distinguish the two usages. English translate is in German übersetzen, when it is transitive ([196]), and übersetzt werden (passive), when it is intransitive ([197]).

[196] **She translates books.**

[197] Water **translates as** eau.

Here the hierarchy yields a good opportunity for selecting translation equivalents on syntactic grounds: The rule for [196] contains a verb variable with a dependent object label, whereas the rule for [197] contains only a verb variable. The former is more specific and prevails over the latter, **if it is applicable**, i.e. if it matches with the tree to be translated, thus if there is an object. However, being transitive does not necessarily mean having an object, but it means only being capable of having an object. The transitive reading can also apply when there is no object:

[198] **What is her profession? She translates.**

The more specific metataxis rule with an object in its input pattern should thus contain both *übersetzen* and *übersetzt werden* in parallel (and, if no additional syntactic criteria are found, the choice should be postponed until it can be made on semantic grounds). The more complex rule, however, still has its function, as it selects the transitive version as soon as there is an object.

Many similar combinations are possible, where one rule selects a single translation, whereas another rule selects several ones, including the one the first rule selects. Staying within the realm of transitivity, the following pairs can be compared. English *begin* translates as Russian *načinat'*, when it is transitive, and as *načinat'sja*, when it is intransitive. This is the same pattern as in *translate*: The verb without an object must be translated to both options, with an object only to one of them. The relation between English *begin* and its Swedish equivalents is different. *Begin* can always be translated as *börja*, whether or not it is transitive. But if it has an object (which is more than just being transitive), it can also be translated as *påbörja*.

[199] English: Russian:

begin -> **načinat'**

begin -> **načinat'sja**

[200] English: Swedish:

begin -> **börja**

The last rule in [200], however, is superfluous. In an English-Swedish metataxis, there is already a rule that translates begin as börja, namely the first one in [200], and there probably is an unmarked rule that transforms an English object into a Swedish object. But if the last rule of [200] is deleted, the second one, with påbörja, always applies, since it is more specific. How can nevertheless both translations, with börja and with påbörja, be received?

This is a more generally interesting problem. In [200], it is a mere question of efficiency which arises because one does not want to repeat information. But also in different cases it is useful to devise a way of allowing for alternatives other than those with equally complex input patterns. If in [200] the third rule is thrown away, the option expressed in that rule amounts to applying both the second and the first one, although the second one has priority and would normally rule out the first one. The solution is simple: It is sufficient to indicate in the more specific rule that is has a parallel alternative. Such rules are called **parallel** metataxis rules. An interesting feature of parallel rules is that it is sufficient to indicate in a rule that it is parallel, but it is not required to point out a particular less specific rule that should be applied in parallel. The general idea of the priority hierarchy is that as soon as one out of the set of applicable rules has been selected, the transformation it prescribes is carried out. Thereafter, the hybrid tree has another form, the borderline has been moved, and the next symbol to be handled is sought. A parallel rule has the same consequences, with the specific effect that in parallel a copy of the tree being translated is handled. But in the search for the highest-ranked applicable rule now the rule already applied is passed by. A parallel rule thus does not point to a certain rule, but just allows for selecting the next one in the hierarchy. If that rule is parallel as well, the process may continue.

The idea of parallel metataxis rules is here introduced as a practical improvement of a metataxis rule system. If rules can be marked as parallel, unnecessary repetition of transformation descriptions can be avoided. In the given example, this possibility is used for a lexical alternative that has structural implications. Thanks to parallel rules, a metataxis system can yield **metatactic ambiguity**. In the first set-up, it is already suited for ambiguity that is bound to lexical choices. Lexical alternatives may imply structural alternatives, and with the help of parallel rules, purely structural alternatives may ultimately be accounted for as well. What is metatactic ambiguity good for? The question can hardly be answered within the scope of a discussion of metataxis itself. The answer has to be sought in the interaction of metataxis and other procedures that carry out parts of the overall translation process. Metatactic ambiguity may for instance be used in a sentence-based metataxis for postponing text level decisions. Several sentences which are more or less equivalent at the level of sentence syntax may be produced in order to later select the one that best fits in with the text coherence requirements - such as the theme-rheme structure - which a text-grammatical combination of sentences may imply.

5.3.4. Transformations and filters

The idea of parallel metataxis rules is in 5.3.3. introduced as a practical improvement, but is then shown to furnish the metataxis rule system with functions it otherwise could not fulfil at all. In principle, the metataxis rule system is ready now. Yet, in view of the number and complexity of rules needed for a single language pair, the system is still undesirably amorphous. In order to ease the practical setting-up of a metataxis system for a language pair, I in this subsection arrange the system of metataxis rules in a more structured way, making use of redundancy on another level. The new structure is imposed upon it in addition to the priority hierarchy.

The number and complexity of transformation rules can be considerably reduced, if the structures they have to handle are simplified. Of course this makes sense only if the scope and the transformational power of the rule system as a whole remain unreduced. The aim is to simplify the rules and to reduce them in number without giving up any part of their functionality. To achieve this goal, two sorts of structures can be addressed: the input and the output structures. Accordingly, both the source and the target language are involved. What can be done is this:

- **Source language**: Syntactic variations irrelevant to translation can be detected and reduced to a standard structure.

- **Target language**: Word-specific restrictions can be used to modify target language trees later.

In these two descriptions there are two process verbs, reduce and modify, that allude to the nature of the facilitations aimed at here: tree manipulation. This is precisely what normal metataxis rules do. So are these words just other labels for the same sort of thing? Not really, because the tree manipulations needed here differ from metataxis rules proper in an important aspect: they are not bilingual. For the sake of terminological clarity I reserve the name **transformation** for metataxis rules proper: Rules that deliver output in a language different from the input language. The rules to be described here modify trees within a single language. I call these rules **filters**.

Simplified in this way, a metataxis rule system consists of three blocks of rules, to be applied subsequently (SL = source language, TL = target language):

[201]

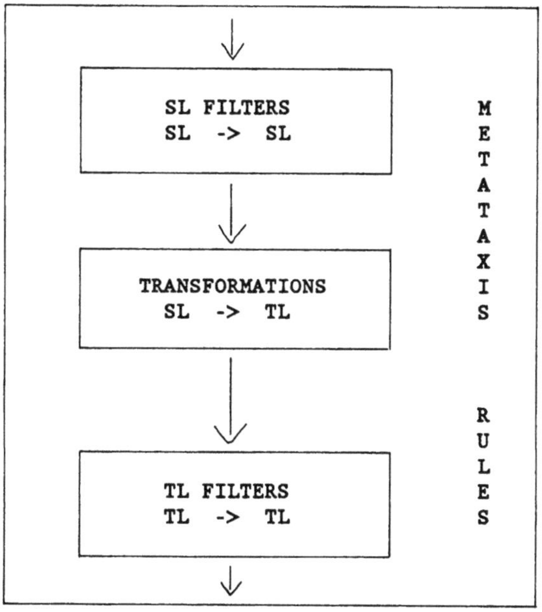

A number of questions should be answered in order to fill in the above scheme. They concern two problems: What are the modifications that can be carried out in filters? And: What are the consequences for the transformation rules?

First consider **source language filters**. If there are a number of different syntactic structures that have a single common translation, it is enough to have a transformation rule for one of them and a filter that transduces the others into the one which can be transformed. In this connection, I am not proposing the reduction of the multitude of possible sentences to a set of kernel sentences or the like. What I have in mind are much smaller modifications. If syntactic analysis does not do this, source language filters in metataxis may split up contractions (see 4.6.) like in [202]:

[202] English: English:

If the correctness of the claim of some authors that in language there is no difference in form without a difference in meaning is assumed, the idea of removing translation-irrelevant structural variety is senseless. Is there a difference in meaning between can't and can not (and cannot)? One certainly has to acknowledge that there might be a difference. And if so, translation should strive to render the difference and should not sacrifice a detectable nuance in meaning to a practical facilitation as the one aimed at here. Differences of this kind, however, are normally not translatable on the level of a word pair, a syntagma or a sentence. The difference between can't and can not does not translate to any language I am aware of as a distinction of two different types of negation in the target language. It is rather a marker of **style**. As such, it can cause totally different choices in the target language - for instance stylistically bound word choices. This is beyond sentence metataxis and also largely beyond syntax in general. Style is a phenomenon of text grammar or text level pragmatics. Differences of this kind should therefore during syntactic analysis be noted as **syntactically detectable style markers** in the same way as syntactic features are noted (see 5.2.), and taken along to the parts of the system which deal with semantic and pragmatic problems. As soon as this extra-syntactic function has been noted, the alternative forms have the same value for sentence level metataxis and can be reduced to a common representation. Which distinction is metataxis-relevant and which is not, is language pair-specific, as is metataxis.

The tree manipulations in source language filters are source language-specific in the sense that they do not yet transform anything into target language, but carry out modifications without making the source language tree hybrid. However, source language filters are language pair-specific in the sense that the decision concerning what they can do depends on translation requirements with respect to a particular target language. These requirements provide the grammarian with the following heuristic: The transformation rules become simpler, if the filters prepare the source language tree for its ultimate objective: translation into a given target language. The ultimate aim is to translate a correct text into a correct text with the same meaning. But this does not imply that all the intermediate representations will be correct in a strict sense. As far as source language filters are concerned, this means that they perhaps can facilitate translation still more, if their output is not confined to correct source language dependency trees.

What can be the use of incorrect trees in metataxis? The objective of metataxis is to translate morphemes and relations. The objective is not to translate syntactic form. Syntactic form plays an important role for the recognition of syntactic relations, but it is not directly translation-relevant. And since syntactic form is subject to the caprices of language development, many relations are identified by a variety of syntactic forms that all signal the same syntactic function. If this variety can be reduced in a reasonable way, metataxis becomes simpler.

An example for the latter idea is found in English comparatives. The question whether or not an English adjective is a comparative is without doubt translation-relevant. Not so relevant, on the other hand, is the question whether the comparative is formed with an -er ending or with a dependent more. The syntactic function of these alternatives is the same, but the syntactic structures they are found in differ. More is an additional word with an additional label, whereas the -er ending is just a part of the adjective. There are two ways out. Either one decides to consider the comparative ending a word of its own, which should be accounted for in syntactic analysis (see 4.6.), or one introduces a source language filter for unifying the two. There are a number of possible ways of filling in the details of this operation. One may leave the more comparatives as they are and change the synthetic ones into analytic forms. Bigger would then become more big with an appropriately labelled additional branch in the tree. Another solution is reducing the two comparative constructions to the positive form of the adjective (big) with a syntactic feature ("degree: comparative").

It is possible to go quite far in the latter approach, and the particulars of the given language pair should determine to what extent it is reasonable to let source language filters prepare the input for metataxis. Verbs are normally carriers of quite a lot of syntactic features. Some of them are identified by the syntactic form of the verb itself, others by complex verb constructions. Again, what has to be translated is not the form directly, but its function. It may therefore be expedient to reduce a finite verb to its infinitive and express tense, aspect, mood, person, number etc. by means of features. It is noteworthy that this can significantly rearrange the tree. [205] could be a filtered version of [203], with the verb in [205] carrying a list of features like [204].

[203]

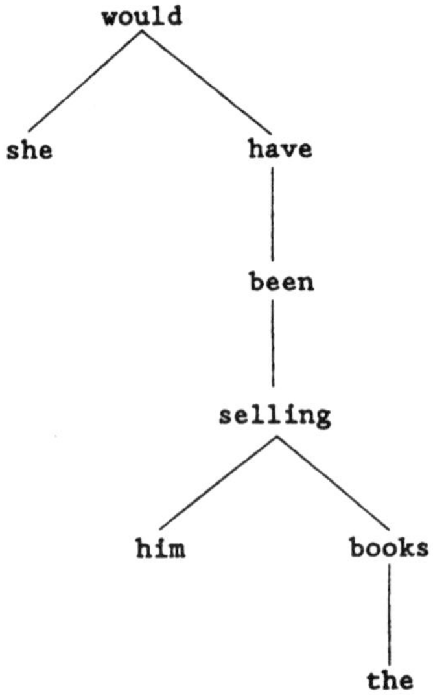

[204] **[(tense: perfect),**
(aspect: progressive),
(mood: conjunctive)]

[205]

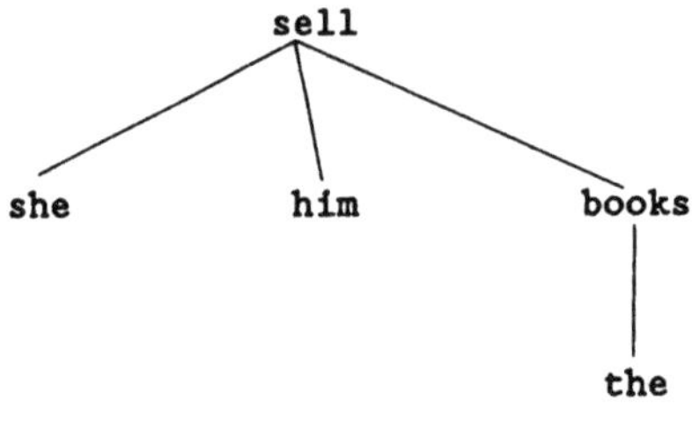

When translating from English into Indo-European languages, it may in most cases be reasonable to filter away the do-supported negations and express them either by the simple "content" verb plus not or a negation feature. But these decisions are language pair-specific. In a translation from English into Finnish, on the contrary, a special verb "do" might be useful, since Finnish also has a finite negation verb with the "content" verb being infinite.

[206] English: **We do not speak Finnish.** -> Finnish:

Me	**emme**	**puhu**	**suomea.**
nom.	finite verb	verb stem	partitive
'we	do-not	speak	Finnish'

[207]

The second type of improvements for metataxis is **target language filters**. As is mentioned in 5.2., one cannot expect that metataxis rules bring about a target language tree that is totally correct even with respect to form government and agreement. The syntactic features are present at least in the feature-determining words, but they have not yet necessarily been distributed from there to all determined words. The provisions for form government and agreement are discussed in 5.5. What is interesting here is the fact that the final products of the metataxis rules are trees that do not yet meet the requirements of the target language syntax. Incorrect trees are to be expected and must be acceptable.

Why are incorrect trees acceptable, and how can they be changed into correct trees, when the translation does not yield the required information? It should be kept in mind that the final objective is not correct trees per se, but correct sentences. A sentence, as opposed to a tree, lacks explicit expression of all the information concerning syntactic relations that makes up a dependency tree. A tree is accordingly a more explicit version of a sentence. Given this explicitness with regard to syntactic relations, syntactic form, indirect signal of these relations, can still be missed. In other words: The information not explicitly yielded by translation is present in the form of syntactic functions and should be made explicit in an appropriate way when the tree is turned into a sentence. Target language filters are needed to distribute the features to their appropriate places.

Just as for source language filters, the insight that a certain preliminary incorrectness is indispensable can be taken as a reason to use and develop the incorrectness for the sake of a simpler metataxis rule system.

In which way can transformation rules become simpler, when well-defined incorrectness is filtered away later? Since an important goal is to save effort, the most effective measures that could be taken are those that reduce the number of word-specific metataxis rules, i.e. transformation rules that have to be entered in the bilingual dictionary. These rules can probably not be totally removed, but if their number can be decreased, this is most welcome. The bilingual dictionary is a dependency dictionary. Most of the idiosyncratic information about the words in it concerns their valency. If, for instance, one has an unmarked metataxis rule that transforms a source language object into a target language object, more specific rules are needed for all cases where the governing verb in the source language is transitive and the corresponding one in the target language is not.

[208]	English: **They attend the conference.**	->	German: **Sie nehmen an der Konferenz teil.**

[209]

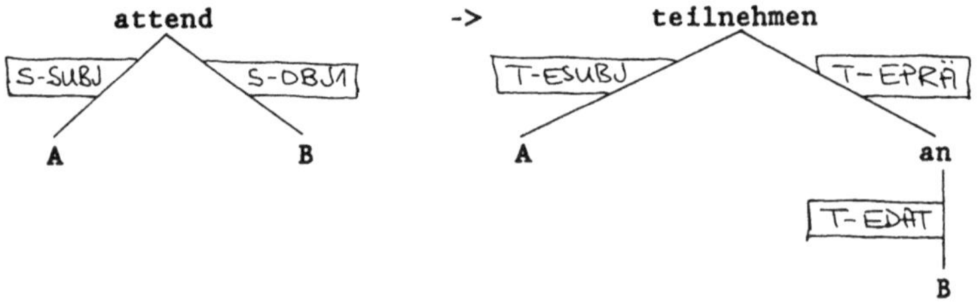

The transformation rule system would be much simpler if one temporarily allowed all verbs to govern an object. A target language filter could then change the object construction into something else, wherever valency forbids an object.

[210] German: German:

This is feasible whenever there is a clear rule for what to do with an incorrect object construction and if this rule does not depend on phenomena in the source language.

In this example, there is, as it were, a direct correspondence between a transformation rule and a target language filter. In a complex rule system, this need not be the case, and it is not even desirable to make the grammarian think about how to establish a link between a transformation and a particular filter. The system of target language filters should therefore be built on the premise that there might be recoverable syntactic incorrectnesses in the tree that is delivered by the transformation rules. This tree is hybrid, and its target language part need not yet be correct. It may require both rearrangements in the constellation of dependency lines, insertion of words and augmentations of the feature lists of the words. At the end of the filtering process, all words should be in their places and all dependency relations should have their final form. The filters that achieve this are only one of two sets of filters. The form government and agreement rules are another set of filters that can be applied later (see 5.5.). All they can do is change the form and the feature list of the words.

In the first set of target language filters that work interleaved with the transformations, there should be filters which examine the appropriate parts of the tree with respect to the following two questions. If the answer to one of the questions is negative, the subtree in question should be transduced into a correct one. The questions are:

- Does the dependency syntax of the target language allow this label to depend on this governor? ([211])
- Does the dependency syntax of the target language allow this word to hang under this label? ([212])

[211]

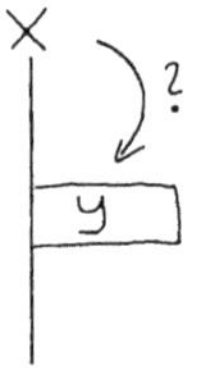

[212]

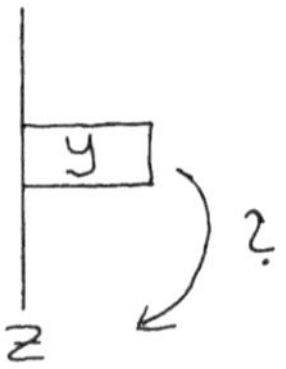

If these questions occur no earlier than in the target language filters, there will be the consequence that transformation rules need not have any access to valency information, whereas the filters need information from a **syntactic dictionary of the target language**. This information may or may not be part of the bilingual dictionary.

What are the changes that target language filters should be able to perform? In principle, as generally in metataxis, everything is allowed. A target language filter for the first question may change the label, move the branch with all that depends on it to another governor, insert a new dependent (e.g. a preposition) and let it govern the branch in question, and so on. A filter for the second question may change the word class of the word, assign it syntactic features (e.g. an accusative for an object) and also do all the things which the first-question filter can do.

In the light of what was said about filters, the figure in [201] can now be refined. The letters "c" and "i" indicate correct and incorrect trees.

[213]

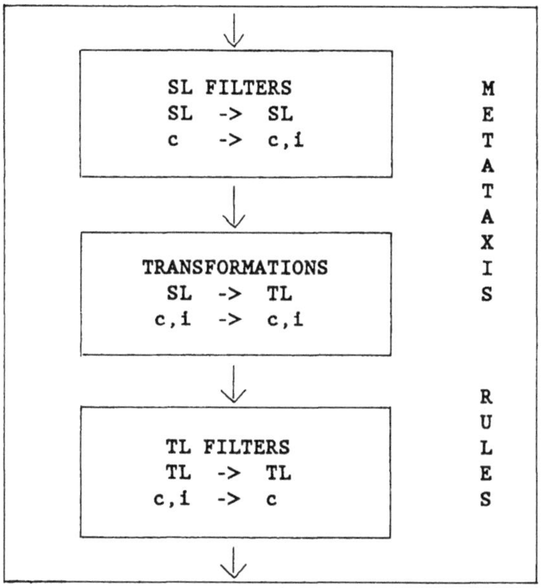

Filtering is a powerful instrument. What are its limitations? There is no hard limit between source language filtering and transformation. Theoretically one could prepare the source language tree until it has the shape of a target language tree and then just insert the words. Obviously this goes too far. But where the limit should be is difficult to say in general terms, since the change is gradual. But there is a good guideline, which is valid for both blocks of filters: Figure [213] should not be interpreted as saying that first the source language filters work on the whole tree, then the transformations and then the target language filters. The idea is that any given part of the tree should pass through all three blocks simultaneously. Thus the source language filters just compete with the transformation rules and are subject to the same search procedure, which is designed to seek applicable rules and select one or more through the hierarchy. If a filter has precedence, it works, not moving the borderline, and the filtered tree re-enters the rule-searching procedure. If a transformation prevails, it changes the tree, moves the borderline and hands over the tree to the target language filters. There an applicable filter is sought and if found, applied. Other applicable target language filters are sought and applied. When no more target language filters are applicable, the whole tree with a moved borderline re-enters the entire process.

This puts limitations on what is feasible in filtering. Firstly, the source language filters must not change the tree so much that the input patterns in the bilingual dictionary no longer match the tree. The entire filtering subsection deals with practical things, so an argument from practice may motivate this orientation in the dictionary. Systems of this kind tend to be very complex. It is necessary that different parts of them be built up independently by different persons. Interface definitions become crucial in this case. A good interface between lexicon and grammar is the provision that the trees in the bilingual dictionary conform with the syntaxes of the two languages. Therefore, also the metataxis rule system should be capable of handling dictionary entries that meet this requirement. They should not change the tree so much that the lexicographer would have to be acquainted with all the details of the metataxis system when devising the input patterns in complex tree-structured dictionary entries.

While source language filtering thus is restricted by the dictionary, target language filtering is restricted by the fact that the whole metataxis process is recursive. The places in the tree changed by the target language filters should be correct with regard to the target language syntax, with the exception of matters related to form government and agreement. This is necessary, because the tree in this form re-enters the process. Source language filters and transformation rules should still match with it. The filters are introduced to facilitate the system of transformation rules. If it were necessary to have peculiarities of filtered target language trees in mind when writing transformation rules, the facilitating effect would generally be lost.

5.3.5. **Metataxis step by step**

The description of how to apply metataxis rules is given scattered over the entire above part of chapter 5., and is intermingled with discussions of ways to structure and refine the metataxis rule system. I therefore resume the metataxis process here in a step-by-step procedure. It begins with a source language dependency tree and is repeated until the whole tree has been transformed into the target language. This point has not yet been reached when, technically speaking, no source language symbols are left, but only when no rule, not even a target language filter, matches the tree.

This is the metataxis process step by step:

1. Scan the tree top-down and left to right.

2. Identify the next source language symbol (word or label).

3. Look for metataxis rules (source language filters or transformation rules) applicable to that symbol.

4. Out of the applicable rules, select the rule with the highest priority. If the rule is marked "parallel", make a copy of the tree and treat it separately with the next-highest rule from the hierarchy.

5. Apply the rule. If it is a transformation rule, apply it inserting the alternative word translations from the bilingual dictionary in as many copies of the tree as are being translated. Henceforth handle these copies separately.

6. Look for target language filters applicable to the changed symbols. (If the rule applied in step 5 was a source language filter, there will be no match.)

7. Out of the applicable target language filters, if any, select the rule with the highest priority.

8. Apply it.

9. Begin again from step 6. If no applicable filters are found, go on.

10. Begin again above. If no applicable metataxis rule is found, stop.

5.4. Text level metataxis

Syntax is in this study defined in a broad sense that includes linguistic signs at all possible levels of analysis, from morphemes to texts (see 2.1.). Until now, however, I have been mainly concerned with the traditional scope of syntax: sentence level. Having taken up word level in 5.2., it is now time to say a few words about metataxis at the text level.

Neither the chapter on dependency syntax (4.) nor the present section, however, can go into too much detail about text level syntax. Text grammar is too wide a field to be handled briefly as a supplement to sentence level grammar, and this is true for text syntax in particular. The remarks I can make here should therefore rather be read as suggestions for more profound text-syntactic research, and maybe they can also provide some very preliminary solutions. This study is written with a practical application in mind, and when in practice a working system is aimed at, some solution must always be found, even when the theoretical basis still is narrow. My remarks thus outline such a preliminary solution that contains working hypotheses for text syntax and connections between sentence and text level, but is not meant to represent the best that can be attained in the field.

There is a subject of syntax which I have not touched very often until now: **word order**. Dependency trees are not projective, so word order was not mentioned in that context. Or to put it more precisely: Word order was not mentioned **explicitly** in the chapter on dependency syntax (4.). That is, quite a lot was said about **syntactic form**, which in a dependency-syntactic analysis is used for detecting **syntactic function**. Syntactic form may find its expression in morphemes, but it may also be found in word order (see 4.4.1.). There is a certain balance between these two aspects of syntactic form. The syntaxes of languages can be ranked on a scale between the two poles "word order-bound" and "morpheme-bound". Of the languages frequently referred to in this study, English is close to the former pole, whereas Russian and Finnish are much closer to the latter. As far as word order is an instrument of syntactic form, indicating syntactic functions such as dependencies, it has been dealt with in the previous chapters.

But as far as word order is not needed as an instrument of syntactic form, it is "free", that is, free to fulfil another function. There is no binary polarity between languages whose syntax is totally word order-bound and languages whose syntax is totally morpheme-bound. As a consequence, there is no polar distinction of languages with a free and languages with a bound word order, but rather a ranking of languages on a scale of freeness. In languages that score high on this scale, word order can fulfil a **text level** function especially well: The communicative structuring of texts as described in the **theme-rheme** and **topic-comment** distinctions. This structure of texts, termed communicative, has a major function in establishing **text coherence**. When the input to a translation process is a coherent text, the target language equivalent should not be just a set of unrelated sentences. A basic working hypothesis on which to base further investigation could read: **When word order expresses a theme-rheme structure, try to preserve this order in the target language.**

Arguing about word order on syntagmatic level, Tesnière (1959/1982: 23) formulates a similar working hypothesis for the translation process when he stipulates that dependency trees should "**respecter l'ordre des relevés horizontaux**". A computational application of Tesnière'ian dependency trees in such an ordering process is described by Mel'čuk (1967) for Russian. His account includes syntagma level tree linearisation (see 5.5.3.).

Two refinements to the above hypothesis can be formulated immediately: Firstly, word order is not as free as one is tempted to believe. Even in "free word order" languages, the freeness is restricted. Normally the most important freeness concerns not the order of all words in a sentence, but the **order of syntagmata**, or, put in terms of dependency trees, the order of entire subtrees. And in addition, not all dependent syntagmata of all possible governors can be ordered freely, but mainly the dependents of **verbs** and **deverbal** words (nominalised verbs, participles etc.).

The second refinement concerns the idea of "preserving" the original syntagma order. Vilém Mathesius (1929), the founder of the theme-rheme analysis (or "functional sentence perspective"), distinguishes subjective and objective word order, or to put in the distinction in Prague School terms, **marked** and **unmarked word order**. An interesting objective of contrastive text level grammar could thus be to establish first descriptions and then transformation rules for analysing and synthesising marked or unmarked word order, respectively.

Also languages which have little or no access to word order as a means of communicative structuring must have some way of providing text coherence. This cannot be worked out in very much detail here, but once word order has been taken up, a few words on syntactic ordering in languages with a "bound" word order may be appropriate.

Where word order is free to fulfil text level functions, most variation is found in the order of verbs and their dependents, i.e. in the basic structure of sentences and clauses. Where verbs, subjects, objects, predicatives etc. cannot be ordered as freely, other ways of changing the order of sentence elements can emerge. Indeed, the more strictly bound word order is, the more productivity is usually encountered in order-changing constructions. These constructions can be seen as sentence level repercussions of text-grammatical needs.

A specific group of these constructions is known under names such as "extrapositions", "gapping constructions", "mise en relief" (French), "emfatisk utbrytning" (Swedish), "sætningskløvning" (Danish) etc. (cf. Schubert 1985b: 471f.)

Another possible instrument of reordering sentence elements is verbal gender (voice). The choice between active and passive constructions can, among other functions, be used to achieve a certain order of verb dependents (Schubert 1982: 104ff.).

If text level metataxis rules can control the choice of these two types of syntactic structures in the target language, and if they can render the choices encountered in the source language text, these are powerful tools for translating text coherence in ways compatible with the working hypothesis.

Contrastive text grammar is a wide field which deserves more profound study.

5.5. A glance at target language synthesis

At the end of the metataxis process the translation is not yet finished. Without going too far into details, I in this section discuss the final steps of the translation process. These form-related steps also have connections to semantic and pragmatic factors in ways which are not taken up in this study (see 5.1.1.).

The final results of the metataxis process so far are alternative target language dependency trees which are syntactically possible translations of the original source language sentence. They conform with the target language syntax to a certain degree. In more precise terms: All the words that should be in the final sentence are now contained in the tree, all words have been put on their correct nodes, and the final choices of dependency branches and their labels have been made. What is not yet in its final shape are the feature lists of the words and accordingly the syntactic form of the words themselves. The words are in part still infinitives, singulars etc. Before the result of the translation can be offered to a user, the tree should be converted into a sentence. Here are the three syntactic processes that should follow the metataxis proper:

- Distribution of inferred **syntactic features**.
- Derivation of **syntactic form** from features.
- Linearisation of the tree: establishing the final **word order**.

They are taken up in the following subsections.

5.5.1. Form government and agreement

Distributing inferred features has to do with two phenomena, often mentioned together in the above discussion: form government and agreement (see 5.2.). Syntactic features often occur in an interrelated way in several words (agreement) or in a single or several words due to influence from a word that does not carry the feature itself (form government). If the syntactic structure of sentences is described in accordance with the dependency-syntactic model adopted for this study (see 4.), the words with common features are syntactically related, although form determination was rejected as a criterion for establishing dependency relations (4.1.1.). These words often govern or depend on one another, directly or indirectly, or they have a common governor. With respect to the syntactic features in question, there is a **determining** word and one or more **determined** words. In the determining word the presence of the feature (in the agreement case) is translation-relevant. A feature in a determining word in the target language has been brought about by metataxis rules and has been triggered by a feature, a morpheme, a word, or another linguistic sign in the source language. The same feature in the determined word, however, is redundant. It is there only by virtue of a language-specific rule on form government or agreement. Since these rules are similar in some languages, a redundant feature might have been attributed to a target language word by metataxis, but this is not a cross-linguistically reliable regularity.

Therefore, the trees delivered by metataxis proper should be filtered once more, this time with respect to form government and agreement. The appropriate rules are another type of **target language filters**. The difference between those described in 5.3.4. and these filters is that the former ones work interleaved with the transformation rules and accordingly handle only a small subtree of the tree being translated, whereas the latter ones work on a complete target language tree. There is also another, less technical difference which, however, is only gradual: The filters needed here use less information from the source language than the target language filters described above. But they do need some information from the source language, and therefore **form government and agreement filters are part of metataxis**.

This may seem surprising. Why do these filters need source language information, when it is their task to distribute redundant syntactic features on purely language-specific grounds? The answer can be found in a more thorough description of how these filters work. They have to be equipped with the form government and agreement rules of the target language and scan the tree, adjusting syntactic features where they do not meet the rules. In order to do so, the filters must first identify determining words and read their feature lists, and then find and examine determined words, adapting their feature lists if necessary. Source language knowledge is required in order to decide which words are the determining ones. A few examples, similar to those used in 5.2., illustrate this:

[214] **My kupili ètu novuju i ètu staruju mašiny.**
sg. sg. sg. sg. pl.
'we bought this new and this old cars'

[215] **My kupili èti novye i èti starye mašiny.**
pl. pl. pl. pl. pl.
'we bought these new and these old cars'

[216] **We bought this new and this old car.**

[217] **We bought these new and these old cars.**

In English, taken as the target language here, number is determined by the noun and occurs redundantly for example in certain attributive pronouns (these cars). In Russian as well, number occurs in nouns and is by agreement imposed on adjectives, attributive pronouns etc. So in a first approach the word mašiny from [214] and [215] is translated into both [216] and [217] as car with the feature list "(number: plural)". Knowledge of the regularities of the source language Russian is required in order to find out that the noun should not impose its plural feature on the attributive pronouns in [216]. [216] becomes correct if the unit of two coordinated singular adjectives is taken to determine the number of its governor, the noun. Here, therefore, the feature found in each of the adjectives determines the feature in the noun. This is due to an English rule, but this English rule is selected on the basis of the Russian sentence.

The filters for form government and agreement are target language filters which presuppose certain information from the source language tree for identifying form-determining words and which then in accordance with rules of the target language distribute syntactically redundant features to the determined words in the target language tree.

5.5.2. Morphological synthesis

When these last rules within the metataxis rule system have accomplished their task, the result is a target language tree in which everything is in final shape except the syntactic form of the words. (Remember that "syntax" includes morphology.) What is needed now is a set of rules for **morphological synthesis** based purely on the target language. They take a word in some form with its feature list and deliver the correct syntactic shape of the word with those features. The morphological synthesis rules thus give a noun its case and number endings, a verb its tense form and an adjective its irregular comparative.

This presupposes that the metataxis rules have prepared the final tree far enough so that no word insertions are required. An English third person singular indicative perfect tense progressive (has been walking) must already have been delivered by metataxis in the shape of a three-word subtree, rather than just walk with the appropriate features. But metataxis need not go further than delivering have be walk with the appropriate features, thus **not** "walk [(tense: perfect), ...]", but "have [(tense: present), ...]" etc.

5.5.3. Tree linearisation

The last step towards a text which is readable for human users is **tree linearisation** (also called "tree-to-string conversion"). Since dependency trees are not projective, some attention should be paid to this process. The rules that determine tree linearisation are mainly concerned with **word order**.

Whereas section 5.4. deals with word order that at sentence level is free to fulfil text level functions, tree linearisation is concerned with word order at the syntagmatic level. When trees are linearised, possible text level rearrangements have already been accomplished. Tree linearisation can in general have a rather narrow scope: It has to decide about the linear sequence to be assigned to a governor and its immediate dependents. This can be done by means of a bottom-up procedure, beginning from those words in a dependency tree that have no dependents. The tree linearisation rules then assign a specific order to these words and their governor. The string of words attained in this way can then be placed on the node formerly occupied by the governor alone, and the process can be pursued recursively. Language-specific characteristics of word order play an important role here, but where there still is some freeness at the syntagmatic level, Tesnière's principle of preserving the encountered order (see 5.4.) can be followed. In this way, the dependency tree is finally reduced to a single node, which carries the whole sentence as a string.

The procedure can be set up to proceed bottom-up in the following way, illustrated with an example from 4.5. (Between [218] and [219], and between [219] and [200], a number of steps have been left out.):

[36]

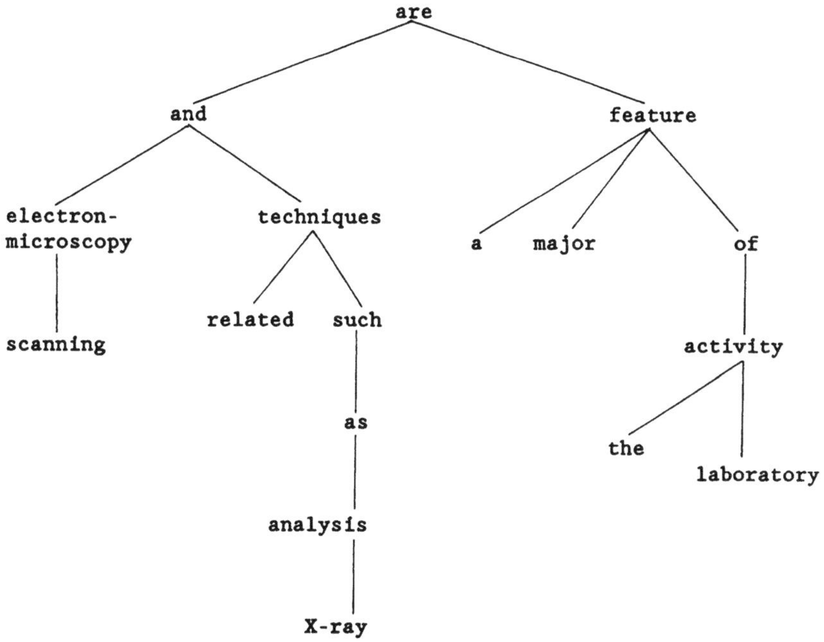
are
and
feature
electron-
microscopy
techniques
a
major
of
scanning
related
such
activity
as
the
laboratory
analysis
X-ray

[218]

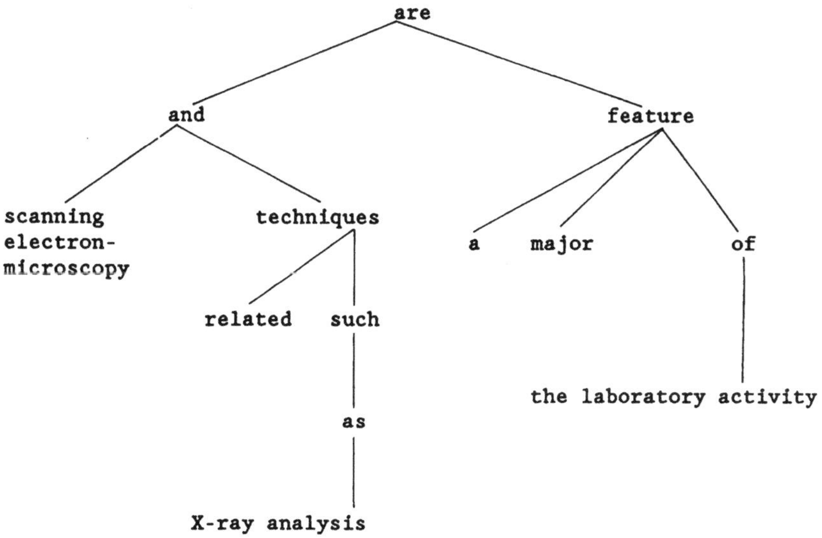
are
and
feature
scanning
electron-
microscopy
techniques
a
major
of
related
such
the laboratory activity
as
X-ray analysis

[219]

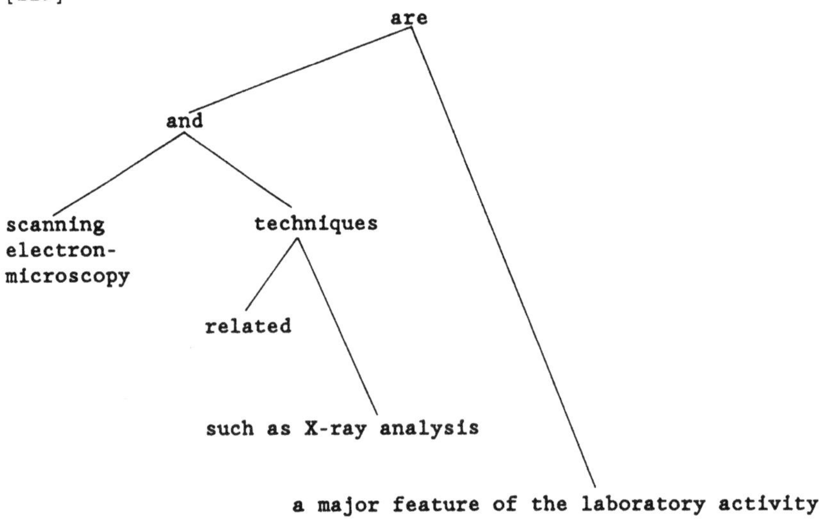

[220]

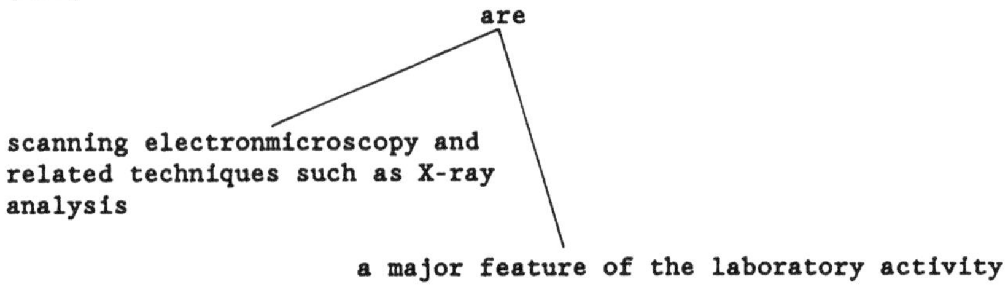

[221] **Scanning electronmicroscopy and related techniques such as X-ray analysis are a major feature of the laboratory activity.**

This procedure works as long as there are no discontinuous governor-dependent pairs. When these are detected, a dependency tree offers a straightforward method for "sending" the concerned syntagmata to their appropriate places. In most cases it is sufficient to send them upwards in the tree to a higher governor and treat them there in linearisation as if they were its immediate (continuous) dependents.

[222] German:
Der Plan hat sich als so unerwartet schwierig und
'the plan has as so unexpectedly difficult and

kostspielig erwiesen, daß das ganze Vorhaben
expensive turned-out that the whole project

abgesagt werden mußte.
cancelled to-be had'

[223]

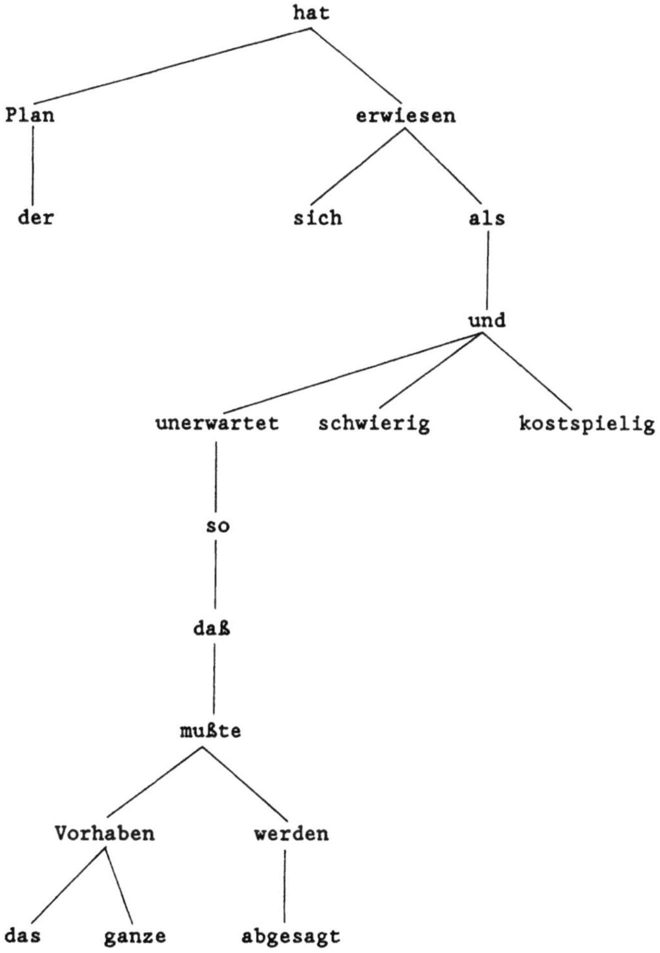

The subtree governed by daß depends on so because of the dependency relation among the two words, but when [223] is linearised, the word string of the daß subtree does not follow so immediately. In fact it should be linearised as if it were the rightmost dependent of the next finite verb that indirectly governs so. This is hat. The string daß das ganze Vorhaben abgesagt werden mußte is linearised in the normal way until it as a whole occupies the node of daß. But then it is not added either to the right or to the left of so, but is marked as a discontinuous dependent. It will be sent upwards recursively by so, unerwartet, und, als and erwiesen. The rules that linearise a finite verb, however, contain a provision that handles a dependent, marked as discontinuous, as a normal dependent and adds it to the string accordingly. (An implementation environment built on these ideas has been devised for the DLT project by Eddie Szulc.)

I said above rather concisely that language-specific regularities determine the word order to be built up by tree linearisation rules. There are numerous languages in which word order at the syntagmatic level, but also at clause and sentence level is restricted quite precisely. In these languages, often there is a residual freeness in placing syntagmata in a linear sequence, but if a decision is made for one syntagma, this inevitably determines the decisions for other syntagmata. The Germanic languages are all more or less obvious examples of this relatedness of sequential places.

Nikula (1986: 109f.) mentions that his account of Swedish has been inspired by Olof Thorell's Swedish grammar, which in turn owes a lot to Paul Diderichsen's Danish grammar (Thorell 1977; Diderichsen 1946). Nikula presents major parts of a dependency grammar, Thorell's standard work is traditionally oriented and Diderichsen's book presents what can be called a position grammar. Investigating the question of what the three seemingly dissimilar works can have to do with each other, one arrives at an interesting solution for the problem of word order in tree linearisation. Nikula's dependency description can borrow ideas from Thorell's grammar, because traditional grammar for a good deal is dependency-minded, albeit not always explicitly and not always stringently. Thorell's traditional account can rely on Diderichsen's string-oriented position grammar, since Diderichsen's famous "sætningsskema" 'sentence scheme' (Diderichsen 1946: 160) accounts for precisely that part of Danish (and, mutatis mutandis, Swedish) syntax in which word order indicates syntactic functions. A model similar to Diderichsen's sentence scheme is familiar in older German linguistics, and not surprisingly, Engel (1982: 202ff.) includes a version of it in his discussion of dependency syntax Sentence schemes are conceptually linked to the "Satzbaupläne" 'construction plans for sentences' of dependency grammar, and it is in this connection interesting to see that the import of sentence construction plans for dependency grammar, and in particular to contrastive dependency grammar, is emphasised by scholars engaged in contrastive comparisons of Germanic languages (e.g. Fabricius-Hansen 1979b; Fabricius-Hansen / Falster Jakobsen / Olsen 1981).

In languages where this is appropriate, tree linearisation rules could therefore be based on a Diderichsen-type sentence scheme. The fact that word order regularities of this kind turn up so late and in so marginal a place in my contrastive dependency-syntactic study, is a repercussion of the role word order plays in the present dependency approach: Where word order is part of syntactic form in a source language, it is used for detecting syntactic function, and where it plays such a role in a target language, it need not be added before the moment when the explicit indications of syntactic function (tree branches and labels) are taken away. When the text level role of word order has been accounted for (5.4.), the remaining role of word order is not translation-relevant.

Tree linearisation, especially when performed with sentence schemes, is the appropriate place to insert so-called **placeholders** or dummies (such as Danish der, German es etc.), since they are required not by syntactic function, but by linear order.

During linearisation, finally, **elision**, **contraction** and other types of positionally conditioned influence should be accounted for. What is still represented as separate words may now have to be merged to a unit. (For examples see 4.6.) It is noteworthy that this is a treatment that should be done **during** or perhaps even **before** tree linearisation proper, but **not in the string-formed sentence**. As contraction and related phenomena are so much position-bound, one might tend to resolve them in the sentence when the tree structure has been abandoned. But it turns out that the right moment for this treatment is reached when the linear sequence is known, but the tree is still available. An example of this need can be seen in Dutch. If the pronouns jij and je (both 'you [singular, informal]') immediately follow the finite verb, they influence both its pronunciation and its written form:

[224] **Je bezoekt een kennis.**
2.person
'you visit an acquaintance'

[225] **Bezoek je een kennis?**
2.person
'visit you an acquaintance ?'

The verb ending t is lost because of this influence, but not for any occurrence of je or jij after the finite verb, but only if one of these pronouns is the subject of the verb. Otherwise, the ending is preserved:

[226] **Je bezoekt je kennis.**
2.person
'you visit your acquaintance'

[227] **Jij koopt je een boek.**
2.person
'you buy yourself a book'

In such cases, a seemingly purely position-bound phenomenon is dependent on syntactic relations. The knowledge about these relations should therefore still be at hand when needed.

5.6. Why dependency?

When discussing dependency and constituency at the beginning of this study, I postponed further discussion of the motivation for the decision to adopt a **dependency syntax** rather than a constituency syntax for machine translation. Now the question left open in 2.3. can be answered. The answer is derived from insights acquired in the discussions from the sections and chapters above concerning the nature of translation and the role of syntax in it.

Constituency syntax is at first hand concerned with **syntactic form**. When analysing a text or sentence, each word is placed in a tree structure under a node that indicates what the word **is**. Immediately above the words, there are verb nodes, noun nodes etc. The "is a" relation is then used for step by step linking up all the words in a sentence. A noun together with a determiner, for example, "is a" noun phrase (NP). A noun phrase, together with a verb phrase (VP), "is a" sentence (S), etc. From these structures of syntactic form, **syntactic function** can be derived. In English, for example, a noun phrase that occurs before the finite verb is normally the subject.

Dependency syntax is at first hand interested in **syntactic function**. It uses **syntactic form** for detecting syntactic function, but what is represented in the tree structure is function. A word is labelled as the subject of a certain verb. Whether this subject is a noun, a pronoun, or a subordinator with a whole subordinate clause as its dependent is not made explicit in tree labels, but can if necessary be seen from the words themselves in connection with a syntactic dictionary.

Leaving aside subtleties for the moment, one may say that the two approaches are equivalent. Both make information about syntactic form and function available. Roughly speaking, in constituency syntax form is explicit and function implicit; matters are the other way round in dependency syntax. Form is immediately available in a constituency approach, and function in a dependency approach.

I do not agree with Manfred Bierwisch (1966/1970: 22), who maintains that Tesnière'ian dependency syntax fails to capture word order and thus is not suitable as a sentence syntax. The counterposition is defended by Richard Hudson (1980: 196), who concludes that "**syntactic analysis needs dependency but does not need constituency**".

The question here, of course, is which of the two is needed for **translation**? After all the discussion above, the answer is short: **syntactic function**. What translation does is transform words and relations from one language into another. These relations are syntactic functions.

To illustrate this in more concrete terms: Translation rules cannot without formulating an intricate network of conditions determine how to translate a German noun in the genitive case (syntactic form) into Finnish. The word class of the translation equivalent is delivered by the dictionary, and the genitive case has no straightforward equivalent on form level. There is no direct path from form to form. It is necessary rather to determine the function of the genitive in the German sentence (object, attribute, argument of a preposition, ...?), find a Finnish syntactic function that corresponds to the detected function in German, and then decide upon the syntactic form of the Finnish word (cf. also Itälä 1986: 73). The path is from **form** to **function** to **function** to **form**. In this path, the steps between form and function and vice versa, are language-specific. The only step that plays a direct role in translation proper is the function to function step. Therefore a syntax that delivers a ready-to-use description of syntactic functions is preferable for the purpose.

When genetically related languages resemble each other in syntactic form, a form-to-form path may present a welcome short cut for a number of problems. But the feasibility of short cuts decreases as the spectrum of languages to be translated becomes broader. A wide-ranging cross-linguistic approach should not need to rely on them.

The insight that a function-to-function step is required for translation, rather than a direct form-to-form link, is indeed common in machine translation research nowadays. But I am not aware of many system designs in which a function-oriented syntax was consequently adopted. Since dependency syntax straightforwardly captures syntactic function, it is a direct approach to translation.

Chapter 6

Metataxis, semantics, pragmatics

Having dwelled for a substantial part of this study on what metataxis is and how it works (5.), and which syntactic model it is based on (4.), it may now be in place to address the question **why** metataxis is included as a major element in a machine translation process. The role of metataxis and possible alternatives can best be assessed when metataxis is placed in a larger framework. As metataxis is a subject of contrastive dependency syntax, at first hand its position within the wider field of **dependency grammar** is considered. Dependency-grammatical elements and concepts are then traced in some alternative grammar models and approaches in 6.1. In 6.2. I return to the question of why translation in the present account so heavily relies on syntax, and thereby on metataxis, and what would be competing solutions.

6.1. Dependency syntax, dependency grammar and related models

The linguistic sign has two sides, form and content, and there is no doubt that both should be described by grammar and that both have to be handled in translation. Syntax in the dependency model proposed in this study is taken to concern the **form** of the linguistic sign, and form only. Accordingly, there should be a semantics to describe the other side.

Dependency and constituency are the two alternative basic concepts for describing grammatical systems, and they are by no means confined to syntax. They are indeed fundamentals of **grammar**, not of syntax only (cf. Baumgärtner 1970: 52). This means that dependency can also be taken as the basic concept of a semantic analysis of linguistic signs, and such an analysis may be expected to yield a description that can be related as closely as possible to the findings of dependency syntax. In short, the best complement for a dependency syntax would be a **dependency semantics**.

Devising a dependency semantics on the basis of some feasible subset of the principles applied here for syntax is far beyond the scope of this study. A look at those principles shows that many of them can as easily be applied to semantics as to syntax. Co-occurrence and directedness are the principal ones, with dependency derived from these. When establishing patterns of semantic dependency relations, one will note that quite often the dependency lines coincide with the syntactic ones, but certainly not always. As far as I can see, semantic dependency structures will not easily yield true trees, at least not without words being restored. Constructions like AcI's (4.8.) suggest double bindings for some words. This may be taken as an indication that the sentence is not such a self-evident unit in semantics as it is often meant to be in syntax.

But these are already introductory ideas about a dependency semantics. Fortunately dependency semantics has for a couple of decennia been much more in the focus of current linguistic interest than dependency syntax was outside a few innovative centres. There are several grammatical schools that more or less closely follow the lines of what in the terms of the present study is called dependency semantics.

A scholar who painstakingly constructs his theories on the basis of explicitly formulated principles is Klaus Heger. His "**Aktantenmodell**" can be read as a thoroughly rethought and augmented Tesnière'ian dependency grammar, with both syntax and semantics. In his earlier works (e.g. Heger 1966), Heger is closer to Tesnière, but by relying on his own premises, he has step by step moved away from that position (cf. for instance Heger 1971, 1971/1976, 1977).

According to Baum (1976: 137), also Halliday's systemic or **systemic functional grammar** (Halliday 1966 and later works) can be seen as a semantically refined offspring of Tesnière's theory.

The best-known dependency semantics is Charles Fillmore's **case grammar**. Fillmore (1968) refers to Tesnière (1959[/1982]) and also to Heger (1966) and says that his aim was to construct a revised version of Tesnière's most famous concept, valency. Fillmore's deep cases are an account of **semantic valency** (Fillmore 1977a: 4). When Fillmore tells the history of his grammatical model (Fillmore 1977a: 3f.; 1987: 29), he repeatedly mentions Tesnière (1959[/1982]) and to works from the German dependency centres on valency (e.g. Helbig / Schenkel 1969[/1980]).

Fillmore's **deep cases** are semantic dependency types. Since Fillmore's 1968 paper, there has been an endless debate on the precise number and nature of these cases. This debate will probably never end except by arbitrary definitions, because the definitions of deep cases are, according to most authors, based on meaning, and in particular, on semantic decomposition. Since meaning never is as clear-cut as form, but essentially is much like a continuum, such approaches are never objective, in the sense that for each solution achieved, always a different solution can always be found that has as much justification. But arbitrariness in grammar need not be a shortcoming. In the present context those case systems that also take a corresponding dependency syntax into account, e.g. the one by Tarvainen (1985c), are most interesting. Tarvainen correctly points out that syntactic valency also has to do with the content side of the linguistic sign (Tarvainen 1985c: 32). In my view, this is true on a much higher level of abstraction, so that I do not let this insight play a visible role in the present study. The semantic anchorage of valency (more precisely: of dependency in general) is in the model of chapter 4. hidden in the fact that dependency is based on co-occurrence, and that co-occurrence is taken as an observable fact without investigation of the premises These premises may well be semantic, or ultimately pragmatic. (For the links between dependency grammar and case grammar, cf. also Helbig 1986: 120ff.)

Halliday, Fillmore, and in a certain sense also Heger are engaged in dependency semantics, as it were, outside the schools of dependency grammar. Accordingly, they give their theories names that do not refer to dependency. In addition to the work of these authors, scholars more closely linked to the mainstream of dependency research have produced numerous publications on dependency-semantic subjects.

Valency works from **Leipzig** have always contained a semantic level (cf. Helbig / Schenkel 1969/1980: 60ff., 93ff.). The **Mannheim** school is engaged in semantics as well (cf. Engel 1980 and many other works), but it is also the origin of an explicit and emphatic distinction between syntax and semantics in dependency grammar. This is most clearly stated by Engel (1982: 49).

Apart from the "schools" many other scholars are engaged in dependency grammar and some of them establish a coherent whole of syntactic and semantic reasonings. I mention only two of them: **Hudson** (1984: 150ff.) includes semantic roles in his multi-level dependency grammar and discusses the relations between his own view and other authors' accounts. **Nikula** (1986: 40ff.) takes the step from syntax to semantics quite straightforwardly. His ideas about meaning and dependency are especially lucid, since he in a well-defined way distinguishes semantic meaning and pragmatic implicature.

The structural centre of a sentence is in dependency syntax the verb. In a dependency tree of the type devised in this study, a look at the main governor of a sentence and its immediate dependents in many cases provides information about the basic structure of the whole sentence. At a semantic level, Fillmore's case frame is very similar to this: A verb and the word groups that fulfil the functions of **arguments** in the **predication** of the verb. The idea of predications and arguments leads directly back to the foundations of European grammar in classical Greek language philosophy. At the same time this way of arguing about **semantic dependency** establishes a connection to a variety of modern approaches in which in philosophical or highly abstract semantic terms **predications** are defined as a basic unit for language theory (e.g. Snell 1952: 14).

A grammatical school that is based on the concept of predications is Simon Dik's **functional grammar** (Dik 1978: 15ff., 25ff.). Leaving details aside, functional grammar can indeed be said to be based on a dependency semantics (cf. Somers 1987: 95). From the starting point of predications and the semantic dependencies they establish, Dik develops all the other parts of grammar. (A schematic overview of Dik's system is found in Dik 1978: 23, a more recent version in Kwee 1987: 317).

From predications, there is also an interesting link to **pragmatics**. Various approaches take as a starting point **events**, thus extralinguistic phenomena. As soon as events are at issue on such an abstract level, there are hardly any familiar terms in everyday language for speaking about them. One of the most ready-to-hand metaphors seems to come from theatre. Tesnière (1959/1982: 102) introduces his "actants" 'complements' with a comparison to "**acteurs**" 'actors' in a drama and Fillmore (1977b) speaks of "**scenes**". The third theatre term comes from Roger Schank: "**scripts**".

Schank's theory bears a name that directly links it to the present discussion: **conceptual dependency** (Schank 1972, 1975; Schank / Abelson 1977 and other works). But not only through its name, but also conceptually Schank's theory is close to dependency semantics. Schank's aim, however, is not semantics proper in the sense of a theory of the meaning of linguistic signs within the grammatical system of language. Schank attempts at a language-independent, unambiguous representation for events. He approaches that aim by means of very deep semantic decomposition with only a handful of semantic atoms and relations of different kinds. Somers (1987: 250) says that conceptual dependency "is never regarded as a serious linguistic model, and indeed Schank never intended it to be, claiming the model to be relevant to cognitive rather than linguistic science". Humans' knowledge about events (or "scenes") is according to Schank and Abelson (1977: 41) stored in "scripts". Scripts contain knowledge or expectations about what is likely to happen in what kind of a situation. These expectations, among other things, tell us which "actors" (to return to Tesnière) play a role (another theatre metaphor!) in a given situation. The link back from here to dependency grammar is established for example by Heringer (1984: 48) under the playful title "Neues von der Verbszene".

Dependency is a concept that applies to many diverse theories. It is impossible here to mention all the theoretical and applicational connections to various models such as diatheses (Cholodovič 1970; Zemb 1987: 109), semantic networks etc.

6.2. Translation - at which level?

The question **why** metataxis is used is still open. It is now time to answer it.

To translate means to find another form side for a given linguistic sign. Both form and content of the linguistic sign are involved in this replacement. But how? Basically, two extremes are possible:

- The content that is linked to the source form is analysed until it can, without further reference to the source form, be assigned a form in the target language.
- The form side is replaced by a corresponding form from another language. For detecting what a "corresponding" form is, it must somehow be ensured that both forms refer to the same content.

The former approach works on content, but makes use of its various links to different forms in different languages. As it handles content and refers to form, I call it content-handling. The latter approach works on forms, but makes use of their link to content. As it handles form and refers to content, I call it form-handling.

The content-handling approach, if realised in such an extreme way as is suggested here, is radical. It is based on the idea that the important thing in texts, and also in texts being translated, is their content. If the content can be given an appropriate form in the target language, translation is accomplished. For detecting what that content is, it is necessary to analyse the source language form of the text, but as soon as this has been found out, the source form no longer plays a role. The synthesis of the target form is fully content-reliant.

The form-handling approach is based on the idea that correspondences between the signs of two languages can be expressed by means of forms, while the content only serves as a tertium comparationis to ensure that the two forms mean the same. If translation can be carried out at such a level, it is not necessary to analyse the content; referring to it is sufficient.

The problem that prevents the two approaches from functioning so ideally, is first of all **semantic ambiguity**. A single form is not linked to exactly one content, but to several distinct or related ones (**homonymy** and **polysemy**). Moreover, even if two forms from two languages refer to "the same" content, these are in fact two contents which to a more or less high degree overlap, but very often do not coincide precisely.

Solutions within the **content-handling approach** usually tackle the problem of semantic ambiguity with an implicit set-theoretical starting point. The contents that are referred to by forms are, often tacitly, assumed to be sets of content atoms. If this is so, a partial overlap of two content sets can be described by enumerating the common elements as opposed to the elements that are specific to one of the sets. The search for **semantic atoms**, **primitives**, whatever they are called, leads towards **semantic decomposition**. A content-handling approach thus in fact does not go the path from form to content to form, but rather from form to content to content to form. There is a source language content and a target language content, and each of them is distinct from the other. Content, which was meant to be the independent connector between the two languages, turns out to be language-specific. More precisely: **Content is divided up in a language-specific way**. This does not necessarily make content-handling translation methods impossible, but it removes a good deal of the safe ground the method was assumed to be built on.

A fundamental problem of an approach that relies on semantic decomposition is the fact that it is impossible to define semantic atoms in a cross-linguistically valid or intersubjectively intuitive way. There are many attempts to define sets of semantic atoms, but there are no reasons to believe that any of the competing systems is truer than others in an absolute sense. In my opinion, the reason for this is simple: **Meaning is not inherently portioned**. Or, to borrow a term from physics, meaning is not quantised.

There is another problem with content-handling approaches which becomes especially obvious in machine translation. This is the problem of **meaning representation**. A computer does nothing but symbol manipulation. It cannot handle content other than by handling its form, and also a human who works on semantic decomposition almost inevitably wants to label semantic atoms and possibly speak about them and write them down. In other words, for analysing linguistic signs into "pure" content, again **signs** are needed to express the content, a **meta-representation**. What is so problematic about a meta-representation? The original idea of the content-handling approach was to strip the content of its source language form and then to generate the target language form in a purely content-based way. Of course during such a translation process the entire content of the text should be preserved. If semantic decomposition is inevitable and if semantic atoms have to be expressed by some sort of signs, these are forms for content, thus **linguistic signs**. The meta-representation thus is a language, or something like a language, though perhaps one not necessarily meant to be used in normal human communication. I use the term **meta-language** in this general sense. The meta-language "text" should contain the entire content of the source language text. This is nothing but **translation** with an intermediate meta-language. The problem is then how to achieve that translation.

A meta-language of the kind described consists of signs for semantic atoms. For the sake of the discussion, I assume that there are semantic atoms or that there is at least some set of content portions which the grammarian decides to consider atoms. Giving form to these atoms produces a meta-language. This is easily said, but, again, serious problems are entailed in each attempt really to give forms to contents. Where shall the forms be taken from? There are two possibilities: They can either come from existing languages, or be artificial. If the meta-forms are taken from existing languages, they are language-bound. The intention was to create a meta-language that would be more expressive and more precise than a human language. But if its forms are language-bound, this cannot be achieved. Should one thus opt for artificial symbols? This is not unproblematic either. Firstly, it is a question of great semantic (and philosophical) bearing whether it is possible to define the meaning of invented symbols other than by means of an existing language. If this question is answered negatively, then even artifical symbol systems are language-bound. Secondly, there is a warning from one of the fundamental thinkers of language science, which to the best of my knowledge has never been disproven: Louis Hjelmslev (1963: 101) says that an artificial symbol system is inherently less expressive than a human language. According to him, an artificial symbol system can always be translated into a human language, but not a human language into an artifical system. Hjelmslev takes this as a (recursive) definition of human language ("dagligsprog"; cf. Schubert 1986c: 148): a language into which every human language can be translated. If Hjelmslev is right, it is impossible to devise a meta-language of semantic atoms that would not be language-bound. As a consequence, a meta-language into which a source language text has to be translated cannot be clearly more explicit than a human language and at the same time convey the complete content.

Can the **form-handling approach** avoid these problems and does it encounter other difficulties? The basic difference between the two approaches (in their extreme variants I am discussing here) is that content handling makes content as **explicit** as possible, whereas form handling keeps content as far as possible **implicit**.

Also the form-handling approach has to cope with the difficulties of **semantic ambiguity**. Often there are no direct form-to-form correspondences because of semantic ambiguity within a language or between the two languages involved in translation. The important difference, however, is the idea that stripping the content of a text of its entire source language form and then generating the target language form in a wholly content-based way goes much too far. There are a good deal of form correspondences, short cuts from form to form, which can and should be used. These correspondences are mostly not found in the directly visible **syntactic form** of texts, but at the next level of abstraction, the level of **syntactic functions** that are inferable from syntactic form. The realisation of this idea is **metataxis**.

It goes without saying that metataxis cannot remove all the semantic problems described in connection with the content-handling approach, but it indeed considerably facilitates the translation process. It does so in two ways. Firstly, syntactic transfer provides a structure of certainty, whereas semantic transfer can ultimately only deliver probabilities. The metataxis process delivers sentence structures, often several alternative ones, in which the possible target language words fulfil exactly defined syntactic functions. The syntactic functions (dependency types) are an important starting point for (semantic) lexical transfer. This is the idea I formulated in 4.4.: If only the syntactic functions are correct, the sentence can be translated. Secondly, by accomplishing part of the translation task on formal grounds, metataxis makes a good deal of the excessive explicitness required in a content-handling approach unnecessary.

When I speak above about making the content of a text explicit by rendering it in a meta-language, this implies two things. Not only do the semantic atoms have to be expressed, but naturally also the semantic relations between them. After all, semantic atoms can only express complex meaning if they are arranged in a **system**, and a system is made up by its elements (the atoms) and their mutual relations. A common way of accounting for the relations between semantic units are Fillmorean **deep cases** (see 6.1.). But since meaning is not quantised, defining deep cases cross-linguistically is as difficult as defining semantic atoms. A number of authors point out that deep cases ultimately are what they were designed not to be: language-specific. Examples are Jochen Pleines (1978: 372), Ulrich Engel (1980: 11), and recently this insight turns up in computational linguistics as well, for instance in a paper by Tsujii Jun-ichi (Tsujii 1986: 656; cf. Schubert 1987: 114).

Metataxis with its emphasis on syntactic relations allows for a different solution. In a metataxis-oriented semantic transfer process, it is possible to keep deep cases **implicit** and use semantic relators that are rather straightforwardly inferable from syntactic functions.

In the machine translation application for which I devise metataxis, such a solution has been adopted. Before giving a very concise sketch of that system, I should emphasise that metataxis as a system of syntactic transfer does not inevitably require lexical transfer to be arranged in the way I outline here. Lexical transfer can complement metataxis regardless of how it is carried out. But of course there are ways that are more directly in harmony with metataxis than others.

Lexical transfer is in the DLT machine translation system (see 1.2. and 7.5.) realised in the following way: Metataxis submits syntactically possible translations with the target language words inserted. From the dependency types made explicit in the trees and from function words, relators are derived which closely follow the dependency types. The trees are chopped up in pairs of two content words connected by a relator. These pairs are compared with similar pairs in a lexical knowledge bank. The most likely solution is chosen. The semantic word choice mechanisms are arranged with an emphasis on keeping content implicit. This is obtained in an elegant way: Meta-language is avoided by allowing only for **linguistic means** in the whole semantic treatment. These need not necessarily be words; also isolated morphemes and morpheme combinations are allowed. I cannot spell out this solution here and therefore refer the reader to the thorough account given by Papegaaij (1986: 75ff.). Only one detail deserves to be mentioned: The DLT translation process does not link two languages directly, but via an intermediate language, a slightly modified version of Esperanto. In a translation process from, say, English to French, metataxis thus takes place two times, first from English to Esperanto, and then from Esperanto to French. The semantic word expert system that performs word choice is arranged in a somewhat more sophisticated manner than I show here: There is only a single lexical knowledge bank in Esperanto, so that the first half of the translation process really works in the way I outline above with the knowledge bank being in the target language of that half of the translation process (Esperanto). For the second half, however, the system is arranged so that even then the Esperanto knowledge bank can be used, thus a knowledge bank in the source language of the second half of the process (cf. Papegaaij 1986: 89).

Neither a content-handling nor a form-handling approach has ever been realised in such an extreme form as I discuss here. The two models should rather be seen as poles with a scale in between. But it is obvious that **metataxis** is close to the form-handling pole. And by using the **implicitness principle** (Schubert 1987: 116), it establishes harmony with a complementary semantic treatment that is also based on implicitness.

Chapter 7

Dependency syntax and metataxis in computational linguistics

Metataxis is in the present study devised as a model for syntactic transfer in machine translation. But although machine translation is alluded to at several times, I do not make a point of it in the body of this study. It is my hope that the previous chapters can be read without knowledge of computational linguistics. I have, indeed, occasionally made arbitrary decisions in these chapters. The motive for these is found in the computational applications I have in mind, but besides this, the computational aspects have not been in the foreground. I have designed the models of dependency syntax (4.) and metataxis (5.) as major elements of a grammar model that is intended to be feasible for the study of language quite generally. This is a choice which I have made not only, and not even mainly, for the ease of readers not interested in computational applications, but as a consequence of my conviction that a theoretical model becomes better when it is tailored only according to the shape of the phenomenon to be described and not according to the possibilities and limitations which an instrument used for carrying out analyses with the model happens to have. Kwee Tjoe-Liong (1987: 315) may feel the same when he writes: "How can we, using a computer, serve best the advancement of general linguistics? In my view, by modeling as faithfully as possible the rules of an **existing** grammatical theory" (emphasis mine).

After much application-free model design, the present chapter establishes the link to computational applications from dependency syntax, including metataxis. In 7.1., I supplement section 3.4. with a more thorough account of the applications dependency grammar has found in computational linguistics, with a look especially at the beginnings and at the situation today. Section 7.2. is an attempt to obtain a clearer view of the various formalisms, formalised grammars, representations and the like that are suggested in the field. I exemplify my distinctions reviewing four current systems. The last two sections deal with connections to the two main types of implementations needed for dependency-syntactic processings: parsers (7.3.) and tree-manipulating "metataxors" (7.4.).

7.1. The way of dependency grammar into computational linguistics

Kwee's opinion (above) is not the most common one in computational linguistics. **Modularity** between grammatical work and programming is not everywhere seen as an essential virtue (see 7.2.). Sometimes one gets the impression that communication between language science and computational linguistics has not been sufficiently frequent. It therefore is not surprising that a theory like dependency grammar has almost since its creation spread along at least two different lines into general and into computational linguistics. The linguistics line has been described for in 3., and the computational one is outlined in this section (see also 3.4.).

Tesnière's ideas became internationally known through his "Éléments" (1959[/1982]). In computational linguistics (which in those years was almost entirely machine translation), dependency grammar seems to turn up before 1959. David Hays (1961: 258 n. 2) refers to an English translation of the (bibliographically not specified) proceedings of a machine translation conference held in May 1958 (apparently in Soviet Union) and says that both dependency and constituency grammar were used in Soviet machine translation work at that time. I have not found any indications as to whether those Soviet applications - Hays quotes the names of Kulagina, Revzin, Mološnaja, Volockaja, Padučeva, Šelimova and Šumilina - have do to with earlier works by Tesnière, e.g. his "Esquisse" (Tesnière 1953). But obviously they (also?) have some roots in an independent dependency theory of Soviet origin. Helbig and Schenkel's account (1969/1980: 21) suggests that tradition lines lead from Kacnel'son (1948) to works in theoretical and computational linguistics around 1960 (Lomtev 1959, 1961; Lejkina 1961; Mel'čuk 1964). Mel'čuk and Percov (1987: 78), however, of whom at least Mel'čuk was personally involved in the Soviet machine translation efforts at an early stage, do not mention any Soviet works on dependency grammar before Tesnière's "Éléments" (1959[/1982]). They see all the Soviet works they refer to in Tesnière's tradition, in which they also place Hays. (On early Soviet research cf. Hutchins 1986: 132ff.; esp. 137.)

The articles by Hays (1961, 1964a,b) stem from a machine translation project at the Rand Corporation in the United States (cf. Hutchins 1986: 78ff.). According to Hays (1961: 258), it is at that time the only project in the United States to use dependency grammar. In his 1961 paper, read at a conference in early 1960, Hays does not say where his acquaintance with dependency grammar comes from, but he does not seem to have invented it himself. In a paper read in 1961, Hays (1964a: 45 n. 3) refers to Tesnière (1953), but he seems also to draw on Soviet sources, since he (Hays 1964b: 511) imports the term "valence" from Iordanskaja (1963).

In view of later developments it is interesting to read that Hays (1961: 259) describes dependency grammar as a rule system that depicts sentences analyses in trees, whereas constituency grammar does not. In the 1961 paper Hays's dependency trees still look similar to the ones drawn in this study, but already in 1961 Hays (1964a: 46) tries to render word order in dependency trees and in 1964 he (Hays 1964b: 519) is aware of Lecerf's and Ihm's works on **projectivity** and draws projective trees (Lecerf 1960; Ihm / Lecerf 1963). Warren Plath (1964) does so already in 1961. A mathematically oriented description of these projective dependency trees is found in an article by Haim Gaifman (1965).

Almost all the early American articles about dependency in computational linguistics compare the two concepts, dependency and constituency, justifying and propagating dependency. But dependency was not in vogue at that time, certainly not in the United States. The first computational linguist to attempt an integration of the two concepts appears to be Jane Robinson (1970). At the same time Klaus Baumgärtner (1970) attempts an integration in theoretical linguistics. In Robinson's opinion, constituency grammar, then prevailingly called transformational grammar, uses dependency ideas when speaking of a head of a phrase (i.e. the internal governor of a syntagma), but cannot in terms of constituency account for the phenomena involved. She therefore advocates an introduction of a phrase level dependency analysis in the wider framework of a transformational grammar. Robinson (1970: 260) categorically declares that dependency grammar is a theory "which was advocated by Tesnière 1953, 1959, and formalized by Hays 1964 and by Gaifman 1965".

The United States and Soviet Union were the first countries where efforts were made in the field of machine translation, and in both dependency grammar was taken up by some scholars. It is only natural that Tesnière's theory attained still more influence on computational applications as soon as French-speaking scholars got involved. Dependency grammar turns up in the CETA project at Grenoble and Paris and at the EURATOM-funded project at Brussels university (see Fourquet's 1965 preface to the second edition of Tesnière [1959/]1982: 7; cf. Hutchins 1986: 128ff.).

Also the direction forwarded by Maurice Gross (1975 and earlier works; see 4.4.1.) seems to be connected with computational linguistics of the sixties (cf. Gross 1964).

An interesting comparison of dependency and constituency syntaxes implemented in parsers is supplied by Wolfgang Klein (1971).

These are the beginnings of dependency grammar in computational linguistics. It is impossible here to include a more detailed history of all the developments this grammatical school has undergone in this particular application. It is noteworthy, however, that there has been a continuous stream of dependency-minded work from early computational linguistics until now. I now skip some 25 years and try to sketch the role of dependency grammar in computational linguistics as it occurs to me in 1987, when this study is being written.

In 1987, dependency grammar is gaining ground in language theory and also in computational linguistics. Because of the high popularity of Fillmore's case grammar in language science, it is no surprise that this form of dependency semantics is a common instrument in computational applications as well. A more recent development is the ongoing breakthrough of dependency syntax. Dependency syntaxes have been implemented in parsers for machine translation, database interfaces etc. (Hellwig 1986; Schubert 1986a: 99ff.). The tradition of projective dependency trees is continued in one of the streams in this field, namely at the East German Academy of Sciences (Kunze 1975; Reimann 1985).

An interesting development is the fact that constituency-based parsing algorithms, due to the bond of constituency to contiguity and word order, in many cases fail to handle "free word order" languages in a comfortable way. This is more and more discovered by researchers engaged in computational treatments of languages like Japanese, Finnish or Czech, so that dependency-syntactic (and -semantic) implementations are spreading especially for these languages. Examples are for Japanese: Sakamoto et al. (1984), Nitta et al. (1984), Muraki et al. (1985), Sakamoto et al. (1986), Nitta (1986), Shirai and Hamada (1986), Sato and Kasuya (forthc.); for Finnish: Nelimarkka et al. (1984), Lehtola et al. (1985), Jäppinen et al. (1986), Valkonen et al. (forthc.) whose dependency syntax derives from Tarvainen (1977; personal communication by Jäppinen); for Czech (and English): Kirschner (1982).

Not only where the syntax of a language, so to speak, enforces its use, dependency syntax is applied. Dependency semantics, especially in the commonly known shape of case grammar, often also in applications for more word order-bound languages suggests analysing sentences in a way that is easily mapped on case frames. From this starting point, quite a number of computational linguists have found their way into valency, and, more generally, dependency approaches in syntax as well. Examples from German are found in the EUROTRA machine translation project (Schmidt 1986:

307ff.) and in speech recognition (Niedermair 1986). Still more word order-bound languages are French and English (Vergne / Pagès 1986; Somers 1986).

Stanley Starosta's Lexicase system (Starosta 1987; Starosta / Nomura 1986) is in many ways dependency-minded, and it is typical that this system derives from applications to very diverse languages.

Within the DLT machine translation system, dependency syntax has been adopted because of its suitability for a metataxis approach to the transfer phase in translation (see 5.6. and 7.5.). Also here, the relatively easy mapping of syntactically analysed sentences onto semantic dependencies is noteworthy (Papagaaij 1986: 100ff.).

7.2. Grammar, formalism, implementation

Computer science uses many terms that originate in linguistics and sometimes have been borrowed from linguistics indirectly, via mathematics, into computer science. It is not always realised that they do not denote the same phenomena in the different disciplines. In computational linguistics, where the terms of computer science and of linguistics meet, it is especially important to be aware of all the vagueness of expression and all the misunderstanding that may be brought about by the **metaphorical** use of linguistic terms in computer science. I therefore began this study with some fundamental definitions (2.1.) and I now return to them in order to make terms clear before I enter more detailed computational-linguistic discussions.

It is useful to establish clearly distinguished levels on which to describe properties of languages on the one hand and computational procedures for analysing, synthesising or simulating some of these properties on the other hand. I therefore establish three distinct levels:

- **grammar**,
- **formalism** and
- **implementation**.

A **grammar** deals with the system of a language. (A language is always taken to be a human language, otherwise the term is used metaphorically; see 2.1.) A grammar describes a language without necessarily referring to computational processing. Writing a grammar of a given language is a task for a **linguist** who is an expert in the particular language.

A **formalism** is a standard notation in which a grammar must be (re)written in order to make it suitable for processing by formal systems (computers). It enforces a degree of precision which often is not achieved in grammar descriptions addressed to humans. There are quite a number of formalisms around, some of which are discussed below.

The rewriting of a grammar from a conventional, non-formalised grammar description into a formalism should be the task of a **computational linguist**. Often the conventional grammar description will not be explicit enough for direct formalisation. It may show inconsistencies etc. and will cause the computational linguist to consult the language expert. It is conceivable that the language expert does not deliver a conventional description first, but directly writes in the formalism. What actually happens all the time in computational linguistics is that computational linguists make up their own grammars, often just tiny "toy" grammars. These shifts between the levels of grammar and of formalism may be good practice in one case and bad practice in another, according to the grammar writer's capability of keeping the formalism requirements from steering the grammatical work. In general, one can say that the modular approach benefits (See the introduction to 7.).

One could conclude that a formalism, as defined here, is the description of a grammar in a form that is amenable to computer processing, but there is more: A formalism is not just a grammar in a computer-friendly form. In practice additional information brought in by a computational linguist is used, instructing the computer how to proceed when using the grammar for a specific task such as parsing or metatactic transformation. This additional amount of information is sometimes called "strategy" or "procedural information". Insofar as it contains this information, a formalism is **dynamic**, whereas the information provided by the grammar (and of course the dictionary) normally is **declarative** or **static**.

The formalism is the interface between the grammar and the third level, the implementation.

An **implementation** is the level nearest to the computer. It consists of computer programs, i.e. sequences of instructions that control the operations of a computer. Designing and writing these programs is the task of **computer scientists** and

programmers. At this level, no language-related knowledge is added.

At the implementation level a distinction can be made between the "shell" proper, and the shell loaded with a specific formalism. A shell is a computer program (or an entire software system of programs) ready to accept a specific formalism. Or stated differently: A shell is ready to accept a formalised grammar with the dynamic information on rule priorities and procedure prescriptions added. The shell performs specific tasks with the filled-in formalism, for instance parsing sentences of the language in question. When one submits a formalism to the computer program, the grammar written in that formalism is usually "compiled" to a specific format, closer to the processing. Often such a software system also includes utilities for creation, correction and updating of the information contained in the formalism.

The shell loaded with the specific formalism could somewhat loosely be called a ready-to-run program (an execution module). It contains all the language-related data, the grammar and the dynamic information, in condensed, computer-processable form.

The background for this threefold level distinction is the idea of **modularity** in system design that was mentioned earlier (introductions to 5. and 7.). In this section, I review in the light of these distinctions five current systems which are in frequent use in computational linguistics for parsing and other applications. (In these paragraphs, I use the term "system" not in the strict sense of 2.2., but just as a vague expression that for the moment leaves open whether the thing in question is a grammar, a formalism or something else.) Thinking about them with dependency grammar in mind sheds a new light on the functionality of some of them. The five systems I take up are often called either grammars or formalisms. Four of them even carry the term grammar in their names:

- Augmented Transition Networks (ATN),
- Augmented Phrase Structure Grammar (APSG),
- Definite Clause Grammar (DCG),
- Lexical-Functional Grammar (LFG) and
- Generalised Phrase Structure Grammar (GPSG).

The main question I try to answer in the following paragraphs is, whether these systems are general-purpose formalisms or restricted formalisms mixed up with a certain type of grammar.

The purpose of this question is by no means only to achieve a clean use of terms. This alone would indeed be welcome in computational linguistics, but my aim goes further. I am interested in the feasibility of these (and other) systems for implementing procedures involving dependency syntax. The grammar-formalism distinction is fruitful in this respect. A grammar is a specific description of a particular language. Several different grammars for the same language can be devised. A formalism should not be bound to a specific language or a specific grammar. As the above definition of a formalism suggests, it should provide the means for expressing different grammars in a way that can be executed in a program. A good criterium therefore is this: If a system is suited for expressing both constituency and dependency syntax (and has the other characteristics of a formalism), it is a true, general-purpose formalism. If a system, however, is bound to one of these grammatical concepts, the modularity between grammar and formalism is violated. Such a mixed system might be called a restricted formalised notation for a grammar or the like. Normally it lacks full cross-linguistic scope and is suited mainly for particular languages that are easily described with the one concept.

Augmented Transition Networks are a system designed for syntactic analysis. They were invented by Woods (1970); a detailed description after a few years of experience is given by Madeleine Bates (1978); a concise overview is provided by Winograd (1983: 195ff.) and an advanced, graphics-supported implementation is described by Doedens (forthc.). ATNs can be used for examining the syntactic correctness of sentences (or other units of text). This is their **recogniser** function. They can also be used for generating an analysed version of the sentence, thus for building up tree structures. This is their **parser** function. They are also said to be suitable for sentence **generation**, and even semantic analyses are sometimes carried out in ATNs.

ATNs have been developed with constituency syntax in mind, and it is certainly not out of place to assume that this was a constituency syntax of English. Of the five systems reviewed here, ATNs give the user most direct access to the sequential order of the steps of analysis, and this feature harmonizes well with the contiguity principle of a constituency-based syntax. A transition network consists of a number of recursively callable subnetworks. How these subnetworks are divided up is ultimately a decision made by the grammarian or programmer, but they cannot be totally avoided, since recursiveness and virtually unlimited combinatorial productivity in language must be accounted for somehow. The subnetworks usually correspond roughly to clauses, phrases and subphrases, the abstract, non-terminal units in constituency syntax.

In short, ATNs are close to the constituency concept and thus seem to be closer to a grammar mixed with a restricted formalism than to a general-purpose formalism. But a closer look shows that this is not so. The structure of a traditional ATN for a particular language is more or less a mirror image of the constituents used in the underlying syntax. But in spite of this, one is by no means obliged to let a parsing ATN generate tree structures that reflect this same constituent structure. It is of course straightforward to do so, but it is not necessary. This can be seen in a practical example: For the DLT machine translation system, Witkam (1983: IV-87ff.) designed an ATN for Esperanto, which is basically constituency-based and for which he had constituency trees in mind (Witkam 1983: IV-72ff.). When dependency syntax was chosen for the DLT system, it was easy to equip this same ATN with tree-building actions for dependency trees (Schubert 1986a: 11f., 99ff.). No rearrangements whatsoever were required in the ATN in order to shift from assumed constituency trees to dependency trees.

At least theoretically no rearrangements were needed.
But in practice faster processing and similar efficiency objectives are attained better when the ATN is tailored in accordance with the structures to be built up (see 7.3.). A dependency ATN works more effectively when its subnetworks correspond to syntagmata. As they lend themselves to procedures with both basic underlying concepts of grammar, ATNs are a general-purpose formalism.

Augmented Phrase Structure Grammar is the name for a group of systems which have much in common with ATNs. The main difference is, according to Winograd (1983: 377ff.), that APSGs do not use a network structure. In the DLT machine translation project, parsers for "Simplified English", a restricted syntax for written English from the aircraft industry, were in parallel formalised (by Bieke van der Korst) in ATNs and in an APSG version provided by the University of Amsterdam. Although the aim of this experimental parallelism was to test the computational efficiency of both systems, it has turned out that much of what was said above about ATNs is also valid for the APSG in question. APSG was certainly developed with (English) constituency syntax in mind, but is suited for dependency parsing as well.

Accordingly, the actual version of APSG is found to be a general-purpose formalism, not linked to either constituency or dependency only.

Definite Clause Grammar is an augmentation of the Prolog programming language. Prolog originates from natural-language processing, especially from Colmerauer's "grammaires de métamorphose" (Colmerauer 1975/1978), and DCGs are still more language-oriented extensions of it (Pereira / Warren 1980). "Damit ist PROLOG eine der wenigen Programmiersprachen, die bereits standardmäßig über die Möglichkeit verfügen, Phrasenstrukturgrammatiken einzugeben und ohne weiteren Aufwand sowohl zum Analysieren, als auch zum Generieren von Sätzen zu verwenden. In analoger Weise wie die DCG's lassen sich in Prolog auch andere Grammatikkonzepte realisieren", says Helmar Gust (1984: 55).

A main feature of Prolog and of DCGs is that they are declarative in the sense that the user has much less direct access to the sequence of steps carried out in analysing a sentence than for instance in ATNs. Pereira and Warren (1980) demonstrate the equivalence of ATNs and DCGs, advocating DCGs, which they find much more effective. This equivalence means that DCGs lend themselves well for constituency syntax ("Phrasenstrukturgrammatiken"), the only type of syntax of which the authors transpose a sample from ATN into DCG form. It also implies that DCGs ought to be suitable for dependency procedures as well. Indeed the declarative character of DCGs is in good harmony with a system of governors with dependent syntagmata, especially if the sequential order of these elements can vary.

I am not aware of an implementation of DCGs involving dependency syntax, at least not for a complete syntax of a language. Within the DLT machine translation project, a small word parser has been implemented (by Job van Zuijlen) which builds up dependency trees for the morphemes of complex Esperanto words.

As a consequence, I conclude that DCG is not a "Grammatikkonzept" but a general-purpose formalism that lends itself for expressing different grammatical rule sets based on different grammatical concepts.

Lexical-Functional Grammar was devised by Ronald Kaplan and Joan Bresnan (1981). LFGs work on constituent structures. What Peter Sells (1985: 80) says about GPSGs is as true for LFGs: They are a sort of mechanism for passing information around trees. An LFG builds up a constituent structure ("c-structure") and a functional structure ("f-structure"). Very roughly these two correspond to what I in this study call syntactic form and syntactic function, respectively. The mechanism relies quite heavily on the dictionary (hence the name "lexical"). Feature values are found there and passed on upwards to various abstract nodes. Wellformedness conditions can then test these features on the appropriate nodes.

Yasukawa (1984) claims that a syntax can be transposed from LFG to DCG form which would suggest equivalence as in the case of DCGs and ATNs (above). Such an equivalence, however, can in my view only be established when both systems are filled in with a constituency-based syntax. The whole mechanism of LFG is so directly bound to the existence of an abstract constituent structure above the words themselves, that an adaptation to a dependency syntax would require such grave rearrangements of the system, that the result would no longer be very similar to LFG.

LFG therefore seems to be a restricted formalism, directly linked to constituency grammar.

Generalised Phrase Structure Grammar derives from work by Gerald Gazdar, the most comprehensive description now being a book by Gazdar, Klein, Pullum and Sag (1985). It is an offspring of transformational generative grammar with the characteristic that it uses neither transformations nor deep structures. These design features seem to conform with a guideline that I try to realise in the syntactic model of this study: The description should deal with actually occurring data, the "surface", as it were. For computational applications, such an approach is welcome, since the input for machine translation and other types of natural-language processing in most cases is a plain text, not deep structures.

Transformations were originally introduced in generative grammar (Chomsky 1957) in order to describe the unlimited productivity of language by a limited set of patterns or rules. GPSG copes with this problem by postulating a set of standardised syntagmata, of which other syntagmata can be "derived". These are called "derived categories" or "slash categories". The latter expression refers to a notation convention: "PP/NP" roughly means "a prepositional phrase from which a noun phrase is missing". The PP is a standardised syntagma with a preposition and an NP, and a preposition alone is described by means of this same pattern with the provision that the NP has been left out and may be found elsewhere in the sentence.

[228]

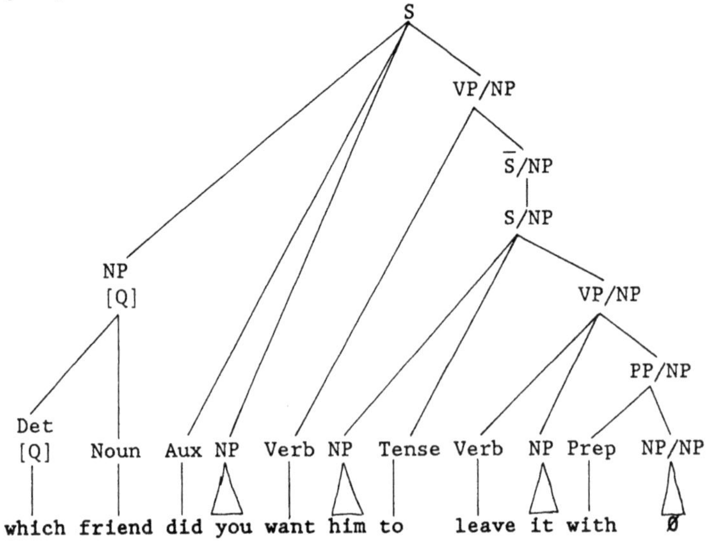

The example is taken from Winograd (1983: 347).

The necessity of saying that something (which friend in [228]) is missing (from with), although it is present elsewhere in the same sentence, points to contiguity as a basic concept. GPSG consequently requires a constituency-based tree structure of abstract nodes, although it does not use a deep structure. As I have already mentioned in connection with Sells' (1985: 80) remark about LFG, GPSG is a theory about how syntactic features are passed on from node to node in such an abstract structure.

As far as I can see, GPSG is too inherently bound to constituency, which it also carries in its name ("phrase structure"), to be a general-purpose formalism that would be open to both basic grammatical concepts. It is certainly possible to devise a theory about feature flow in dependency trees, but the result would no longer be GPSG. I therefore consider GPSG to be a restricted formalism linked to constituency grammar.

These are only five of many systems used in parsers and similar computational applications of syntax. The brief diagnoses I give here may suggest how other systems can be assessed with respect to their suitability for the notion of dependency.

7.3. Dependency parsing

Parsing means carrying out by means of computer programs an analysis of the syntax (or generally the grammar) of a piece of text. Parsing, as opposed to recognising, implies that output of some kind is created in which the analysis found is made explicit. Parsing a sentence with a dependency syntax thus means producing a dependency tree. There are many parsing techniques, some of them suited for dependency parsing. In 7.2. I have reviewed five in computational linguistics generally known systems on which parser implementations often are based, and found that three of them, ATNs, APSG and DCG, lend themselves well to dependency parsing. Other dependency-oriented parsers are used by various scholars (see 7.1.; cf. Klein 1971).

I have earlier discussed a number of technical details about how an ATN can work as a dependency parser (Schubert 1986a: 99ff.). This discussion is not repeated here, but I outline a few principles which, in ATNs as well as in other formalisms, may be taken as a guideline for writing dependency parsers. It should be kept in mind that different solutions are always possible. The present sketch is meant to provide parsing efficiency by devising the main structure of the parsing algorithm as closely as possible with the trees to be built up.

A parser should ideally be able to cope with all syntactically correct sentences of a given language. It should of course be emphasised that the definition of what is "correct" is up to the grammarian. The **correctness definition** one finds desirable for a given application may well be much wider than what ordinary school grammar accepts. Especially in speech recognition the "incorrect", "incomplete" and "ill-formed" utterances of current spoken language certainly belong to the range a parser should cover. In addition to the possibility of a wider correctness definition, analyses may be assigned even to input strings that fall outside the scope of the correctness definition, but only if one can be sure that such structures are never offered to the parser. This is possible if the parser is used as a parser only, i.e. if a separate recogniser ensures that only input that is in concord with the correctness definition will arrive at the parser. In many applications, however, a parser is used as a parser and a recogniser simultaneously, in which case it should reject exactly those sentences that violate the definition.

Whether or not it is necessary to ensure that incorrect sentences be rejected, the condition remains valid that a parser should produce appropriate trees for all correct input. When the correctness definition is a dependency syntax, there is a direct route to a description of all possible correct sentences. This route was described in terms of the generative productivity of a dependency syntax (4.12.) and can now be applied. The complete, but virtually unlimited, set of correct sentences is obtained by recursively inserting the maximal government patterns of word classes into the dependent slots of other government patterns of word classes, starting with the possible main governors of sentences. The most straightforward way of building up a parser is to divide up the formalisation of the syntax into recursively callable subroutines, each of which describes the government pattern of a word class. For instance a verb with all its possible dependents. The descriptions of the dependents can test the identifying characteristics of words that signal their syntactic function (dependency type). These characteristics are the syntactic form of words, thus either morphological markings or word order (see 4.4.1.). Word order may play a role either with respect to the governor or to other dependents. Diderichsen-type sentence schemes may be used where appropriate (see 5.5.3.). Since there may be many different word classes that can alternatively function as a particular dependency type, it can become efficient to group them into one subroutine.

For the Danish example used in 4.12., such a procedure would yield the following basic structure of a parser. I use an ATN-like notation in which the boxes denote subroutines and the box-less symbols words to consume. The arrows indicate where to continue the process. To begin with, the main governor is the verb.

[229]

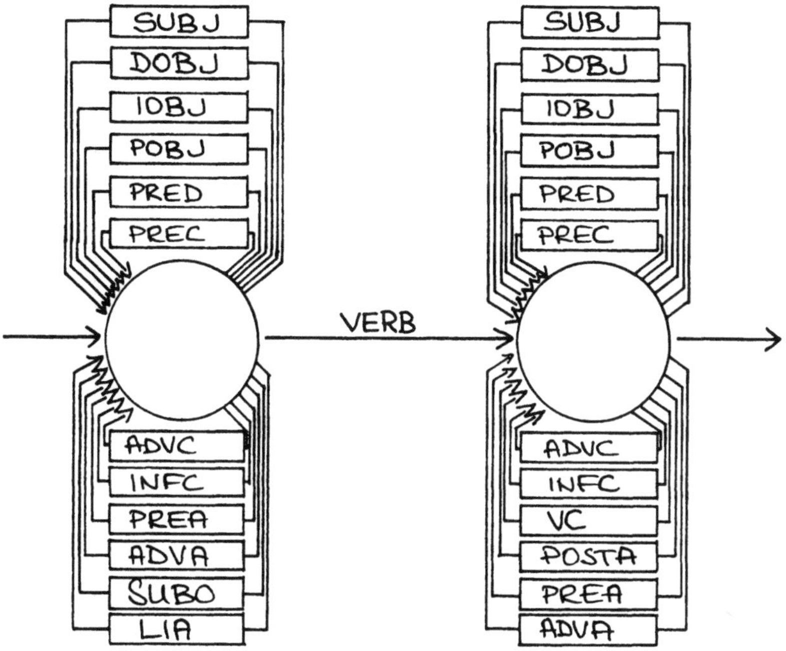

The subroutine for subjects contains the following possibilities:

[230]

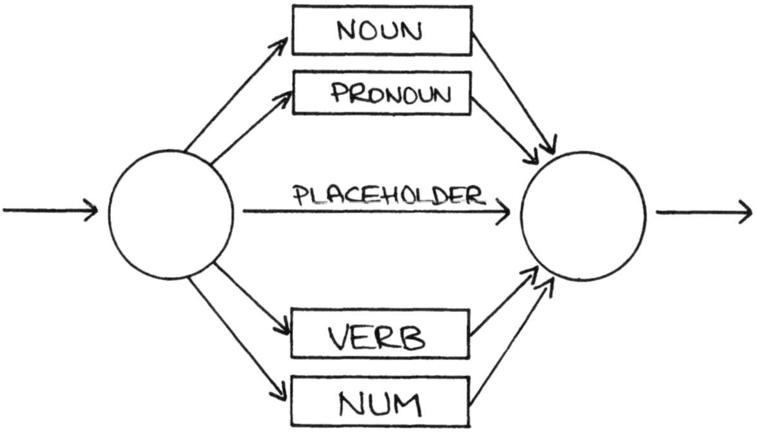

The subroutines of [230] again are word class analyses, for example the one for the noun:

[231]

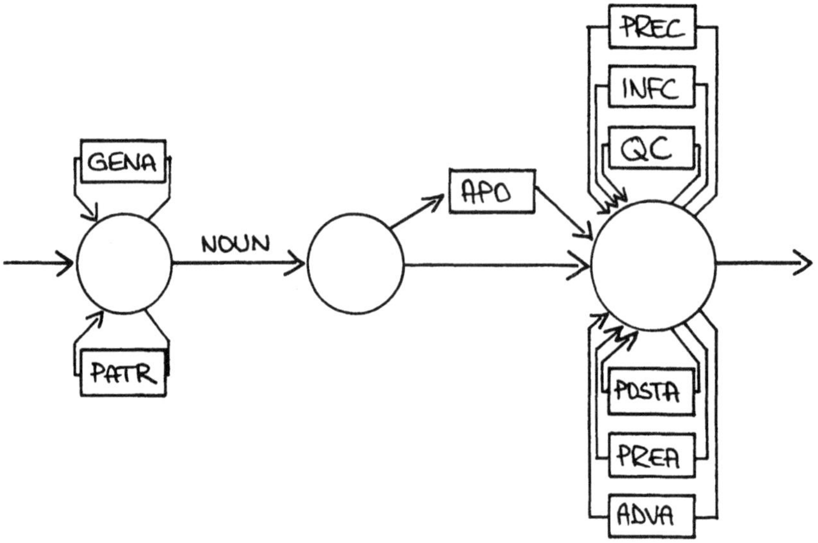

All the routines shown here are meant to illustrate my point rather than being a complete account of Danish. Especially [231] is very sketchy.

This is a straightforward method for designing a dependency parser. It may be adapted to the restrictions of a given parsing technique and to the particulars of a specific syntax. Many different refinements are possible, but if the basic idea is maintained, the tree-building process will work virtually without the need of any bookkeeping about where to continue building the tree. Even discontinuous elements can be handled and placed in a dependency tree in this way. However, a fast and efficient treatment may in practice require a method similar to the connection point technique in metataxis rules (5.1.2.).

7.4. Formalising metataxis

As soon as a parser has delivered a dependency tree for a sentence, all the rest of the syntactic processing until the final target language sentence is **tree manipulation**. Therefore a uniform formalism can be used for formalising all the syntactic steps that follow parsing. These steps are **metataxis** and **target language synthesis** (see 5.).

A look at the metataxis process (summarised in 5.3.5.) shows the main functions that should be catered for:

- **Scanning** trees and distinguishing source and target language symbols.
- **Matching** subtrees of the tree being translated with the input trees of metataxis rules.
- **Comparing** metataxis rules as regards their hierarchic status.
- **Applying** metataxis rules.

An important additional function which is not dealt with here is dictionary look-up. Tree manipulation is a well-known exercise which has a number of applications in computer science, even outside language processing. Scanning and matching trees are common functions in tree manipulation. The same is valid for applying metataxis rules, which amounts to replacing nodes or subtrees by other subtrees. All these functions require metataxis-oriented implementations for efficient processing, but the basic requirements for this are not foreign to programming.

Comparing metataxis rules and selecting rules by virtue of their hierarchic priority status is a somewhat more specific function that is created by the design of the metataxis system. Are the criteria for hierarchic ordering easily expressed in formalism level properties of trees? In 5.3.3. the hierarchy of metataxis rules was formulated in such a way as to render the basic idea of layered rules in metataxis: Metataxis rules usually have too large a coverage, but more specific, overriding rules ensure that a more general rule is not applied unless the form change it describes is the desired one. This is an ordering based on grammatically relevant properties. In a formalisation of metataxis, it turns out that the criteria chosen on language-related grounds are well-suited for the selection process on a formalism level. This is not surprising, first of all because the relationship between specific and general rules has a much wider validity than just in syntax, and secondly because the entire syntax (and thereby the metataxis) in this study is based on form, which facilitates formal and formalised processing. The priority hierarchy of metataxis rules can accordingly be used directly in a formalisation. The algorithm there counts the number of nodes in trees and compares variables on the one hand with specifically given words and labels on the other hand.

There is no fundamental difference between metataxis rules in the rule system and in the dictionary (5.1.). For formalisation, however, it is useful to have a simple criterion by which a rule can be assigned its place (dictionary or redundancy rule system) and a matching rule for a given tree found quickly. Indeed this distinction can be made in a formal way as well, and remains in good harmony with the grammatical properties of rules. Those rules are taken to be in the bilingual dictionary, that have as the internal governor of their input tree a word. Rules with input trees governed by labels or variables belong to the rule system.

In a practical formalisation it is possible that the adopted hierarchy principles do not in every possible case select exactly one applicable metataxis rule, but several ones which are equally specific. If in such cases an arbitrary choice is made, e.g. by taking the first rule found, the result is in my experience always a valid translation. If results in this respect are unsatisfactory, the hierarchy principles should be applied more deeply and a finer selection mechanism should be devised by extending the principle of specificity. It seems less likely that new principles will be needed to supplement the specificity criterion.

7.5. Metataxis and the design of machine translation systems

Metataxis has become a characterising feature of the DLT machine translation system (see 1.2.). At first sight, this seems to be contradictory. Where is the contradiction? Indeed, it is not an obvious contradiction, but a hidden one. Nevertheless it seems worthwhile to find and dismantle it.

Metataxis is specific for a language pair and a translation direction (see 5.). As is shown in 6.2., metataxis heavily relies on the **implicitness principle**. Metataxis is an attempt to perform as much as possible of the translation process on a form-to-form path, keeping content implicit and only referring to it as a tertium comparationis. Such a **form-oriented** translation method makes use of form correspondences between the source and the target language and in this way establishes a structure of certainty which restricts the enormous freedom of choice that otherwise would prevail in semantic and pragmatic translation.

In the well-known triple distinction of designs for machine translation systems - direct, transfer or interlingual - metataxis thus must be placed with **direct translation**. The highest degree of implicitness can be achieved in direct translation.

This is the contradiction: Metataxis belongs to direct translation, whereas DLT is always attributed to the **interlingual** machine translation systems. Due to the fact that DLT uses as its intermediate language not just an artificial symbol system, but a full-fledged human language (although a special one, Esperanto), it is often said to be an interlingual system par excellence. So, how can metataxis work in DLT?

The answer is simple: The **content side** of the translation process in DLT is interlingual, but the **form side** is not. Since DLT's intermediate language in itself is suited for human communication, the form-transforming part of translation is not interlingual. It is **double-direct**. The DLT system in fact translates a text two times, and both of these steps profit from the benefits of form-oriented direct translation. This seemingly double effort becomes meaningful against the background of DLT's basic design ideas as a whole: Fully automatic high-quality translation is generally held to be impossible, or - as some scholars assert - impossible for the time being. In order to live with this situation, DLT has been conceived as a **knowledge-based, interactive** MT system. First, a human-aided machine translation process from a source language into the intermediate language takes place. During this process the content of the text is made clearer and more precise by combined means of a semantic-pragmatic word expert system (knowledge bank) and an interactive dialogue with the user. This is the **information enrichment** of DLT. The intermediate text, then, is in a human language, but in an especially clear one, Esperanto. The intermediate text in this form is suited for **fully automatic** translation into a target language.

In a nutshell, the syntactic side of the DLT machine translation system is double-direct thanks to the special qualities of Esperanto as an intermediate language, and because of this property, DLT can make use of the implicity-based advantages of **metataxis**.

Translation is not confined to form. It has a content side as well, which consists entirely of steps involving semantics and pragmatics. In DLT, these are carried out entirely in the intermediate language, for both the translation into and from it. The double-direct part of the overall translation process (metataxis) delivers a large number of syntactically possible translation alternatives. The content part then on **semantic-pragmatic** grounds selects the one alternative that should be taken as the correct translation. Both the form and the content side of the process together accomplish the complete translation process. Since the semantic-pragmatic interpretation and selection procedure is carried out entirely in the intermediate language, the DLT system as a whole is an **intermediate-language** system. As such, it may with another word be called **interlingual**, but it should be borne in mind that the term "interlingual" is often used for designs that do not incorporate a full-fledged intermediate **language** but rather an abstract symbol system involving logic or semantics for the pivotal function.

Chapter 8

Prospects

What are the advantages of metataxis as it now stands and how can it be further developed?

The outstanding characteristics of metataxis as compared to similar mechanisms are rooted in its theoretical foundations in two fields. The basic ideas that metataxis is built on are:

- **dependency**

  and

- **implicitness**.

Dependency as the fundamental concept of the syntax model devised in this study essentially enhances the aim of **cross-linguistic** validity of the syntax model, and thereby, of the contrastive syntactic rules that make up metataxis. In principle dependency and its counterpart constituency are equivalent in their descriptive and explanatory capacity. But as long as constituency has to remain in the definitorial bonds of contiguity, it fails to cover all that is needed in a complete cross-linguistic syntax model. Dependency, which relies on the concept of **syntactic function** as indicated by language-specific **syntactic form**, is cross-linguistically valid.

Implicitness as the guiding principle of the method of translation described here crucially promotes the interplay of form and content in translation. Implicity is a fruitful guideline on several levels. As far as metataxis is concerned, the implicity principle guarantees that the translation procedure makes use of the amount of certainty that derives from form correspondences between languages. In this way a basic structure is established which makes up the framework for choices among semantic options and even takes a steering role with respect to what is possible and what is not in pragmatic reinterpretation.

Metataxis, built on this twofold foundation, is a powerful and efficient instrument of machine translation.

A number of goals for further research have been alluded to throughout this study. In my view, there are three types: immediate, medium-term and long-term goals.

An immediate goal for further development of metataxis is to broaden the scope of syntax. I define syntax as an area of language containing the word, sentence, and text levels (2.1.). This study mainly deals with the sentence level. Word level syntax is included, but is taken up here only inasmuch as it has an effect on sentence level. Much more can be said about word grammar (cf. also Schubert forthc. a). But to extend syntax to the text level, a good deal of work remains to be done. Text syntax, and when semantics is included, **text grammar**, is a fundamental desideratum in language theory and for machine translation as a practical application, it is an indispensable instrument for transferring text coherence from source to target language.

A medium-term goal of a somewhat more formal nature is a thorough investigation into the **reversibility of metataxis**. This question is not only of immediate relevance to multilingual machine translation, but has a bearing also on the theoretical implications of the question whether grammar is, or rather whether an individual grammar should be, **static** or **dynamic**.

A long-term goal which leads profoundly into the core of language theory is the question of a possible semantic anchorage of syntax and of a possible pragmatic anchorage of semantics.

Index

References

Allerton, D. J. (1982): Valency and the English verb.
London etc.: Academic Press

Appelo, Lisette (1986): The machine translation system Rosetta.
In: I. International Conference on the State of the Art in Machine Translation in America, Asia and Europe (Proceedings of IAI-MT 86). Tom C. Gerhardt (ed.). Saarbrücken: IAI/Eurotra-D, pp. 34-50

Bates, Madeleine (1978): The theory and practice of Augmented Transition Network grammars.
In: Natural language communication with computers. Leonard Bolc (ed.). Berlin / Heidelberg / New York: Springer, pp. 191-259

Baum, Richard (1976): "Dependenzgrammatik". Tesnières Modell der Sprachbeschreibung in wissenschaftsgeschichtlicher und kritischer Sicht.
(= Beihefte zur Zeitschrift für romanische Philologie 151)
Tübingen: Niemeyer

Baumgärtner, Klaus (1965): Spracherklärung mit den Mitteln der Abhängigkeitsstruktur [Review of Tesnière 1959].
In: Beiträge zur Sprachkunde und Informationsverarbeitung 5, pp. 31-53

Baumgärtner, Klaus (1970): Konstituenz und Dependenz.
In: Vorschläge für eine strukturale Grammatik des Deutschen.
Hugo Steger (ed.). Darmstadt: Wissenschaftliche Buchgesellschaft, pp. 52-77

Bierwisch, Manfred (1966): Aufgaben und Form der Grammatik.
In: II. Internationales Symposium.
Vol. 3: Zeichen und System der Sprache.
Berlin: Akademie-Verlag, pp. 28-69
[here quoted from:]
(1970):
In: Vorschläge für eine strukturale Grammatik des Deutschen.
Hugo Steger (ed.). Darmstadt: Wissenschaftliche Buchgesellschaft, pp. 1-51

Brinkmann, Hennig (1962): Die deutsche Sprache. Gestalt und Leistung.
Düsseldorf: Schwann

Busse, Winfried / Jean-Pierre Dubost (1977); Französisches Verblexikon.
Stuttgart: Klett-Cotta

Cholodovič, A. A. (1970): Zalog.
In: Kategorija zaloga.
Leningrad: AS SSSR, Institut jazykoznanija, pp. 2-26

Chomsky, Noam (1957): Syntactic structures.
's-Gravenhage: Mouton

Chomsky, Noam (1965): Aspects of the theory of syntax.
Cambridge [USA]: MIT Press

Colmerauer, A. (1975): Les grammaries de métamorphose.
Marseille: Groupe d'Intelligence Artificielle, Université de Marseille-Luminy
[here quoted from:]
(1978): Metamorphosis grammars.
In: Natural language communication with computers.
Leonard Bolc (ed.). Berlin / Heidelberg / New York: Springer, pp. 133-189

Diderichsen, Paul (1946): Elementær dansk Grammatik.
København: Gyldendal

Dik, Simon C. (1978): Functional grammar.
Amsterdam / New York / Oxford: North-Holland

Doedens, Crist-Jan (forthcoming): On-screen ATN parsing.
In: [Proceedings of the International Conference on Machine and Machine-Aided Translation (Birmingham 1986)]

Eckert, H. (1985): Valences Ltd. vs. Valences Associated. Comments on Heringer's association experiment as a basis for valence theory.
In: Journal of Semantics 4, pp. 257-263

Emons, Rudolf (1974): Valenzen englischer Prädikatsverben.
Tübingen: Niemeyer

Emons, Rudolf (1978): Valenzgrammatik für das Englische.
Tübingen: Niemeyer

Engel, Ulrich (1980): Fügungspotenz und Sprachvergleich. Vom Nutzen eines semantisch erweiterten Valenzbegriffs für die kontrastive Linguistik.
In: Wirkendes Wort 30, pp. 1-22

Engel, Ulrich (1982): Syntax der deutschen Gegenwartssprache.
Berlin: Schmidt [2. ed.; major changes from 1. ed. 1977]

Engel, Ulrich / Helmut Schumacher (1976): Kleines Valenzlexikon deutscher Verben.
Tübingen: Narr

Erben, Johannes (1958): Abriß der deutschen Grammatik.
Berlin: Akademie-Verlag
[quoted from:]
(1972): Deutsche Grammatik. Ein Abriß.
München: Hueber [11. ed.]

Eroms, Hans-Werner (1981): Valenz Kasus und Präpositionen.
Heidelberg: Winter

Fabricius-Hansen, Cathrine (1977): Projektet "Dänisch-deutsche kontrastive Grammatik".
In: Kontrastiv grammatik i Danmark.
København: Statens humanistiske forskningsråd, pp. 170-183

Fabricius-Hansen, Cathrine (1979a): Valenztheorie und kontrastive Grammatik (Dänisch-Deutsch).
In: Osloer Beiträge zur Germanistik 3

Fabricius-Hansen, Cathrine (1979b): Die Relevanz der Satzbaupläne für den Fremdsprachenunterricht. Überlegungen zu einer Deutschgrammatik für Skandinavier.
In: Jahrbuch Deutsch als Fremdsprache 5, pp. 156-174

Fabricius-Hansen, Cathrine (1980): Plan einer dänisch-deutschen kontrastiven Grammatik.
- KONTRA, Dänisch-deutsche kontrastive Grammatik, Arbeitsbericht 1. København: Københavns Universitet, Institut for Germansk Filologi

Fabricius-Hansen, Cathrine / Lisbeth Falster Jakobsen / Jørgen Olsen (1981): Die Satzbaupläne im Dänischen und Deutschen.
1: Vorüberlegungen.
= KONTRA, Dänisch-deutsche kontrastive Grammatik, Arbeitsbericht 4. København: Københavns Universitet, Institut for Germansk Filologi

Fillmore, Charles J. (1968): The case for case.
In: Universals in linguistic theory.
E. Bach / R. T. Harms (eds.). New York: Holt, Rinehart & Winston, pp. 1-88

Fillmore, Charles J. (1977a): The case for case reopened.
In: Kasustheorie, Klassifikation, semantische Interpretation.
Klaus Heger / János S. Petöfi (eds.). Hamburg: Buske, pp. 3-26

Fillmore, Charles J. (1977b): Scenes-and-frames semantics.
In: Linguistic structure processing.
Antonio Zampolli (ed.). Amsterdam: North-Holland, pp. 55-81

Fillmore, Charles J. (1987): A private history of the concept "frame".
In: Concepts of case.
René Dirven / Günter Radden (eds.). Tübingen: Narr, pp. 28-36

Gaifman, Haim (1965): Dependency systems and phrase-structure systems.
In: Information and Control 8, pp. 304-337

Garey, Howard B. (1954): [Review of Tesnière 1953]
In: Language 30, pp. 512-513

Gazdar, Gerald / Ewan Klein / Geoffrey Pullum / Ivan Sag (1985): Generalized phrase structure grammar.
Oxford: Blackwell

Groot, A. W. de (1949): Structurele syntaxis.
Den Haag: Servire

Gross, Maurice (1964): The equivalence of models of language used in the fields of mechanical translation and information retrieval.
In: Information Storage and Retrieval 2, pp. 43-57

Gross, Maurice (1975): Méthodes en syntaxe.
Paris: Hermann

Gust, Helmar (1984): Ein Grammatiklabor in Prolog.
In: Probleme des (Text-)Verstehens. Ansätze der Künstlichen Intelligenz.
Claus-Rainer Rollinger (ed.). Tübingen: Niemeyer, pp. 55-66, 271-286

Halliday, M. A. K. (1966): Some notes on "deep" grammar.
In: Journal of Linguistics 2, pp. 57-67

Harris, Zellig (1982): A grammar of English on mathematical principles.
New York etc.: Wiley

Hays, David G. (1961): Grouping and dependency theories.
In: Proceedings of the national symposium on machine translation (1960).
H. P. Edmundson (ed.). Englewood Cliffs: Prentice-Hall, pp. 258-266

Hays, David G. (1964a): Valeurs à attribuer aux différents types de rapports de dépendance.
In: Traduction automatique et linguistique appliquée.
Paris: Presses Universitaires de France, pp. 43-59

Hays, David G. (1964b): Dependency theory: a formalism and some observations.
In: Language 40, pp. 511-525

Heger, Klaus (1966): Valenz, Diathese und Kasus.
In: Zeitschrift für romanische Philologie 82, pp. 138-170

Heger, Klaus (1971): Monem, Wort und Satz.
Tübingen: Niemeyer
[augmented edition:]
(1976): Monem, Wort, Satz und Text.
Tübingen: Niemeyer [2. ed.]

Heger, Klaus (1977): Aktantenfunktionen und abstrakte Kasus.
In: Kasustheorie, Klassifikation, semantische Interpretation.
Klaus Heger / János S. Petöfi (eds.). Hamburg: Buske, pp. 43-69

Helbig, Gerhard (1965): Der Begriff der Valenz als Mittel der strukturellen Sprachbeschreibung und des Fremdsprachenunterrichts.
In: Deutsch als Fremdsprache, pp. 10-23

Helbig, Gerhard (1973): Geschichte der neueren Sprachwissenschaft.
München: Hueber [2. ed.; 1. ed. Leipzig: Enzyklopädie 1971]

Helbig, Gerhard (1982): Valenz - Satzglieder - semantische Kasus - Satzmodelle.
Leipzig: Enzyklopädie

Helbig, Gerhard (1986): Entwicklung der Sprachwissenschaft seit 1970.
Leipzig: Bibliographisches Institut

Helbig, Gerhard / Wolfgang Schenkel (1969): Wörterbuch zur Valenz und Distribution deutscher Verben.
Leipzig: Bibliographisches Institut [5. ed. 1980]

Hellwig, Peter (1986): Dependency unification grammar.
In: 11th International Conference on Computational Linguistics. Proceedings of Coling 86.
Bonn: Institut für angewandte Kommunikations- und Sprachforschung, pp. 195-198

Herbst, Thomas (1983): Untersuchungen zur Valenz englischer Adjektive und ihrer Nominalisierungen.
Tübingen: Narr

Heringer, Hans-Jürgen (1970a): Theorie der deutschen Syntax.
München: Hueber [2.ed. 1973]

Heringer, Hans-Jürgen (1970b): Deutsche Syntax.
Berlin / New York: de Gruyter [2.ed. 1972]

Heringer, Hans Jürgen (1984): Neues von der Verbszene.
In: Pragmatik in der Grammatik.
Gerhard Stickel (ed.). Düsseldorf: Schwann, pp. 34-64

Heringer, H.J. (1985): The verb and its semantic power: association as a basis for valence theory.
In: Journal of Semantics 4, pp. 79-99

Heringer, Hans Jürgen / Bruno Strecker / Rainer Wimmer (1980): Syntax.
München: Fink

Hjelmslev, Louis (1963): Sproget.
København: Berlingske forlag [2. ed.]

Hockett, Charles F. (1958): A course in modern linguistics.
New York

Hudson, Richard A. (1980): Constituency and dependency.
In: Linguistics 18, pp. 179-198

Hudson, Richard (1984): Word grammar.
Oxford / New York: Blackwell

Hutchins, William John (1986): Machine translation: past, present, future.
Chichester: Horwood / New York etc.: Wiley

Ihm, P. / Y. Lecerf (1963): Éléments pour une grammaire générale des langues projectives.
Bruxelles: Communauté européenne de l'energie atomique

Iordanskaja, L. N. (1963): O nekotorych svojstvach pravil'noj sintaksičeskoj struktury.
In: Voprosy jazykoznanija [4], pp. 102-112

Isaac, Luc (1986): Syntaxe dépendantielle du français.
Unpublished report. Utrecht: BSO/Research

Itälä, Marja-Leena (1986): Verbvalenz - Valenzsemantik.
- Turun yliopiston julkaisuja \ Annales Universitatis Turkuensis B 172, Turku

Jäppinen, H. / A. Lehtola / K. Valkonen (1986): Functional structures for parsing dependency constraints.
In: 11th International Conference on Computational Linguistics, Proceedings of Coling 86.
Bonn: Institut für angewandte Kommunikations- und Sprachforschung, pp. 461-463

Joshi, Aravind K. (1987): The relevance of tree adjoining grammar to generation.
In: Natural language generation.
Gerard Kempen (ed.). Dordrecht / Boston / Lancaster: Nijhoff, pp. 233-252

Kacnel'son, S. D. (1948): O grammatičeskoj kategorii.
In: Vestnik Leningradskogo Universiteta (Serija istorii, jazyka i literatury) [2], pp. 114-134

Kaplan, Ronald M. / Joan Bresnan (1982): Lexical-Functional Grammar: a formal system for grammatical representation.
In: The mental representation of grammatical relations.
Joan Bresnan (ed.). Cambridge [USA]: MIT Press

Kirschner, Zdeněk (1982): A dependency-based analysis of English for the purpose of machine translation.
(- Ėksplicitnoe opisanie jazyka i avtomatičeskaja obrabotka tekstov \ Explizite Beschreibung der Sprache und automatische Textbearbeitung 9)
Praha: Matematicko-fyzikální fakulta UK

Klein, Wolfgang (1971): Parsing. Studien zur maschinellen Satzanalyse mit Abhängigkeitsgrammatiken und Transformationsgrammatiken.
Frankfurt a.M.: Athenäum

Korhonen, Jarmo (1977, 1978): Studien zu Dependenz, Valenz und Satzmodell.
Vol. 1-2. Bern / Frankfurt am Main / Las Vegas: Lang

Korst, Bieke van der (1986): A dependency syntax for English.
Unpublished report. Utrecht: BSO/Research

Kunze, J. (1972): Die Auslaßbarkeit von Satzteilen bei koordinativen Verbindungen im Deutschen.
Berlin

Kunze, Jürgen (1975): Abhängigkeitsgrammatik.
Berlin: Akademie-Verlag

Kwee Tjoe-Liong (1987): A computer model of functional grammar.
In: Natural language generation.
Gerard Kempen (ed.). Dordrecht / Boston / Lancaster: Nijhoff, pp. 315-331

Lecerf, Y. (1960): Programme des conflits, modèle des conflits.
In: Traduction automatique 1 [4], pp. 11-18, [5], pp. 17-36

Lehtola, A. / H. Jäppinen / E. Nelimarkka (1985): Language-based environment for natural language parsing.
In: Second Conference of the European Chapter of the Association for Computational Linguistics, (Proceedings of the conference; Geneva 1985).
s.l.: Association for Computational Linguistics, pp. 98-106

Lejkina, B. M. (1961): Nekotorye aspekty valentnosti.
In: Doklady na konferencii po obrabotke informacii, mašinnomu perevodu i avtomatičeskomu čteniju teksta [5], pp. 1ff.

Lobin, Henning (1987): Dependenzsyntax des Deutschen.
Unpublished report. Utrecht: BSO/Research

Lomtev, T. P. (1959): O nekotorych voprosach struktury predloženija.
In: Naučnye doklady Vysšej školy (Filologičeskie nauki) [4]

Lomtev, T. P. (1961): Priroda sintaksičeskich javlenij.
In: Naučnye doklady Vysšej školy (Filologičeskie nauki) [3]

Maas, Utz (1974): Dependenztheorie.
In: Grundzüge der Literatur- und Sprachwissenschaft.
Heinz Ludwig Arnold / Volker Sinemus (eds.).
Vol. 2: Sprachwissenschaft.
Arnold / Sinemus / Rolf Dietrich / Siegfried Kanngießer (eds.). München: Deutscher Taschenbuch-Verlag, pp. 257-275

Mathesius, Vilém (1929): Zur Satzperspektive im modernen Englisch.
In: Archiv für das Studium der neueren Sprachen und Literaturen 84, pp. 202-210

Maxwell, Dan (1986): Dependency trees for English for use in DLT.
Unpublished report. Utrecht: BSO/Research

Maxwell, Dan (1987): Metataxis English-IL.
Unpublished report. Utrecht: BSO/Research

Megen, J. van (1985): Dependency grammar, valence and the bilingual lexicon.
In: Meaning and the lexicon.
G.A.J. Hoppenbrouwers / P.A.M. Seuren / A.J.M.M. Weijters (eds.). Dordrecht / Cinnaminson: Foris, pp. 170-178, 483-509

Melby, Alan K. (1986): Lexical transfer: a missing element in linguistics theories.
In: 11th International Conference on Computational Linguistics, Proceedings of Coling 86.
Bonn: Institut für angewandte Kommunikations- und Sprachforschung, pp. 104-106

Mel'čuk, Igor' A. (1964): Avtomatičeskij sintaksičeskij analiz.
Novosibirsk: Akademija nauk

Mel'čuk, I. A. (1967): Ordre des mots en synthèse automatique des textes russes.
In; TA Informations [2], pp. 65-84

Mel'čuk, Igor A. (1979a): Dependency syntax.
In: Mel'čuk: Studies in dependency syntax.
Ann Arbor: Karoma, pp. 3-21

Mel'čuk, Igor A. (1979b): Types of surface-syntactic relations: three distinction criteria.
In: Mel'čuk: Studies in dependency syntax.
Ann Arbor: Karoma, pp. 91-161

[Mel'čuk, Igor' Aleksandrovič / Nikolaj Viktorovič Percov] Igor A. Mel'čuk / Nikolaj V. Pertsov (1987): Surface syntax of English.
Amsterdam / Philadelphia: Benjamins

Moilanen, Markku (1985): Zum Begriff der Notwendigkeit bei der Satzgliedanalyse.
In: Grammatik im Unterricht.
(= Meddelanden från Stiftelsens för Åbo Akademi forskningsinstitut 103)
Kurt Nyholm (ed.). Åbo: Åbo Akademi, pp. 185-198

Munniksma, F. et al. (1975): International business dictionary in nine languages \ Internacia komerca-ekonomika vortaro en naŭ lingvoj.
Deventer / Antwerp: Kluwer

Muraki, Kazunori / Shunji Ichiyama / Yasutomo Fukumochi (1985): Augmented dependency grammar: a simple interface between the grammar rule and the knowledge.
In: Second Conference of the European Chapter of the Association for Computational Linguistics,
(Proceedings of the conference; Geneva 1985).
s.l.: Association for Computational Linguistics, pp. 198-204

Nelimarkka, Esa / Harri Jäppinen / Aarno Lehtola (1984): Two-way finite automata and dependency grammar: a parsing method for inflectional free word order languages.
In: 10th International Conference on Computational Linguistics, 22nd Annual Meeting of the Association for Computational Linguistics (Proceedings of Coling 84, Stanford 1984).
s.l.: Association for Computational Linguistics, pp. 389-392

Newmark, Peter (1981): Approaches to translation.
Oxford etc.: Pergamon

Newmark, Peter (1987): The application of case grammar to translation.
In: Concepts of case.
René Dirven / Günter Radden (eds.). Tübingen: Narr, pp. 162-176

Niedermair, Gerh. Th. (1986): Divided and valency-oriented parsing in speech understanding.
In: 11th International Conference on Computational Linguistics, Proceedings of Coling 86.
Bonn: Institut für angewandte Kommunikations- und Sprachforschung, pp. 593-595

Nikula, Henrik (1976): Verbvalenz. Untersuchungen am Beispiel des deutschen Verbs mit einer kontrastiven Analyse Deutsch-Schwedisch.
(= Acta Universitatis Upsaliensis, Studia Germanistica Upsaliensia 15)
Uppsala: Almqvist & Wiksell

Nikula, Henrik (1986): Dependensgrammatik.
Malmö: Liber

Nitta, Yoshihiko (1986): Idiosyncratic gap: a tough problem to structure-bound machine translation.
In: 11th International Conference on Computational Linguistics. Proceedings of Coling 86.
Bonn: Institut für angewandte Kommunikations- und Sprachforschung, pp. 107-111

Nitta, Yoshihiko / Atsushi Okajima / Hiroyuki Kaji / Touichi Hidano / Koichiro Ishihara (1984): A proper treatment of syntax and semantics in machine translation.
In: 10th International Conference on Computational Linguistics. 22nd Annual Meeting of the Association for Computational Linguistics (Proceedings of Coling 84, Stanford 1984).
s.l.: Association for Computational Linguistics, pp. 159-166

Papegaaij, B. C. (1986): Word expert semantics.
(= Distributed Language Translation 1)
V. Sadler / A.P.M. Witkam (eds.). Dordrecht / Riverton: Foris

Papegaaij, B. C. / V. Sadler / A. P. M. Witkam (1986): Experiments with an MT-directed lexical knowledge bank.
In: 11th International Conference on Computational Linguistics. Proceedings of Coling 86.
Bonn: Institut für angewandte Kommunikations- und Sprachforschung, pp. 432-434

Pereira, Fernando C. N. / David H. D. Warren (1980): Definite Clause Grammars for language analysis - a survey of the formalism and a comparison with Augmented Transition Networks.
In: Artificial Intelligence 13, pp. 231-278

Plath, Warren (1964): Construction automatique du diagramme d'une phrase.
In: Traduction automatique et linguistique appliquée.
Paris: Presses Universitaires de France, pp. 23-42

Pleines, Jochen (1978): Ist der Universalitätsanspruch der Kasusgrammatik berechtigt?
In: Valence, semantic case, and grammatical relations. Werner Abraham (ed.). Amsterdam: Benjamins, pp. 335-376

Reimann, Dorothee (1985): Aŭtomata sintaksa analizo de la germana lingvo.
In: Perkomputila tekstoprilaboro. Ilona Koutny (ed.). Budapest: Scienca Eldona Centro, pp. 125-144

Robinson, Jane J. (1970): Dependency structures and transformational rules.
In: Language 46, pp.259-285

Sakamoto, Yoshiyuki / Tetsuya Ishikawa / Masayuki Satoh (1986): Concept structure of semantic markers for machine translation in Mu-project.
In: 11th International Conference on Computational Linguistics. Proceedings of Coling 86. Bonn: Institut für angewandte Kommunikations- und Sprachforschung, pp. 13-19

Sakamoto, Yoshiyuki / Masayuki Satoh / Tetsuya Ishikawa (1984): Lexicon features for Japanese syntactic analysis in Mu-Project-JE.
In: 10th International Conference on Computational Linguistics. 22nd Annual Meeting of the Association for Computational Linguistics (Proceedings of Coling 84, Stanford 1984). s.l.: Association for Computational Linguistics, pp. 42-47

Sato, Shigeru / Hideki Kasuya (forthcoming): Automatic translation / speech synthesis of Japanese from written Esperanto incorporating a linguistic knowledge base editor.
In: Conference proceedings of the European Conference on Speech Technology (Edinburgh 1987)

Saussure, Ferdinand de (1916): Cours de linguistique générale. Paris: Payot [new ed. 1969]

Schank, Roger C. (1972): Conceptual dependency: a theory of natural language understanding.
In: Cognitive Psychology 3, pp. 552-631

Schank, Roger C. (1975): Conceptual information processing. Amsterdam: North-Holland

Schank, Roger C. / R. P. Abelson (1977): Scripts, plans goals and understanding: an inquiry into human knowledge structures.
Hillsdale: Erlbaum

Schmidt, Paul (1986): Valency theory in a stratificational MT-system.
In: 11th International Conference on Computational Linguistics, Proceedings of Coling 86.
Bonn: Institut für angewandte Kommunikations- und Sprachforschung, pp. 307-312

Schubert, Ingrid (1987): Dänische Dependenzsyntax für DLT.
Unpublished report. Utrecht: BSO/Research

Schubert, Klaus (1982): Aktiv und Passiv im Deutschen und Schwedischen.
= SAIS Arbeitsberichte aus dem Seminar für Allgemeine und Indogermanische Sprachwissenschaft 5 [Kiel]

Schubert, Klaus (1985a): Ist Höflichkeit ungrammatisch? Über formale und begriffliche Einheiten im Bereich der Personendeixis.
In: Sprachtheorie, Pragmatik, Interdisziplinäres (Akten des 19. Linguistischen Kolloquiums, Vechta 1984, vol. 2).
Wilfried Kürschner / Rüdiger Vogt / Sabine Siebert-Nemann (eds.). Tübingen: Niemeyer, pp. 151-162

Schubert, Klaus (1985b): Svenskan som ett möjligt målspråk i halvautomatisk översättning.
In: Svenskans beskrivning 15 (Förhandlingar vid sammankomst för att dryfta frågor rörande svenskans beskrivning, Göteborg 1985).
Sture Allén et al. (eds.). Göteborg: Göteborgs universitet, pp. 464-473, p. 572

Schubert, Klaus (1986a): Syntactic tree structures in DLT.
Utrecht: BSO/Research

Schubert, Klaus (1986b): Wo die Syntax im Wörterbuch steht. Esperanto als Brückensprache der maschinellen Übersetzung.
In: Pragmantax (Akten des 20. Linguistischen Kolloquiums, Braunschweig 1985).
Armin Burkhardt / Karl-Hermann Körner (eds.).
Tübingen: Niemeyer, pp. 449-458

Schubert, Klaus (1986c): Linguistic and extra-linguistic knowledge. A catalogue of language-related rules and their computational application in machine translation.
In: Computers and Translation 1, pp. 125-152

Schubert, Klaus (1987): Wann bedeuten zwei Wörter dasselbe? Über Tiefenkasus als Tertium comparationis.
In: Linguistik in Deutschland (Akten des 21. Linguistischen Kolloquiums, Groningen 1986). Werner Abraham / Ritva Århammar (eds.). Tübingen: Niemeyer, pp. 109-117

Schubert, Klaus (forthcoming a): Interlingual terminologies and compounds in the DLT project.
In: [Proceedings of the International Conference on Machine and Machine-Aided Translation (Birmingham 1986)]

Schubert, Klaus (forthcoming b): [Review of Nikula 1986].
In: Nysvenska studier

Sells, Peter (1985): Lectures on contemporary syntactic theories: An introduction to Government-Binding Theory, Generalized Phrase Structure Grammar, and Lexical-Functional Grammar. Stanford: Center for the Study of Language and Information

Shirai, K. / T. Hamada (1986): Linguistic knowledge extraction from real language behavior.
In: 11th International Conference on Computational Linguistics, Proceedings of Coling 86. Bonn: Institut für angewandte Kommunikations- und Sprachforschung, pp. 253-255

Smereka, Krystyna (1986): Valenztheorie und Sprachvergleich im Bereich ausgewählter Verbfelder des Deutschen und Polnischen.
(= Acta Universitatis Wratislaviensis 696, Germanica Wratislaviensia 54)
Wrocław: Wydawnictwo Uniwersytetu Wrocławskiego

Snell, Bruno (1952): Der Aufbau der Sprache.
Hamburg: Claassen, [3.ed.]

Somers, Harold L. (1984): On the validity of the complement-adjunct distinction in valency grammar.
In: Linguistics 22, pp. 507-530

Somers, Harold L. (1986): The need for MT-oriented versions of case and valency in MT.
In: 11th International Conference on Computational Linguistics, Proceedings of Coling 86. Bonn: Institut für angewandte Kommunikations- und Sprachforschung, pp. 118-123

Somers, H. L. (1987): Valency and case in computational linguistics.
Edinburgh: Edinburgh University Press

Sommerfeldt, Karl-Ernst / Herbert Schreiber (1974): Wörterbuch zur Valenz und Distribution deutscher Adjektive.
Leipzig: Bibliographisches Institut [3. ed. 1983]

Sommerfeldt, Karl-Ernst / Herbert Schreiber (1977): Wörterbuch zur Valenz und Distribution deutscher Substantive.
Leipzig: Bibliographisches Institut [2. ed. 1980]

Starosta, Stanley (1987): A place for (Lexi-)Case.
In: Concepts of case.
René Dirven / Günter Radden (eds.). Tübingen: Narr, pp. 54-74

Starosta, Stanley / Hirosato Nomura (1986): Lexicase parsing: a lexicon-driven approach to syntactic analysis.
In: 11th International Conference on Computational Linguistics. Proceedings of Coling 86.
Bonn: Institut für angewandte Kommunikations- und Sprachforschung, pp. 127-132

Tamis, Dorine (1986): De afhankelijkheidssyntaxis van het Frans.
Unpublished report. Utrecht: BSO/Research

Tamis, Dorine (1987a): Contribution à la synthèse automatique du français.
Unpublished report. Utrecht: BSO/Research / Unpublished doctorandus thesis. Amsterdam: Vrije Universiteit

Tamis, Dorine (1987b): La métataxe IL-français.
Unpublished report. Utrecht: BSO/Research

Tarvainen, Kalevi (1977): Dependenssikielioppi.
Helsinki

Tarvainen, Kalevi (1981): Einführung in die Dependenzgrammatik.
Tübingen: Niemeyer

Tarvainen, Kalevi (1983a): Principles and problems of English dependency grammar.
In: Tarvainen (1983): Two papers on dependency grammar.
- Umeå Papers in English 6, Umeå, pp. 1-28

Tarvainen, Kalevi (1983b): The object as a syntactic category: A contrastive analysis of German, English and Swedish.
In: Tarvainen (1983): Two papers on dependency grammar.
- Umeå Papers in English 6, Umeå, pp. 29-52

Tarvainen, Kalevi (1985a): Kontrastive Syntax Deutsch - Finnisch.
Heidelberg: Groos

Tarvainen, Kalevi (1985b): Kielioppia kontrastiivisesti. Suomesta saksaksi.
= Jyväskylän yliopisto, Saksan kielen laitoksen julkaisuja \ Veröffentlichungen des germanistischen Instituts, Universität Jyväskylä 4

Tarvainen, Kalevi (1985c): Semantic cases in the framework of dependency theory.
(= LAUT A 145)
Trier: Linguistic Agency, University of Trier
also (1987):
In: Concepts of case.
René Dirven / Günter Radden (eds.). Tübingen: Narr, pp. 75-102

Tarvainen, Kalevi (1986): Deutsche Satzstruktur und ihre Entwicklung. Dependenzgrammatik des Deutschen mit historischen Erläuterungen.
= Jyväskylän yliopisto, Saksan kielen laitoksen julkaisuja \ Veröffentlichungen des germanistischen Instituts, Universität Jyväskylä 5

Tarvainen, Kalevi (1987): Formale Dependenzgrammatik des Finnischen.
Unpublished report. Utrecht: BSO/Research

Tesnière, Lucien (1953): Esquisse d'une syntaxe structurale.
Paris: Klincksieck

Tesnière, Lucien (1959): Éléments de syntaxe structurale. Paris: Klincksieck [2.ed., 4.print. 1982]

Teubert, Wolfgang (1979): Valenz des Substantivs.
Düsseldorf: Schwann

Thorell, Olof (1977): Svensk grammatik.
Stockholm / Göteborg / Lund: Esselte [2. ed.; 1.ed. 1973]

Tsujii, Jun-ichi (1986): Future directions of machine translation.
In: 11th International Conference on Computational Linguistics. Proceedings of Coling 86.
Bonn: Institut für angewandte Kommunikations- und Sprachforschung, pp. 655-668

Valkonen, K. / H. Jäppinen / A. Lehtola / M. Ylilammi (forthcoming): Declarative model for dependency parsing - a view into blackboard methodology.
In: [Third Conference of the European Chapter of the Association for Computational Linguistics, Proceedings (Copenhagen 1987)]

Vater, Heinz (1978): On the possibility of distinguishing between complements and adjuncts.
In: Valence, semantic case, and grammatical relations. Werner Abraham (ed.). Amsterdam: Benjamins, pp. 21-45

Vergne, Jacques / Pascale Pagès (1986): Synergy of syntax and morphology in automatic parsing of French language with a minimum of data.
In: 11th International Conference on Computational Linguistics, Proceedings of Coling 86.
Bonn: Institut für angewandte Kommunikations- und Sprachforschung, pp. 269-271

Vijay-Shanker, K. / David J. Weir / Aravind K. Joshi (1986): Tree adjoining and head wrapping.
In: 11th International Conference on Computational Linguistics, Proceedings of Coling 86.
Bonn: Institut für angewandte Kommunikations- und Sprachforschung, pp. 202-207

Weissgerber, Monika (1983): Valenz und Kongruenzbeziehungen. Ein Modell zur Vereindeutigung von Verben in der maschinellen Analyse und Übersetzung.
Frankfurt am Main / Bern / New York: Lang

Winograd, Terry (1983): Language as a cognitive process.
Vol. 1: Syntax.
Reading etc.: Addison-Wesley

Witkam, A. P. M. (1983): Distributed Language Translation. Feasibility study of a multilingual facility for videotex information networks.
Utrecht: BSO

Woods, W. A. (1970): Transition network grammars for natural language analysis.
In: Communications of the Association for Computing Machinery 13 [10], pp. 591-606

Yasukawa, Hideki (1984): LFG system in Prolog.
In: 10th International Conference on Computational Linguistics, 22nd Annual Meeting of the Association for Computational Linguistics (Proceedings of Coling 84, Stanford 1984).
s.l.: Association for Computational Linguistics, pp. 358-361

Zampolli, A. (1977): Statistique linguistique et dépouillements automatiques.
In: Lexicologie. Een bundel opstellen voor F. de Tollenaere. P. G. J. van Sterkenburg et al. (eds.). Groningen: Wolters-Noordhoff, pp. 325-358

Zasorina, L. N. / V. P. Berkov (1961): Ponjatie valentnosti v jazyke.
In: Vestnik Leningradskogo Universiteta (Serija istorii, jazyka i literatury) 8 [2]

Zemb, Jean-Marie (1987): Zum Begriff des "Prädikats".
In: Maschinelle Übersetzung - Methoden und Werkzeuge. Wolfram Wilss / Klaus-Dirk Schmitz (eds.). Tübingen: Niemeyer, pp. 101-111

Bei Fragen zur Produktsicherheit wenden Sie sich bitte an:
If you have any questions regarding product safety,
please contact:

Walter de Gruyter GmbH
Genthiner Straße 13
10785 Berlin
productsafety@degruyterbrill.com